EZRA POUND

Modern Critical Views

Henry Adams
Edward Albee
A. R. Ammons
Matthew Arnold
John Ashbery
W. H. Auden
Jane Austen
James Baldwin
Charles Baudelaire
Samuel Beckett
Saul Bellow
The Bible
Elizabeth Bishop
William Blake
Jorge Luis Borges
Elizabeth Bowen
Bertolt Brecht
The Brontës
Robert Browning
Anthony Burgess
George Gordon, Lord
    Byron
Thomas Carlyle
Lewis Carroll
Willa Cather
Cervantes
Geoffrey Chaucer
Kate Chopin
Samuel Taylor Coleridge
Joseph Conrad
Contemporary Poets
Hart Crane
Stephen Crane
Dante
Charles Dickens
Emily Dickinson
John Donne & the Seven-
    teenth-Century Meta-
    physical Poets
Elizabethan Dramatists
Theodore Dreiser
John Dryden
George Eliot
T. S. Eliot
Ralph Ellison
Ralph Waldo Emerson
William Faulkner
Henry Fielding
F. Scott Fitzgerald
Gustave Flaubert
E. M. Forster
Sigmund Freud
Robert Frost

Robert Graves
Graham Greene
Thomas Hardy
Nathaniel Hawthorne
William Hazlitt
Seamus Heaney
Ernest Hemingway
Geoffrey Hill
Friedrich Hölderlin
Homer
Gerard Manley Hopkins
William Dean Howells
Zora Neale Hurston
Henry James
Samuel Johnson and
    James Boswell
Ben Jonson
James Joyce
Franz Kafka
John Keats
Rudyard Kipling
D. H. Lawrence
John Le Carré
Ursula K. Le Guin
Doris Lessing
Sinclair Lewis
Robert Lowell
Norman Mailer
Bernard Malamud
Thomas Mann
Christopher Marlowe
Carson McCullers
Herman Melville
James Merrill
Arthur Miller
John Milton
Eugenio Montale
Marianne Moore
Iris Murdoch
Vladimir Nabokov
Joyce Carol Oates
Sean O'Casey
Flannery O'Connor
Eugene O'Neill
George Orwell
Cynthia Ozick
Walter Pater
Walker Percy
Harold Pinter
Plato
Edgar Allan Poe
Poets of Sensibility & the
    Sublime

Alexander Pope
Katherine Ann Porter
Ezra Pound
Pre-Raphaelite Poets
Marcel Proust
Thomas Pynchon
Arthur Rimbaud
Theodore Roethke
Philip Roth
John Ruskin
J. D. Salinger
Gershom Scholem
William Shakespeare
    (3 vols.)
    Histories & Poems
    Comedies
    Tragedies
George Bernard Shaw
Mary Wollstonecraft
    Shelley
Percy Bysshe Shelley
Edmund Spenser
Gertrude Stein
John Steinbeck
Laurence Sterne
Wallace Stevens
Tom Stoppard
Jonathan Swift
Alfred, Lord Tennyson
William Makepeace
    Thackeray
Henry David Thoreau
Leo Tolstoi
Anthony Trollope
Mark Twain
John Updike
Gore Vidal
Virgil
Robert Penn Warren
Evelyn Waugh
Eudora Welty
Nathanael West
Edith Wharton
Walt Whitman
Oscar Wilde
Tennessee Williams
William Carlos Williams
Thomas Wolfe
Virginia Woolf
William Wordsworth
Richard Wright
William Butler Yeats

These and other titles in preparation

Modern Critical Views

EZRA POUND

Edited and with an introduction by

Harold Bloom
Sterling Professor of the Humanities
Yale University

CHELSEA HOUSE PUBLISHERS ◇ 1987
New York ◇ New Haven ◇ Philadelphia

© 1987 by Chelsea House Publishers, a division of Chelsea
House Educational Communications, Inc.
133 Christopher Street, New York, NY 10014
345 Whitney Avenue, New Haven, CT 06511
5014 West Chester Pike, Edgemont, PA 19028

Introduction © 1987 by Harold Bloom.

Printed and bound in the United States of America

∞ The paper used in this publication meets the minimum
requirements of the American National Standard for
Permanence of Paper for Printed Library Materials,
Z39.48-1984.

Library of Congress Cataloging-in-Publication Data
Ezra Pound.
(Modern critical views)
Bibliography: p.
Includes index.
1. Pound, Ezra, 1885–1972—Criticism and
interpretation   I. Bloom, Harold.   II. Series.
PS3531.082Z6214   1986   811'.52   86-17088
ISBN 0-87754-634-7 (alk. paper)

Contents

Editor's Note

This volume gathers together what I judge to be the best criticism so far
available on the writings of Ezra Pound, arranged in the chronological order
of its original publication. I am grateful to Margaretmary Daley for her
erudition and judgment in helping me choose these essays.

My introduction centers upon Pound's relation to Walt Whitman, particularly as manifested in *The Pisan Cantos*. The chronological sequence begins
with Pound's canonical exegete, Hugh Kenner, whose account of *Hugh Selwyn
Mauberley* may prove to be definitive. Eva Hesse, an equally learned and
devoted scholarly critic of Pound, follows with an analysis of *Drafts &
Fragments*, the end of *The Cantos*. Her Pound is tragic and Dionysiac, a return
of the repressed, while Kenner's Pound is rather a classical ironist.

Daniel D. Pearlman, whose criticism invariably helps me to read *The
Cantos* in the sequence's larger contours, emphasizes Pound's poetic argument
in Canto 5 as a polemic on time's decay in the cultural decline (as Pound
saw it) from troubadour poetry to the supposed aesthetic disorder of the
Renaissance. Pound's early poems are viewed by the eminent scholar of
meditative poetry, Louis L. Martz, as a movement from Rossetti and Swinburne to *Cathay*. *Personae*, Pound's poetry through 1926, is explored by Max
Nänny in terms of Roman Jakobson's distinction between metaphoric and
metonymic modes of discourse.

A second essay by Daniel D. Pearlman takes as its vexed subject Pound's
anti-Semitism. Pearlman concentrates on the psychodynamics of Pound's
obsession, which he terms "unfortunate" and ascribes to an "incapacity for
introspection, leading to the most unwitting and dangerous sort of *projection*."
One might choose harsher terms, historically, than Pearlman's, but his will
suffice, unacceptable as they would have been to the anti-Freudian Pound.

Fred C. Robinson, the distinguished scholarly critic of Anglo-Saxon
poetry, refreshingly turns us to a reading of Pound's eloquent version of
"The Seafarer" in relation to the poet's Anglo-Saxon studies. We come back

to *The Cantos* in Donald Davie's analysis of *Rock-Drill* and some later parts, which shrewdly balances the use of Structuralist criticism against the claims of a more Poundian mimetic criticism in arriving at a proper apprehension of Pound's major work.

Christine Froula intricately attempts to relate Pound's stance in regard to the errors in *The Cantos*, to what she hopes might become a more open stance of readers and critics towards Pound, who thus would learn from the poet's sacrificial eloquence the error of all ways whatsoever. More modestly, Michaël André Bernstein finds in Pound's imagery, as drawn from the visual arts, evidence for the poet's sense of fragmentation and dispersal, in his psyche and in his culture alike.

Pound's intense struggle with American tradition is the subject of Kathryne V. Lindberg's complex reading of how Pound read the native strain in his literary lineage. In the final essay here, George Kearns reads Pound writing Chinese, analyzing a page from *Rock-Drill*, and strongly defending the *praxis* of *The Cantos*, while lamenting the anti-Semitism that has caused many readers to close the door on Pound, as Kearns phrases it. As one of those readers, I have said what I could say in my introduction to this volume.

Introduction

I

I have brought the great ball of crystal;
who can lift it?
                                    —Canto 116

Pound's prime explainer, Hugh Kenner, commenting on *The Cantos*, writes of "the paradox that an intensely topical poem has become archaic without ever having been contemporary: archaic in an honorific sense." Kenner accounts for the paradox by insisting that: "There is no substitute for critical tradition: a continuum of understanding, early commenced. . . . Precisely because William Blake's contemporaries did not know what to make of him, we do not know either. . . . " As the greatest of antiquarian Modernists, Kenner's authority in these judgments is doubtless unassailable. His Pound may well be *the* Pound, even if his Joyce somehow seems less Dublin's Joyce than T. S. Eliot's Joyce. I in any case would not care to dispute any critic's Pound. They have their reward, and he has them.

I do not know many readers who have an equal affection for *The Cantos* and for, say, Wallace Stevens's *An Ordinary Evening in New Haven* or *The Auroras of Autumn*. Doubtless, again, such differences in poetic taste belong to the accidents of sensibility, or to irreconcilable attitudes concerning the relation of poetry to belief. They may indeed belong to more profound distinctions; in judgments as to value that transcend literary preferences. I do not desire to address myself to such matters here. Nor will I consider Pound's politics. *The Cantos* contain material that is not humanly acceptable to me, and if that material is acceptable to others, then they themselves are thereby less acceptable, at least to me.

My subject here, in necessarily curtailed terms, is Pound's relation to poetic tradition in his own language, and to Whitman in particular. Pound's

1

critics have taken him at his word in this regard, but no poet whatsoever can be trusted in his or her own story of poetic origins, even as no man or woman can be relied on to speak with dispassionate accuracy of his or her parents. Perhaps Pound triumphed in his agon with poetic tradition, which is the invariable assertion of all of his critical partisans. But the triumph, if it occurred, was a very qualified one. My own experience as a reader of *The Cantos*, across many years, is that the long poem or sequence is marred throughout by Pound's relative failure to transume or transcend his precursors. Their ancestral voices abound, and indeed become more rather than less evident as the sequence continues. Nor is this invariably a controlled allusiveness. Collage, which is handled as metaphor by Marianne Moore and by the Eliot of *The Waste Land*, is a much more literal process in Pound, is more scheme than trope, as it were. The allusive triumph over tradition in Moore's "Marriage" or *The Waste Land* is fairly problematical, yet nowhere near so dubious as it is in *The Cantos*. Confronted by a past poetic wealth in figuration, Pound tends to resort to baroque elaborations of the anterior metaphors. What he almost never manages is to achieve an ellipsis of further troping by his own inventiveness at metaphor. He cannot make the voices of Whitman and Browning seem belated, while his own voice manifests what Stevens called an "ever early candor."

I am aware that I am in apparent defiance of the proud Poundian dictum: *Make It New*. Whitman made it new in one way, and Browning in another, but Pound's strength was elsewhere. Anglo-American Poetic "Modernism" was Ezra Pound's revolution, but it seems now only another continuity in the long history of Romanticism. Literary history may or may not someday regard Pound as it now regards Abraham Cowley, John Cleveland, and Edmund Waller, luminaries of one era who faded into the common light of another age. But, as a manneristic poet, master of a period style, Pound has his deep affinities to Cowley, Cleveland, and above all Waller. He has affinities also though to Dante Gabriel Rossetti, a permanent poet who suffered from belatedness in a mode strikingly akin to that of Pound. Poundian critics tend to regard Rossetti as a kind of embarassing prelude to their hero, but I certainly intend only a tribute to Pound in comparing him to Rossetti. It is, after all, far better to be called the Dante Gabriel Rossetti than the Edmund Waller of your era.

II

Mr. Eliot and I are in agreement, or "belong to the same school of critics," in so far as we both believe that existing works form a complete order which is changed by the introduction of the "really new" work.

—POUND, *Active Anthology*

Timeless, or complete, orders are beautiful idealizations, and have not the slightest relevance to the actual sorrows of literary influence. Time's disorders are the truth of poetic tradition. Eliot, child of Whitman and Tennyson, preferred to see himself in the timeless order of Virgil and Dante, Pascal and Baudelaire. Pound, brash and natural child of Whitman and Browning, found his idealized forerunners in Arnaut Daniel and Cavalcanti, Villon and Landor. Oedipal ambivalence, which marks Pound's stance towards Whitman, never surfaces in his observations on Cavalcanti and Villon, safely remote not only in time and language, but more crucially isolated from the realities of Pound's equivocal relation to his country and compatriots.

I find Whitman quite unrecognizable in nearly every reference Pound makes to him. Our greatest poet and our most elusive, because most figurative, Whitman consistently is literalized by Pound, as though the Whitmanian self could be accepted as a machine rather than as a metaphor. What can be construed in the weird piece of 1909, "What I Feel about Walt Whitman," is a transference so ambivalent that the positive and negative elements defy disentanglement:

> From this side of the Atlantic I am for the first time able to read Whitman, and from the vantage of my education and—if it be permitted a man of my scant years—my world citizenship: I see him America's poet. The only Poet before the artists of the Carmen-Hovey period, or better, the only one of the conventionally recognised 'American Poets' who is worth reading.
>
> He *is* America. His crudity is an exceeding great stench, but it *is* America. He is the hollow place in the rock that echoes with his time. He *does* 'chant the crucial stage' and he is the 'voice triumphant.' He is disgusting. He is an exceedingly nauseating pill, but he accomplishes his mission.
>
> Entirely free from the renaissance humanist ideal of the complete man or from the Greek idealism, he is content to be what he is, and he is his time and his people. He is a genius because he has vision of what he is and of his function. He knows that he is a beginning and not a classically finished work.
>
> I honour him for he prophesied me while I can only recognise him as a forebear of whom I ought to be proud.
>
> In America there is much for the healing of the nations, but woe unto him of the cultured palate who attempts the dose.
>
> As for Whitman, I read him (in many parts) with acute pain,

but when I write of certain things I find myself using his rhythms. The expression of certain things related to cosmic consciousness seems tainted with this maramis.

I am (in common with every educated man) an heir of the ages and I demand my birth-right. Yet if Whitman represented his time in language acceptable to one accustomed to my standard of intellectual-artistic living he would belie his time and nation. And yet I am but one of his 'ages and ages' encrustations' or to be exact an encrustation of the next age. The vital part of my message, taken from the sap and fibre of America, is the same as his.

Mentally I am a Walt Whitman who has learned to wear a collar and a dress shirt (although at times inimical to both). Personally I might be very glad to conceal my relationship to my spiritual father and brag about my more congenial ancestry— Dante, Shakespeare, Theocritus, Villon, but the descent is a bit difficult to establish. And, to be frank, Whitman is to my fatherland (*Patriam quam odi et amo* for no uncertain reasons) what Dante is to Italy and I at my best can only be a strife for a renaissance in America of all the lost or temporarily mislaid beauty, truth, valour, glory of Greece, Italy, England and all the rest of it.

And yet if a man has written lines like Whitman's to the *Sunset Breeze* one has to love him. I think we have not yet paid enough attention to the deliberate artistry of the man, not in details but in the large.

I am immortal even as he is, yet with a lesser vitality as I am the more in love with beauty (if I really do love it more than he did). Like Dante he wrote in the 'vulgar tongue,' in a new metric. The first great man to write in the language of his people.

Et ego Petrarca in lingua vetera scribo, and in a tongue my people understood not.

It seems to me I should like to drive Whitman into the old world. I sledge, he drill—and to scourge America with all the old beauty. (For Beauty *is* an accusation) and with a thousand thongs from Homer to Yeats, from Theocritus to Marcel Schwob. This desire is because I am young and impatient, were I old and wise I should content myself in seeing and saying that these things will come. But now, since I am by no means sure it would be true prophecy, I am fain set my own hand to the labour.

It is a great thing, reading a man to know, not 'His Tricks are not as yet my Tricks, but I can easily make them mine' but 'His message is my message. We will see that men hear it.'

Whitman is at once crude, disgusting, nauseating, and to be read with acute pain, but also America's poet, indeed America itself, a genius more vital than the equally immortal Pound, and a father one has to love. Let us read this Oedipal fragment just a touch more closely. Its subject is hardly Whitman at all, but rather the United States in 1909, viewed as a country that does not acknowledge its self-exiled bard, Ezra Pound, who had taken up residence in London the year before. As a country that needs to be scourged with/by beauty (a conceit perhaps more Sacher-Masoch than Whitman), the United States (or Whitman) becomes a castrated father, even as the passionate Pound assumes the male function of driving the American vitality into the old world. If this seems crude, it is, but the crudity is certainly not Walt Whitman's.

Though he once assured the world that "Whitman goes bail for the nation," Pound seems to have meant that no one could bail out the nation. Many Poundians have quoted as evidence of their hero's esteem of Whitman a bad little poem of 1913:

A Pact
I make a pact with you, Walt Whitman—
I have detested you long enough.
I come to you as a grown child
Who has had a pig-headed father;
I am old enough now to make friends.
It was you that broke the new wood,
Now is a time for carving.
We have one sap and one root—
Let there be commerce between us.

"Truce," the original word in the first line, is more accurate than "pact," because truly there was a failure in commerce between Whitman and Pound. Whether Pound remembered that Whitman's father was a carpenter, and that Whitman himself had worked, with his father, at the trade, is beyond surmise. The root, as Pound perhaps knew, was Emerson. It is no accident that Whitman and Emerson return to Pound together in *The Pisan Cantos*, with Whitman central in the eighty-second and Emerson in the eighty-third of *The Cantos*. Emerson, I think, returns in his own trope of self-identification, the Transparent Eyeball, yet in Pound's voice, since Emerson was at most

Pound's American grandfather. But Whitman returns in Whitman's own voice, and even in his own image of voice, the "tally," because the obstinate old father's voice remains strong enough to insist upon itself:

> "Fvy! in Tdaenmarck efen dh' beasantz gnow him,"
>> meaning Whitman, exotic, still suspect
> four miles from Camden
>> "O troubled reflection
>> "O Throat, O throbbing heart"
> How drawn, O GEA TERRA,
>> what draws as thou drawest
>>> till one sink into thee by an arm's width
>> embracing thee. Drawest,
>>> truly thou drawest.
> Wisdom lies next thee,
>> simply, past metaphor.
> Where I lie let the thyme rise
>
> . . . .
>
>> fluid XΘONOΣ, strong as the undertow
>> of the wave receding
> but that a man should live in that further terror, and live
> the loneliness of death came upon me
>> (at 3 P.M., for an instant)   δακρύων
>>   ἐντεῦθεν
>
> three solemn half notes
>> their white downy chests black-rimmed
> on the middle wire
>> periplum

Pound begins by recalling his German teacher at the University of Pennsylvania, forty years before, one Richard Henry Riethmuller, author of *Walt Whitman and the Germans*, an identification I owe to Roy Harvey Pearce. Riethmuller (Pound got the spelling wrong) had contrasted Whitman's fame in the professor's native Denmark to the bard's supposed obscurity in the America of 1905, a contrast that leads Pound to a recall of Whitman's "Out of the Cradle Endlessly Rocking." Whitman's poem is an elegy for the poetic self so powerful that any other poet ought to be wary of invoking so great a hymn of poetic incarnation and disincarnation. Whitman's "O troubled reflection in the sea!/O throat! O throbbing heart!" is revised by Pound into "O troubled reflection/O throat, O throbbing heart," with "in the sea" omitted. These are the last two lines of the penultimate stanza of the song of the bird lamenting his lost mate:

> *O darkness! O in vain!*
> *O I am very sick and sorrowful.*
> *O brown halo in the sky near the moon, drooping upon the sea!*
> *O troubled reflection in the sea!*
> *O throat! O throbbing heart!*
> *And I singing uselessly, uselessly all the night.*

Canto 82 rather movingly has shown the incarcerated poet studying the nostalgias of his early literary life, while meditating upon the unrighteousness of all wars. A vision of the earth now comes to him, in response to his partly repressed recall of Whitman's vision of the sea. Marrying the earth is Pound's counterpart to Whitman's marrying the sea, both in "Out of the Cradle Endlessly Rocking" and in "When Lilacs Last in the Dooryard Bloom'd," and both brides are at once death and the mother. "Where I lie let the thyme rise," perhaps repeating William Blake's similar grand pun on "thyme" and "time," is a profound acceptance of the reality principle, with no more idealization of a timeless order. Whitman returns from the dead even more strongly in the closing lines of Canto 82, where Pound lies down in a fluid time "strong as the undertow/of the wave receding," which invokes another great elegiac triumph of Whitman's, "As I Ebb'd with the Ocean of Life." The two song-birds of "Out of the Cradle," with Whitman their brother making a third, utter "three solemn half notes" even as the loneliness of death came, for an instant, upon Whitman's son, Pound. Most powerful, to me, is Pound's recall of Whitman's great image of voice, the tally, from "Lilacs," "Song of Myself," and other contexts in the poet of night, death, the mother, and the sea. In Whitman, the tally counts up the poet's songs as so many wounds, so many auto-erotic gratifications that yet, somehow, do not exclude otherness. Pound, marrying the earth, realizes his terrible solitude: "man, earth: two halves of the tally/but I will come out of this knowing no one/either they me."

Kenner is able to read this as commerce between Whitman and Pound, and insists that "the resources in the Canto are Pound's, as are those of Canto 1." But Homer, ultimate ancestor in Canto 1, was safely distant. Whitman is very close in Canto 82, and the resources are clearly his. Pound does better at converting Emerson to his own purposes, a canto later, than he is able to do with Whitman here. Would the following judgment seem valid to a fully informed and dispassionate reader?

Pound's faults are superficial, he does convey an image of his time, he has written histoire morale, as Montaigne wrote the history of his epoch. You can learn more of 20th-century America from Pound than from any of the writers who either refrained from perceiving, or limited their record to what they had been taught to consider suitable literary expression. The only way to enjoy Pound thoroughly is to concentrate on his fundamental meaning.

This is Pound on Whitman from the *ABC of Reading*, with Pound substituted for Whitman, and the 20th for the 19th century. Pound was half right about Whitman; Whitman does teach us his country in his century, but his form and his content are not so split as Pound says, and his fundamental meaning resides in nuance, beautifully shaped in figurative language. Pound's faults are not superficial, and absolutely nothing about our country in this century can be learned from him. He conveys an image only of himself, and the only way to enjoy him is not to seek a fundamental meaning that is not there, but to take his drafts and fragments one by one, shattered crystals, but crystalline nevertheless. He had brought the great ball of crystal, of poetic tradition, but it proved too heavy for him to lift.

HUGH KENNER

Mauberley

Firmness,
Not the full smile,
His art, but an art
In profile.

With the partial exception of the *Cathay* sequence, the *Personae* volume up to page 183 may be said to be implicit in *The Cantos*. The early poems are deficient in finality; they supplement and correct one another; they stand up individually as renderings of moods, but not as manifestations of mature self-knowledge; they try out poses. They are leading their author somewhere; the reader may be excused if his interests are not wholly engaged, if he finds himself separating the technique from the value of the presented state. . . .

The volume ends, however, with two great self-justifying poems. *Homage to Sextus Propertius* and *Hugh Selwyn Mauberley* would, had not a single Canto been finished, dispel any doubt of Pound's being a major poet.

It will be convenient to shorten our discussion by referring the reader to Dr. Leavis's tributes to *Mauberley* in *New Bearings in English Poetry*. That the poem moves him as it does, and that he registers his admiration so adequately and with such economical power of inciting others to comprehension, may, considering the intrinsic resistance of the Bloomsbury-Cambridge milieu to all but certain types of subtly-discriminated moral fervors, be taken as some gauge of the emotional weight, the momentum of essential seriousness, massed in these seventeen pages of disrupted quatrains.

Yet the reader will infer correctly from this way of describing Dr. Leavis's dealings with *Mauberley* that the highly selective vision of that honest

From *The Poetry of Ezra Pound*. © 1951 by Hugh Kenner. New Directions, 1951.

and irascible critic has screened out certain essential elements. Pound emerges from his account as a man of one poem; the early work is uninteresting, *The Cantos* a monument of elegant dilettantism. In *Mauberley*, for a few pages, under urgent and unhappily transient personal pressures, he found himself with precision and sincerity. Dr. Leavis's view of Pound's career is introduced here as representative of the most respectable critical thought. Setting aside journalistic opportunism of the kind that has no real concern for letters, attacks on Pound are generally attacks on *The Cantos*. The isolated success of *Mauberley* is generally conceded. The dispraise even of Mr. Winters is qualified somewhat at this point.

Mauberley, that is, is a tricky poem. It is difficult for men of a certain training not to misread it subtly, to select from its elements certain strings that reverberate to an Eliotic tuning fork. A taste for contemporary poetry that has shaped itself almost entirely on Mr. Eliot's resonant introspections has no difficulty in catching what it has come to regard as the sole note of contemporary poetic sincerity in:

> For three years, out of key with his time,
> He strove to resuscitate the dead art
> Of poetry: to maintain 'the sublime'
> In the old senses. Wrong from the start—

It is easy to see how this chimes with such passages as:

> So here I am, in the middle way, having had
>   twenty years—
> Twenty years largely wasted, the years of *l'entre deux
>   guerres*—
> Trying to learn to use words, and every attempt
> Is a wholly new start, and a different kind of failure
> Because one has only learnt to get the better of words
> For the thing one no longer has to say, or the way in which
> One is no longer disposed to say it.
>
>   *(East Coker, 5)*

It may briefly be said that there has been a muddle about "impersonality." Mr. Eliot's impersonality is Augustinian; a dispassionate contemplation of the self which permits without romantic impurities a poetic corpus of metamorphosed personae. Pound's impersonality is Flaubertian: an effacement of the personal accidents of the perceiving medium in the interests of accurate registration of *moeurs contemporaines*. As we have said, the adoption of various personae is for such an artist merely a means to ultimate depersonalization, ancillary and not substantial to his major work. J. Alfred Pruf-rock is not Mr. Eliot, but he speaks with Mr. Eliot's voice and bears intricate analogical relations with the later Eliot persona who is the speaker of *Four Quartets*. Hugh Selwyn Mauberley, on the other hand, does not speak with Mr. Pound's voice, and is more antithetically than intimately related to the poet of *The Cantos*. It would be misleading to say that he is a portion of Mr. Pound's self whom Mr. Pound is externalizing in order to get rid of him (like Stephen Dedalus); it would be a more accurate exaggeration to say that he is a parody of Pound the poet with whom Mr. Pound is anxious not to be confounded.

The sort of critic we have been mentioning, the one who finds the note of sincerity in *Mauberley* as nowhere else in Pound, pays unconscious tribute to the accuracy with which Pound, in quest of devices for articulating this quasi-Prufrockian figure, has echoed the intonations and gestures of a char-acteristic Eliot poem. (The primary echo is as a matter of fact with Corbière.) Such a critic has been known to quote in confirmation of his view of Pound Mr. Eliot's remark, "I am sure of *Mauberley*, whatever else I am sure of." Mr. Eliot has not, however, the perceptive limitations of his disciples; in the same essay he insists that the entire *Personae* collection is to be read as a process of exploration leading up to *The Cantos*, "which are wholly himself."

It may be helpful to remark that Joyce is in this respect like Pound, an artist of the Flaubertian kind; his Stephen Dedalus is a parody of himself, not an artist but an aesthete, at length mercilessly ridiculed in *Finnegans Wake*. The analogy is reasonably exact; Stephen is partly an aspect of Joyce himself which Joyce is trying to purify; his horror of bourgeois civilization echoes Joyce's much as *Mauberley's* "sense of graduations,"

> Quite out of place amid
> Resistance of current exacerbations,

echoes Pound's. But Joyce refrains from unambiguous sympathy with Ste-phen's desire for Shelleyan sunward flight; he involves Stephen in an Icarian fall into the sea of matter just as Pound reduces Mauberley to

> Nothing, in brief, but maudlin confession,
> Irresponse to human aggression,
> Amid the precipitation, down-float
> Of insubstantial manna,
> Lifting the faint susurrus
> Of his subjective hosannah.

This cannot be taken as an account of the poet of *The Cantos* any more than Stephen's fastidious shrinking away from common noises can be regarded as characteristic of the author of *Ulysses*. Both men channelled their disgust into patient sifting of immense sottisiers; Pound has been, significantly, almost alone in perceiving the continuity between *Ulysses* and *Bouvard et Pécuchet*. In *Ulysses* Stephen is the focus of spectacular technical sonorities, sympathized with and rejected; the same is true of the Lotus-eaters in *The Cantos*.

It may be remarked that the critic who thinks of *Mauberley* as Pound's one successful poem commonly sees Stephen Dedalus as the hero of *Ulysses*, perceives in both figures elements of failure, and takes as dim a view of Joyce as of the author of *The Cantos*.

Against what may be mistaken for the drift of the above paragraphs, it should be insisted that the process of creating and disowning Hugh Selwyn Mauberley had not the personal importance for Pound that the purgation of the Dedalian aspects of himself had for Joyce. No such trauma was involved in the Idaho poet's flight from America as in the Irish novelist's disentanglement from Church and Motherland. It is not true, on the other hand, to say that Joyce could do nothing until he had focused and gotten rid of Stephen: the bulk of *Dubliners* was written in 1904, in Joyce's twenty-third year. But even when we have balanced *Dubliners* with the social observations in *Lustra*, and *Chamber Music* with the first volume of *Personae*, the excernment of Stephen Dedalus remains of crucial importance to Joyce's future achievement in a way that the writing of *Mauberley* probably was not to Pound. It was probably necessary that he focus in some such oblique way the tension between popular demands and his earlier poetic activities before embarking on *The Cantos;* but the process need not be thought to have coincided with a spiritual crisis from which, as it suits the critic, he emerged either crippled or annealed.

Mauberley does not mark in that way a hurt awakening from aesthetic playgrounds into thin cruel daylight. Its postures and conflicts continue, as we have indicated, those of *Propertius*, the *robustezza* of which could scarcely be confounded with hurt awakening. If a decisive point of maturation must be found, it is to be found in *Propertius*, the earlier poem, it is not always remembered, by some three years. It is easy, for that matter, to over-estimate the reorientation there involved *vis-à-vis* the earlier work. There need be nothing traumatic about supervening maturity; the bulk of *Personae* is the work of a young man in his twenties. The earliest *Personae*, dated 1908, belong therefore to *aetat.* 23. He published "The Seafarer" translation at 27; *Lustra* at 30, *Cathay* at 31. The next year saw *Propertius* and the first drafts of the earliest *Cantos*. He published *Mauberley* at 35. *The Pisan Cantos* are the work of a man of 60. Emotional maturation may be seen going on in the

Lustra volume; and there is enough difference between the monolinear intensity of "The Needle":

> Come, or the stellar tide will slip away,
> Eastward avoid the hour of its decline,
> Now! for the needle trembles in my soul!

and the calm detached emotion of "Gentildonna" (*Lustra*, 1915):

> She passed and left no quiver in the veins, who now
> Moving among the trees, and clinging
>   in the air she severed,
> Fanning the grass she walked on then, endures:
> Grey olive leaves beneath a rain-cold sky.

to preclude any suggestion of a cataclysmic reorientation a few years later.

These pages will have performed their function if they can arm the reader against the too-easy supposition that Pound found in *Mauberley* an eloquence of disillusion. The subtle balance of diverse strong emotions in that poem will be utterly destroyed by too ready a response to one or two elements. We may now look, belatedly, at the text.

The subtitle ("Life and Contacts") and the title-page footnote (". . . distinctly a farewell to London") furnish a perspective on the title of the first of the eighteen poems: "E. P. Ode Pour L'Election de son Sepulchre." This is largely Pound's career in London seen through the eyes of uncomprehending but not unsympathetic conservers of the "better tradition": a strenuous but ineffectual angel, his subtleties of passion "wrong from the start," accorded the patronizing excuse of having been born "in a half savage country, out of date," and given to Yankee intensities ("bent resolutely on wringing lilies from the acorn") of an unclubbable sort. The epitaph modulates into grudging admiration for the pertinacity of this dedicated spirit—

> His true Penelope was Flaubert,
> He fished by obstinate isles;
> Observed the elegance of Circe's hair
> Rather than the mottoes on sun-dials.

The first line of this stanza renders with astonishing concision an intricate set of cultural perspectives. Pound's voyages to China, to Tuscany, to Provence, his battles with Polyphemic editors and his dallyings with pre-Raphaelite Sirens, are transformed, as in *The Cantos*, into an Odyssey of discovery and frustration, imposed, for jealous and irrelevant reasons, by the ruler of the seas (a neat fusion of the chaotic state of letters with English mercantile smugness; the "obstinate isles" are both the British Isles and recalcitrant aesthetic objectives.) The irony with which the British mortician of reputations is made to utter unambiguous truths about artistic effort (cf. the "Beauty is difficult" motif of *The Pisan Cantos*) at the same time as he vaunts his national obstinacy and imperception, is carried on with the mention of Flaubert, the "true Penelope" of this voyage. For Pound, Flaubert is the true (= faithful) counterpart, entangling crowds of suitors (superficial "realists") in their own self-deceit while she awaits the dedicated partner whose arm can bend the hard bow of the "mot juste." Flaubert represents the ideal of disciplined self-immolation from which English poetry has been too long estranged, only to be rejoined by apparently circuitous voyaging. For the writer of the epitaph, on the other hand, Flaubert is conceded to be E. P.'s "true" (= equivalent) Penelope only in deprecation: Flaubert being for the English literary mind of the first quarter of the present century a foreign, feminine, rather comically earnest indulger in quite un-British preciosity; "wrong from the start," surrounded by mistaken admirers, and very possibly a whore; a suitable Penelope for this energetic American. England was at that time preparing to burn and ban *Ulysses* exactly as France had sixty years before subjected *Madame Bovary* to juridical process; it was the complaint of the tribunal against Flaubert that he had spent pains on the elegance of his Circe's hair that might better have been diverted to honester causes.

The implications of line after line, irony upon irony, might be expanded in this way; the epitaph concludes with a superbly categorical dismissal of this *impetuus juventus* from the cadres of responsible literary position:

> Unaffected by "the march of events,"
> He passed from men's memory in *l'an trentiesme*
> *De son eage;* the case presents
> No adjunct to the Muse's diadem.

The echo of Villon is of course the crowning irony. *His* passage from the memory of his contemporaries has if anything augmented his place in the history of poetry.

As soon as we see that this epitaph is not (except at the level at which it transposes Corbière) being written by Pound, the entire sequence falls into focus. The eleven succeeding poems (2–12) present an ideogrammic survey of the cultural state of post-war England: of the culture which we have just heard pronouncing upon the futility of Pound's effort to "resuscitate the dead art of poetry." The artist who was "unaffected by the march of events" offers his version of this criterion:

> The age demanded an image
> Of its accelerated grimace;

the third poem, with its audacious closing counterpoint from Pindar's *Second Olympic*, generalizes with a more austere bitterness:

> All things are a flowing,
> Sage Heracleitus says;
> But a tawdry cheapness
> Shall outlast our days.

Poems 4 and 5 are similarly paired. Poem 4 surveys with compassion the moral dilemmas of the war:

> These fought in any case,
> and some believing,
>> pro domo, in any case . . .

poises sacrifice against domestic cheapness:

> walked eye-deep in hell
> believing in old men's lies, then unbelieving
> came home, home to a lie,
> home to many deceits,
> home to old lies and new infamy;
> usury age-old and age-thick
> and liars in public places.

and closes with a quick evocation of the pullulating new artistic soil, entrapping the artist in an opportunity for defined and significant passions that all but swamp his Flaubertian criteria:

> frankness as never before,
> disillusions as never told in the old days,
> hysterias, trench confessions,
> laughter out of dead bellies.

Poem 5 intensifies the antithesis between sacrifice and gain:

> Charm, smiling at the good mouth,
> Quick eyes gone under earth's lid,
>
> For two gross of broken statues,
> For a few thousand battered books.

The cultural heritage has been reduced to the status of a junkman's inventory by the conservators of tradition mobilized behind the epitaph of poem 1; the superimposed tension of the apparent incommensurability, at best, of human lives and civilized achievements brings the sequence to a preliminary climax that prepares for the change of the next six sections into a retrospective key.

"Yeux Glauques" poises the pre-Raphaelite purity,

> Thin like brook water,
> With a vacant gaze

against the bustle of Gladstone and Buchanan (whose attack on "The Fleshly School of Poetry" was answered by Rossetti and Swinburne). The painted woman of the poem contains in her "questing and passive" gaze the complex qualities of passion, between the poles of Swinburne and Burne-Jones, which the aesthetic movement of the nineteenth century mobilized against a world in which "The English Rubaiyat was still-born." The picturesque reminiscences of the nineties in the next poem intensify the personal tragedies of the inheritors of that movement; "Dowson found harlots cheaper than hotels." This struggle and rebuttal is, we see, still being carried on; a new dimension of tradition and conflict is added to the efforts of the epitaphed E. P. of the first poem. The success of official literary history in discrediting the vitality of the century of Rossetti, Swinburne, and Fitzgerald and turning it instead into the century of Ruskin, Carlyle, and Tennyson is epitomized in the final stanza:

> M. Verog, out of step with the decade,
> Detached from his contemporaries,
> Neglected by the young,
> Because of these reveries.

M. Verog, "author of *The Dorian Mood*," is a pseudonym for Victor Plarr, who appears in Canto 74 "talking of mathematics."

The next three poems are vignettes of three contrasting literary careers. "Brennbaum" (? Max Beerbohm) embodies what passes for the cult of "style":

> The stiffness from spats to collar
> Never relaxing into grace.

This style is neo-classical, not that of the leaping arch; Brennbaum's motive is simply to prepare a face to meet the faces that he meets; such emotional intensity as he knows is not only repressed almost to imperceptibility, its dynamic is private, alien, and accidental to the traditions of Latin Europe: "The heavy memories of Horeb, Sinai, and the forty years."

Mr. Nixon, exhibit number two, is the successful public man of letters
(? Arnold Bennett). The forced rhymes (reviewer/you are) enact his hearty
grimaces; his drawled climactic maxim,

> as for literature
> It gives no man a sinecure,

unites the pretentious popular philosophy of a Wells, a Shaw, a Bennett
with the smug generalizations of commercial success and the hard-boiled
saws of *Poor Richard's Almanac*.

> 'And give up verse, my boy,
> 'There's nothing in it.'

The third exhibit is the genuine stylist in hiding, an anti-climactic
redaction of the Lake Isle of Innisfree:

> The haven from sophistications and contentions
> Leaks through its thatch;
> He offers succulent cooking;
> The door has a creaking latch.

These are not *poèmes à clef*; but the post-war fortunes of Ford Madox Ford
are entirely apropos. Ford, the collaborator of Conrad and in the decade
pre-war the long enunciator of the Flaubertian gospel in England, on his
discharge from the army retired in disgust to Sussex to raise pigs, and
ultimately, at about the same time as Pound, left England. His detailed
account of the cultural state of post-war London in the first third of *It Was
the Nightingale* can be made to document *Mauberley* line by line. The reviewing
synod hastened to write his epitaph, so effectively that his reputation is only
beginning to quicken a quarter of a century after the publication of his best
work. Pound has never made a secret of his respect for Ford, and Ford has
testified that Pound alone of the young writers he could claim to have "discovered" about 1908 did not amid his later misfortunes disown and castigate
him. It pleases at least one reader to suppose that it is the spectacle of Ford's
disillusion that animates these three extraordinary stanzas.

Poems 11 and 12 present a postwar contrast to the intricate contempla-
tive passion of "Yeux Glauques." The twelfth closes the survey of the London
situation with an image of grotesquely effusive aristocratic patronage;
"Daphne with her thighs in bark" dwindles to the Lady Valentine in her
stuffed-satin drawing-room, dispensing "well-gowned approbation of literary
effort" in sublime assurance of her vocation for a career of taste and
discrimination:

> Poetry, her border of ideas,
> The edge, uncertain, but a means of blending
> With other strata
> Where the lower and higher have ending;
>
> A hook to catch the Lady Jane's attention,
> A modulation toward the theatre,
> Also, in the case of revolution,
> A possible friend and comforter.

Dr. Johnson's letter to Lord Chesterfield stands as the archtypal repudiation of the vague, vain, and irrelevant claims of patronage; but the street of literary commerce to which Johnson turned has also lost its power to support the artist:

> Beside this thoroughfare
> The sale of half-hose has
> Long since superseded the cultivation
> Of Pierian roses.

The *Envoi* which follows is a consummate ironic climax; against these squalors is asserted the audacious Shakespearean vocation of preserving transient beauty against the tooth of time (cf. the end of the first *Propertius* poem); against the halting and adroitly short-winded quatrains of the "dumb-born book" is set a magnificently sustained melodic line:

> Go, dumb-born book,
> Tell her that sang me once that song of Lawes:
> Hadst thou but song
> As thou hast subjects known,
> Then were there cause in thee that should condone
> Even my faults that heavy upon me lie,
> And build her glories their longevity.

Seventeenth-century music, the union of poetry with song, immortal beauty, vocalic melody, treasure shed on the air, transcend for a single page the fogs and squabbles of the preceding sections in a poem that ironically yearns for the freedom and power which it displays in every turn of phrase, in triumphant vindication of those years of fishing by obstinate isles. The poet who was buried in the first section amid such deprecation rises a Phoenix to confront his immolators, asserting the survival of at least this song

When our two dusts with Waller's shall be laid,
Siftings on siftings in oblivion,
Till change hath broken down
All things save Beauty alone.

There follows a five-part coda in which the Mauberley *persona* comes to the fore; gathering up the motifs of the earlier sections, the enigmatic stanzas mount from intensity to intensity to chronicle the death of the Jamesian hero who might have been Pound. Part two is practically a précis of the flirtation with passionate illusion of Lambert Strether in *The Ambassadors*. "Of course I moved among miracles," said Strether. "It was all phantasmagoric." The third part contains the essential action; having postulated Mauberley's "fundamental passion":

This urge to convey the relation
Of eye-lid and cheek-bone
By verbal manifestations;

To present the series
Of curious heads in medallion,

and implied a context of opportunities missed—

Which anaesthesis, noted a year late,
And weighed, revealed his great affect,
(Orchid), mandate
Of eros, a retrospect.

—Pound particularizes on the Propertian conflict between the aesthetic martyr and the demands of the age.

Contemplation is weighed against Shavian strenuousness:

The flow of porcelain
Brought no reforming sense
To his perception
Of the social inconsequence.

Thus if her colour
Came against his gaze,
Tempered as if
It were through a perfect glaze

He made no immediate application
Of this to relation of the state
To the individual, the month was more temperate
Because this beauty had been.

In Canto 13 Confucius provides a cross-light:

> And Kung raised his cane against Yuan Jang,
>   Yuan Jang being his elder,
> For Yuan Jang sat by the roadside pretending to
>   be receiving wisdom.
> And Kung said
>   'You old fool, come out of it,
> Get up and do something useful.'

The serious artist does not "pretend to be receiving wisdom"; we have heard Pound dilating on his quasi-automatic social functions. It is the essence of the artist's cruel dilemma that his just reaction against politicians' and journalists' canons of usefulness drives him so perilously close to

> an Olympian *apathein*
> In the presence of selected perceptions.

The descent into this Nirvana of the fastidious moth with the preciously-cadenced name is chronicled with elaborate subtlety. The validity of his perceptions is played off against "neo-Nietzschean clatter"; but meanwhile the directness of the opening images, the red-beaked steeds, the glow of abstractions: "isolation," "examination," "elimination," "consternation," "undulation," "concentration." The tone shifts from the sympathetic to the clinical:

> Invitation, mere invitation to perceptivity
> Gradually led him to isolation
> Which these presents place
> Under a more tolerant, perhaps, examination.

The preservation of a critical distance both from the inadequacies of Mauberley and from the irrelevantly active world of Mr. Nixon, Nietzsche, and Bishop Bloughram, with its "discouraging doctrine of chances," the realization of an impersonality that extracts strength from both of the anti-thetical cadres of the first twelve poems, is the major achievement of these final pages. Mauberley's disappearance into his dream-world is related without approbation and without scorn:

> A pale gold, in the aforesaid pattern,
> The unexpected palms
> Destroying, certainly, the artist's urge,
> Left him delighted with the imaginary
> Audition of the phantasmal sea-surge,

and we are warned by commas in the next stanza against adopting too readily
the standpoint of pontifical criticism:

> Incapable of the least utterance or composition,
> Emendation, conservation of the 'better tradition',
> Refinement of medium, elimination of superfluities,
> August attraction or concentration.

That "better tradition" interjects the accent of a Buchanan or an Edmund
Gosse; the other canons are Flaubertian. Mauberley is not simply a failure
by Mr. Nixon's standards of success, he is a failure *tout court*; he is the man
to whom that initial epitaph might with justice be applied; the man for whom
the writer of the epitaph has mistaken "E. P." It is the focusing of this that
guarantees the closing irony:

> Ultimate affronts to
> Human redundancies;
>
> Non-esteem of self-styled 'his betters'
> Leading, as he well knew,
> To his final
> Exclusion from the world of letters.

The irrelevancy of the canons of "the world of letters," for once right but
from utterly wrong reasons, very efficient in guillotining the already defunct,
could not be more subtly indicated.

As a technical marvel this poem cannot be too highly praised. Only
Pound's economical means were sufficiently delicate for the discriminations
he sought to effect: "perhaps" and "we admit" belong to one mode of perception, "the month was more temperate because this beauty had been" to
another, the concessive "certainly" and the clinical "incapable" and "in brief "
to a third. The technique of distinguishing motivations and qualities of
insight solely by scrupulous groupings of notes on the connotative or etymological keyboard has never been brought to greater refinement. One cannot
think of another poet who could have brought it off.

The sequence is refocused by a vignette of hedonistic drift protracting
the coral island imagery that had troubled Mauberley's reverie, ending with
an epitaph scrawled on an oar—

> 'I was
> And I no more exist;
> Here drifted
> An hedonist'

—pathetic echo of the elaborate opening "Ode Pour L'Election de son Se-pulchre." The final "Medallion," to be balanced against the "Envoi" of the first part, recurs in witty disenchantment to the singing lady. Neither the Envoi's passion:

> Tell her that sheds
> Such treasure on the air,
> Recking naught else but that her graces give
> Life to the moment

nor Mauberley's "porcelain reverie":

> Thus if her colour
> Came against his gaze,
> Tempered as if
> It were through a perfect glaze

is denied by the paradoxical dispassion of the final picture:

> Luini in porcelain!
> The grand piano
> Utters a profane
> Protest with her clear soprano.

But the tone is "objective" in a way that detaches the "Medallion" from the claims of the various worlds of perception projected in earlier parts of the poem. There are witty echoes of those worlds: the "profane protest" of heavy-fingered clubbably professional letters; an ambrosial Mauberleian dream of braids

> Spun in King Minos' hall
> From metal, or intractable amber;

but the closing stanza is pitched to a key of quasi-scientific meticulousness that delivers with Flaubertian inscrutability a last voiceless verdict of inadequacy on all the human squinting, interpreting, and colouring that has preceded: fact revenging itself on art and artists—

> The face-oval beneath the glaze,
> Bright in its suave bounding-line, as,
> Beneath half-watt rays,
> The eyes turn topaz.

Beauty? Irony? Geometrical and optical fact?

And this last poem yields a final irony. "To present the series / Of curious heads in medallion" was, we remember, Mauberley's ambition, and this sample Medallion in its very scrupulousness exemplifies his sterility. His imagination falls back upon precedents; his visual particularity comes out of an art-gallery and his Venus Anadyomene out of a book. The "true Penelope" of both poets was Flaubert, but Pound's contrasting Envoi moves with authority of another order. Mauberley cringed before the age's demands; he wrote one poem and collapsed. Pound with sardonic compliance presents the age with its desiderated "image" (poems 3–12); then proves he was *right* from the start by offering as indisputable climax the "sculpture of rhyme" and the "sublime in the old sense" which the epitaph-writer had dismissed as a foolish quest. And he adds a sympathetic obituary and epitaph of his own for the *alter ego*.

This thin-line tracing of the action of *Mauberley* is offered with no pretence to fulness. It is possible, as we have seen, to spend a page meditating on a line. The writer professes two objectives in proceeding as above. First, it seemed profitable to trace the "intaglio method" through an entire work, with a detail which will be impossible when we come to *The Cantos*. Secondly, it seemed important to guide the reader towards an apprehension of *Mauberley* in terms that will not falsify his notion of Pound's later or earlier work. The poem has commended itself too readily as a memorable confession of failure to those whom it comforts to decide that Pound has failed. Anyone to whom the above pages are persuasive will perhaps agree that a less obvious perspective augments, if anything, the stature of this astonishing poem.

EVA HESSE

The End of The Cantos

Composed of a palimpsest of ever shorter units of intelligence, fractured quotations and fleeting allusions, many of which become fully comprehensible only when considered in relation to the human tragedy of their author's return to Italy in 1958, Ezra Pound's *Drafts & Fragments of Cantos CX-CXVII* (first published in book form in 1969) were all written in the years 1958 and 1959, directly after the completion of *Thrones*. Despite the heading "Notes for Canto 117 et seq." which appears on the penultimate page above three short fragments discarded from earlier versions of 113 and 116 no reader having a general familiarity with the overall conception of *The Cantos* is likely to be misled into believing that Pound's "forty-year epic" does not end quite irrevocably—and magnificently—with Canto 116.

Where these valedictory cantos—here to be referred to for convenience as the Final Cantos—differ surprisingly from preceding sections of the long poem is in Pound's sudden abandonment of his former habitual reserve about things private in order, it would seem, to seize this one last opportunity to "place on the record" certain of his more intimate thoughts. And as was to be noticed earlier in *The Pisan Cantos*, which also contained a personal note albeit far more restrained, the unfailing sign of the poet's "going private" is his trick of alienating the emotion by switching to a strange language.

The Cantos as a whole are conceived as a poem written from outside of Western civilization, their point of departure being Pound's break with narrow Western thinking and their goal a cultural renewal. Any such break must inevitably lead back to the East, i.e., Asia Minor and the Far East,

Published for the first time in this volume. © 1987 by Eva Hesse.

which throughout the history of European ideas has been envisaged as the antipode to Western colonizing rationality that holds out the promise of a return to beginnings, a rejuvenation of the mind and a broadening of outlook. This approach to Asia, however, has time and again been halted by the stumbling block of Western "logic," which persists in seeing as antagonistic opposites what the Chinese have always realized to be complementary pairs. Pound's own treatment of Plotinus as well as Buddhism and Taoism are, as we intend to show, highly illustrative of the intractability of the problem and of the general inability of Westerners—but for a few notable exceptions among whom the most outstanding is Joseph Needham—to cross this cognitive threshold.

Pound's second break with the idea of civilization, this time not merely with Western civilization, occurs in the Final Cantos, in which he turns instead to nature and nature rites as mankind's most hopeful source of purification and renewal. Thus we see that while the goal of the renewal of the people—in Confucian terms, *hsin min*—remains unchanged, the method adopted to achieve it goes back far beyond Confucius. Renewal is now to be realized not so much under the guidance of neo-Confucian thinking as through invocations and the observance of animistic rites.

Pound is here identifying with Ch'ü Yüan (332–295 B.C.), author of the famous poem *Li Sao*, which though conventionally translated as "Falling into Trouble" is perhaps more accurately rendered as "Separation from Sorrow"; the Chinese characters allow either interpretation, while the context favours the latter. Ch'ü Yüan is the Chinese prototype of a loyal servant of the state. While in the service of Prince Huai of Ch'u State, he drew upon himself the hostility of the ambitious politician Chang I by, among other things, advising the Prince against making war on the neighbouring State of Ch'in. A victim of unending court intrigue, Ch'ü Yüan eventually went into itinerant exile in the Yingtu region, now known as Wuchang, where he stayed for 15 years composing the 187 long verses or distichs of the *Li Sao* as well as certain other elegies later collected in the *Ch'u Tz'u*. Ch'ü Yüan's central theme is the realization of an ideal state. First he tells of his vain search for a just ruler who will listen to his counsels and describes his visions of paradise. Failing to find such a ruler even in paradise, he finally decides to "embrace a stone" and "repair to the home of P'êng Hsien," or in other words to drown himself in the Mi-lo river in emulation of the prehistoric statesman of that name who committed suicide in protest against the iniquities of Chou Hsin, last ruler of the Yin dynasty. In a festival commemorating Ch'ü Yüan's suicide, traditionally held on the fifth day of the fifth moon of the ancient Chinese calendar, the ceremonies include the throwing of rice dumplings wrapped in leaves into the river and the launching of dragon-boats in a symbolic search for the body of Ch'ü Yüan. These ceremonies, which are thought to derive from some far earlier Spring fertility rite, may very possibly be associated in Pound's mind with the Adonis / Tammuz rite and the Eleusinian Mysteries of Asia Minor invoked so often in earlier cantos, for in the preceding line we find a reference to the Kalenda Maya, a Provençal dance measure signifying the ritual union of mankind and nature as in the earlier Greek dithyrambos. But *Li Sao* certainly also exemplifies for Pound a classic case of political sincerity and opposition to unjust war leading to suicide. Nor do we have to look far for the thematic rhyme on suicide which a knowledge of Pound's technique teaches us to expect. It appears right at the beginning of Canto 110 in the reference to the rites of the Na-khi montagnards which Pound had read about in the prolific anthropological writings of the Vienna-born American botanist Joseph F. Rock.

Originally a tribe native to Tibet, the Na-khi migrated southeast to Li-chiang in the present province of Yünnan when the animistic Bön cult was displaced in Tibet by Buddhism. Although over the centuries Bön assimilated some elements of Burmese Nat worship, Chinese Taoism and Tibetan Buddhism, it survived until the first half of the present century as an essentially animistic religion admixed with aboriginal tribal shamanism. The independent Na-khi kingdom lasted until 1723, when the Li-chiang region waas incorporated into the Chinese Empire under Manchu rule. Hitherto regular marriages had been restricted to members of ruling Na-khi families, while the common people practiced free love. The sudden institution of marriages arranged by parents for their children caused untold misery among these simple folk, and many young couples who saw themselves compelled to marry partners they had never seen or perhaps disliked preferred to go up the mountain slopes to commit suicide on some lovely alpine meadow, having been told by the shamans (²dto ¹mba in Canto 101) that by so doing they would be reunited in paradise. Hardly any family was spared the loss of some of its members in these suicide pacts.

It is to such a suicide—this time for love, not a political expiatory self-sacrifice— that Pound alludes in Canto 110/7:

> che paion' si al vent'
> ²Har-²la-¹llü ³k'ö
> of the wind sway,
> The nine fates and the seven,
> and the black tree was born dumb,
> The water is blue and not turquoise
> When the stag drinks at the salt spring
> and sheep come down with the gentian sprout,

can you see with eyes of coral or turquoise
                    on walk with the oak's root?

. . . .

Quercus on Mt Sumeru
             can'st'ou see with the eyes of turquoise?
         heaven   earth
                   in the center
                        is
                     juniper
The purifications
             are snow, rain, artemisia,
             also dew, oak and the juniper

And in thy mind beauty, O Artemis,
             as of mountain lakes in the dawn

The invocation "che paion' si al vent' " means "that she might appear in the
wind"; "^{2}Har-^{2}la-^{1}llü ^{3}k'ö" are Na-khi words (the superscript numerals indicating the tone in which they are to be spoken) meaning literally "wind
sway perform" and referring to a wind rite traditionally performed to pro-
pitiate the spirits of those who have died by suicide without exhaling their
last breath in the presence of relatives. The Na-khi believe that unless this
rite is performed the dead will turn into headless wind demons that bring
hailstorms and disease. In the ^{2}Har-^{2}la-^{1}llü ^{3}k'ö rite a chicken is strangled
and its last breath taken as substitute for that of the suicide, whose spirit
can now be escorted to the realm of his or her ancestors and finally to the
realm of the gods. Also according to Na-khi beliefs a young man has nine
fates and a young girl seven. Seven girls rule the wind and have in their
train all the demons of those who have died by suicide whose spirits have
not been propitiated. The reference to the black tree comes from a suicide
song in the romance "^{2}K'a ^{2}mâ-^{1}gyu-^{3}mi-^{2}gkyi" in which a girl contemplating
suicide approaches a black tree to ask whether she should take her life. But
the tree, having been born without a mouth, or "born dumb" as the song
has it, cannot answer and so the girl returns home. In another suicide song
the girl's boyfriend asks her how it will be with her after death: "If I give
you turquoise and coral eyes, will you again be able to see? If I attach to
you the roots of the pine and the oak, will you again be able to walk? if I
give you silver and gold teeth, will you again be able to laugh?"

The Na-khi say that when the stag drinks at the salt spring, the taste
remains with him and he yearns for more. And in autumn the sheep come
down from the alpine meadows where a species of gentian opens before the

first frost comes and flowers once more after it has disappeared. The sheep remember the taste of the gentian, just as an old man may dimly remember love.

Quercus is the *Quercus semicarpifolia*, an evergreen oak that grows in the foothills of Li-chiang. Ancient groves of oaks mark the place of worship of the Na-khi, to whom the oak represents both heaven and earth. Between heaven and earth is the juniper, the *juniperus religiosa* of the Himalayas, the crown of which holds up the vast sky, while its foot holds down the earth. Standing thus between heaven and earth, the juniper symbolizes divine authority.

Most Na-khi ceremonies are purification rites concerned with snow, rain, dew and various plants and herbs; we shall see later how the almost compulsive theme of purification in the Final Cantos is bound up with Pound's special conception of evil. Mt. Sumeru, the Throne of the Gods mentioned in Canto 110/8—Mt. Meru in the *Tibetan Book of the Dead*—is symbolized for the Na-khi by ^{3}Shi-^{2}lo, more commonly known as Mt. Kailas, the mystic Tibetan mountain of the Bön cult.

While on the private level of understanding the alpine region of Li-chiang is obviously associated with the Italian Tyrol where Pound lived for a time after his return to Italy in 1958, on the philosophical level it stands for the timeless world in which life's basic needs are not eclipsed by civilization's distracting clutter:

> And over Li Chiang the snow range is turquoise
> Rock's world that he saved us for memory
>   a thin trace in high air
>
> (Canto 113/16)

>   white wind, white dew
> Here from the beginning, we have been here
>   from the beginning
> From her breath were the goddesses
> ^{2}La ^{2}mun ^{3}mi
>
> (Canto 112/14)

> The Gods have not returned. They have never left us.
>   They have not returned.
>
> (Canto 113/17)

Artemis, the "Mountain Mother," the Cretan Mistress of the Wilds, the solitary goddess of mountains, woods, meadows, springs, and lakes, with power over all living creatures, the goddess of shapely ankles (KALLIA-

STRAGALOS in Canto 110/10) is, along with Neptune, the presiding deity
of these final cantos. In her reside all those forces of renewal, purification
and propitiation which Pound seeks for both himself and mankind. Greek
mythology, which appropriated her from the Cretan cultural cycle, attributes
to Artemis the power of annually renewing her virginity by a ritual bath.
This would explain why in Canto 110/10 her name is juxtaposed with the
Chinese character *hsin*[1], denoting renewal, which Pound has taken from the
make-it-new inscription on T'ang's bathtub.

If we assume that Pound in his early seventies read or reread Giordano
Bruno, who in Canto 114/21 he places in opposition to Plotinus, the repeated
invocation "And in thy mind beauty, O Artemis" (110/8 and 113/20) further
reveals Artemis as nature incarnate and, at the same time, as the source of
poetic creativity. According to Giordano Bruno the "hero," as he calls him,
meaning the man of exceptional sensibility capable of apprehending the
primary shape of things, is passionately in quest of "divine objects," which
represent in turn to the heroic philosopher truth, to the heroic poet beauty,
and to the heroic statesman order. These objects—platonic ideas or, as Pound
would say, *formae*—are not so much rational and abstract entities existing
on a higher plane of being as traditional Neoplatonic thinking would have
it, but rather modes of seeing which lay hold of man, spiritual forces which
act upon him to endow him with creative power. Bruno illustrates his point
by classical allegory: the "hero's" fate is that of the hunter Actaeon, who set
out to discover Artemis/Diana naked in her pool but "as soon as he sets
eyes on such great beauty was transported beyond himself and himself turned
into a quarry, so that he saw himself metamorphosed into that which he had
sought; and he came to realize that he himself had become the quarry of his
own dogs, i.e., his thoughts, for since he now possessed the quintessence of
the deity in his mind he did not have to pursue it further outside of himself."
Or as Pound observes: the verb is "see," not "walk on" (116/26)

These remarks of Bruno also throw, I think, a significant light on
Pound's statements about *hypostasis* as against *persona* in Cantos 76 and 114/
23. Truth, says Bruno, is thought of as something inaccessible, "as an ab-
straction which not only cannot be conceived but also as something which
cannot be hypostatized, for no one believes it is feasible to look directly into
the sun and to see the ever-shining Apollo in his most extreme and perfect
quintessence of absolute light; yet it is possible to perceive his shadow, Diana,
the world, the universe, nature . . . to see Diana naked, to arrive at the point
where the beautiful form of love that is nature will possess the hunter utterly,
so that through the very eyes which have perceived the shining of divine
beauty . . . he will be metamorphosed into a stag and will be the hunted

instead of the hunter." Ideas in man's mind consequently cannot belong to the individual: the individual is merely the locus where objective reality is apprehended. When we experience difficulty in following the words of a philosopher, a poet, or a statesman of heroic stature, this difficulty, Bruno tells us, is not due to any subjective arbitrariness on the part of the author, but rather to the measure of his objectivity surpassing our normal standards. The "hero" will therefore be subject to a communication gap; his passion transforms him from a normal human being into a creature living in divine loneliness in forests, the caves of mountains, or at the source of the great streams; he is free of the entanglements of thought and sense, all mental barriers disappear for him, so that he, with the vast boundless horizon of nature before him, becomes nothing but a seeing eye; *to see again*, intones Pound (116/26), to see, that is, the goddess who is at the source of the *forma* and "of all numbers, all species, all ideas: she who is the Monas, the true essence at the core of all existence. From that Monas which is the godhead this Monas which is nature, the universe, the world, emanates. In her the godhead perceives and mirrors itself as the sun does in the moon, and this [second] Monas is Diana."

In Canto 114/21 "this moving is from the inward" is Giordano Bruno's assertion of the divinity of matter as *natura naturans* and *natura naturata* requiring no extra-mundane mover; "*o di diversa natura*" is Bruno quoting Albertus Magnus on the heavenly spheres, which in Pound's context takes on the meaning of Bruno's assertion of the relativity of space and movement as well as of the plurality of worlds; "and in these triangular spaces" refers to Bruno's speculation as to the content of the interstitial triangles formed by contiguous spheres. How Pound relates this to Plotinus is treated in another section of this analysis which must here be omitted for reasons of space.

Artemis then is nature, the force of renewal and the prevailing archetype which includes as one of its subdivisions love on the human level. It is on this private level that the nonclassical name "Marcella" appears (in 113/16 along with numerous characterizing allusions throughout the Final Cantos as well as in "Conversations in Courtship," a verse translation made in 1958) in whom students of comparative literature will recognize a parallel to Goethe's Ulrike. Written by Pound at the age of 72/73, the Final Cantos have a genetic element in common with the "Marienbader Elegie," the sole issue from an unconsummated romantic interlude that occurred in Marienbad when Goethe had reached precisely the same age. It is also in this context that we are definitely to understand the reference to the stag and the sheep in Canto 110/7.

It should be noted that Pound's early conception of Artemis/Diana in *Patria Mia*, which still adheres to the stock typology of the Classics while already manifesting an impulse to break family bonds, underwent considerable modification and expansion under the influence of later anthropological studies. The myth of Diana and Actaeon, first treated in Canto 4, becomes in later cantos a vital theme that is functional on various levels, one of which is discernible in Giordano Bruno's philosophical treatment of the myth as the relation between the inspired artist and his divine object, while on another level Artemis is seen anthropologically as the Triple Earth Goddess: the hard, inviolate virgin of Canto 30, the orgiastic nymph of the Ephesian fertility cult, and the witch and sibyl of chthonic provenance. The Artemis trinity is the mother of the living as well as of the dead. In her latter aspect as Goddess of the Gate and female counterpart to Janus, she prevails in the Layamon passage of Canto 91. In these Final Cantos she is to be understood in her total triadic aspect, for only thus can she represent the great theme of Nature incarnate.

Concretely Artemis symbolizes for Pound his second major break, the return to nature. This includes among other things his repudiation of civilization's repressive marriage contracts and family commitments. His views on family life have in fact undergone a series of fluctuations during the course of his long life which run parallel to his changing definitions of order in the field of politics. While in his poem "Commission," written when he was still in his early thirties, he led off with a downright rejection of the bourgeois conception of family, from his early forties to his early seventies he gradually went over to advocating a family concept which commonly passes for Confucianism although Confucius himself had sought, if anything, to democratize family relations—his advice in *Lun yü* 4/18 that children might permissibly chide their parents as long as they do so gently will have sounded ominously subversive in early China. Indeed Confucius can aptly be quoted in favor of anti-authoritarian education; in Canto 13 Pound glosses *Lun yü* 9/22 very nearly as: "Respect a child's faculties/From the moment it inhales the clear air,/But, a man of fifty who knows nothing/Is worthy of no respect."

It was this middle period of Pound's life which marked the first change in his attitude towards the concept of family. In 1913 a bohemian Pound had deplored in his poem "Commission" the fate of "the adolescent who are smothered in family," likening the hideous sight of "three generations of one house gathered together" to "an old tree with shoots,/and with some branches rotted and falling." Towards the end of the 1920s he had begun to take at least a theoretical interest in the upbringing of a second generation, and towards the end of the 1940s we find him still more preoccupied with the aesthetic future of the third. Also as late as *Thrones* (in Cantos 98/99/107/ 108) we see him insistently rocking the theme of pen^3 yeh^4 (a Chinese term meaning the hereditary family vocation) as a covert injunction to the youngest generation of his own family to follow the Loomis-Weston-Pound tradition, which he evidently saw as distinguished by a special sensibility: "Our dynasty came in because of a great sensibility" (85) is not a quotation or paraphrase from the *Shu-ching* but pure Pound. The passage in an inauthentic section of the book from which the elaborate $ling^2$ character, standing for sensibility, has been excerpted, merely records Fa (Wu Wang), first sovereign of the Chou dynasty, reciting a formula to the effect that heaven and earth are as the father and the mother of all creatures, that among all creatures only humans are endowed with reason, and that the man who is of superior sensibility will become the supreme ruler. Pound's resonant opening line does not in fact express the kind of thought to which any Chinese ruler, as far as the records show, ever gave utterance. Wearing the mask of Fa, he is speaking at this particular moment very much for himself. This covert orientation of so many of his pedagogical quotations from the Book of Records (*Shu-ching*) in *Thrones* is overtly paralleled in his prose by the dedication of the 1951 edition of his English versions of the *Ta Hsüeh* and *Chung-yung* to a grandson.

Yet in the Final Cantos—especially 114—he suddenly abandons this patriarchism to take a very hard look at the Western institution of marriage with its concomitant "encroachment of one personality upon another in the sty of the family." An abrupt return to his original refractory mood is signaled by the terse observation "Veritas, by anthesis, from the sea depth" (111/13). This oblique way of informing us that truth resides in full sexual flowering *(anthesis)* is a clear reference to the heterogenesis of the anthomedusa, a marine organism which, during its free-swimming sexual phase of reproduction, is called "Eleutheria," the Greek word for freedom that Pound has already used earlier in this sense in Canto 2. The motif recurs in Canto 29 to illustrate what the poet regards as the two antipodal modes of female existence.

In its asexual, parthenogenetic phase of budding, the anthomedusa will remain as stationary as a tree of coral or attached like seaweed to the bed of the sea, whereas in its sexual phase of anthesis it will swim in the water as freely as algae "fleeing what band of Tritons" (Canto 29). The basic zoological information would seem to derive from Louis Agassiz, while Pound's anthropological interpretation is more reminiscent of Remy de Gourmont.

Two historical concubines, Cunizza da Romano and Pernella, mistress of Count Pitigliano of the House of Orsini, are brought in by Pound to illustrate his point. Pernella, intent on consolidating her hold on her lover and staking claims for her offspring, represents the static mode of female existence, while Cunizza, who transferred her favor from one lover to another without any thought of hanging on either to them or to her possessions— well demonstrated by her manumission of her slaves—stands for the dynamic, "free-swimming" mode. It may be recalled that Dante placed Cunizza, despite her free way of living, in his *terzo cielo*, the third heaven to which he assigned those whose sins are pardoned for the sake of their love. In Canto 29 (1930) the nature of womankind is likened to the hydromedusa's heterogenesis: "Sea weed dried now, and now floated, / mind drifts, weed, slow youth, drifts, / Stretched on the rock, bleached and now floated; / Wein, Weib, TAN AOIDAN / Chiefest of these the second, the female / Is an element, the female / Is a chaos / An octopus / A biological process / and we seek to fulfill . . . TAN AOIDAN, our desire, drift . . . She is submarine, she is an octopus, she is / A biological process."

On the social level this ambivalent nature of womankind, static in the asexual phase when the female acts as the conservatrix of property and social conventions, dynamic in the sexual phase when she acts as the subverter of both, is referred to for a last time in Canto 114/21, 22: "Their dichotomies (feminine) present in heaven and hell. / Tenthrils trailing: caught in rocks under wave. / Gems sunned as mirrors, alternate." It is apparent that, to Pound, the female is capable of alternating between a divine and a diabolical state of mind, which ambivalence makes itself felt to her partner throughout love and marriage. His sympathies at this particular juncture lie with feminine vagrancy. On the cultural rather than the social level we discover this theory reinforced in Canto 114/22 by the introduction of Fu Hsi, the first of China's five legendary rulers. Fu Hsi's emblem is the T-square, symbol of all the arts, and in the Table of Correspondences his reign is governed by the phase of metamorphosis associated with wood, which explains "Governed by wood (the control of) / $mu^{4,5}$. / Another by metal (control of) / Fu Hi, etcetera".

As the founder of Chinese culture, Fu Hsi is associated *a fortiori* with ethics and the institution of marriage, and is traditionally depicted together with his wife, their limbs entwined. Much in line with Pound's ideas about the anthomedusa, Fu Hsi's mother is said to have been impregnated by a wooden peg floating in the water.

As against this, the conservative female mode is contemned for "Pride, jealousy and possessiveness / 3 pains of hell" (113/17), leaving scant doubt about the poet's feelings in 1959 when it was committed to paper. The "pains of hell" all derive, as we see, from the right of private property, which among other things includes a claim to ownership over members of the family as human chattels. Since it is the essential cell on which any society is based, Pound's late reappraisal of the concept of the family unit and, more particularly, of the institution of marriage, led him quite logically back to his lifelong and, as we have shown elsewhere, highly equivocal preoccupation with order and, above all, his search for a new order for human society. The fleeting reference to the "man of Oneida" (114/22), either a paternal uncle on the Loomis side or the founder of Oneida Community himself, which follows in the next canto, invokes a further deep-rooted American tradition, that of way-out social experiment.

It should here be called to mind that during the early and middle nineteenth century the United States was a hotbed of social and sexual experimentation; the many small hippie communities in America today can be better understood when seen in the light of this tradition. At least 178 experimental social communities sprang up in America over the past century, some twelve of which owed their origin to the teachings of Robert Owen and forty to the ideas of Fourier. The number of members of these individual communities ranged between 15 and 900. All sought to rethink the premises which govern society and set up models based on radically revised attitudes towards the concepts of private property and sex. Depending on the teaching of their founders, the main emphasis was placed on economics, sex, or religion. The most successful of these communities was the one commended by Pound, the communistic Oneida Community founded in 1847 by John Humphrey Noyes (of Vermont) in York State. Hence "York State" or "Paris" in 114/23; the parallel with Paris relates autobiographically to the Paris of the years 1921–1923.

In his *History of American Socialisms* (1870) Noyes asserts that the relation of male and female was the first social relation. As such it is at the root of all other social relations. Earlier social experiments had failed because they confined their attention either to the "rectifying of the industrial system" or to a revival of faith, whereas Noyes held that neither religion nor socialism by themselves were sufficient, for in order to change society "the true scheme of redemption begins with reconciliation with God, proceeds first to the restoration of true relations between the sexes, then to a reform of the industrial system, and ends with victory over death . . . The sin-system, the mar iage-system, the work-system and the death-system, are all one and must be abolished together." The human heart, he believed, is capable of loving any number of times and any number of persons: "This is the law of nature, thrust out of sight and condemned by common consent, and yet secretly known to all." The sexual urge is here understood as being necessary to provide the "afflatus," or energy, necessary to decompose the old family unit and to re-assemble its members in the new organization. To achieve this, Noyes institutionalised polygamy in the form of what he called Complex Marriage; the cardinal sin for members of the community was Special Affection either for a sexual partner or for a child born of the Complex Marriage, for Special Affection means the assertion of a claim of individual ownership over a member of the community and "the possessive pronoun *mine* is the same in essence when it relates to persons as when it relates to money or any other property . . . From *I* comes *mine*, and from the I-spirit comes exclusive appropriation of money, women, etc. From *we* comes *ours*, and from the We-spirit comes universal community of interests."

Like the "man of Oneida" who "fought against jealousy" (114/22), Pound is "all for Verkehr without tyranny" (110/7), a line in which he uses quite correctly the German term *Verkehr* for sexual intercourse, characteristically switching to a foreign language as is his wont whenever he wishes to record some intimate thought that readers are not supposed to grasp straight off.

By reducing the danger of conception through the practice of *coitus reservatus*, Noyes was able to place sex on a new communal basis. His most amazing achievement in this connection was perhaps his success in dissociating the idea of sex from that of hell-fire in the minds of his followers, the majority of whom were converted Presbyterian or Congregationalist descendants of New England Puritans. He even held up sexual enjoyment as a sure step towards salvation on earth. Indeed it should not be necessary to die in order to achieve salvation; man should be able to rid himself of sin while still alive. Like Noyes, Pound has also set his sights upon an earthly paradise, a *"paradiso terrestre"* (117 et seq./32), and, as if in spiritual communion with Noyes, mutters under his breath: "As to sin, they invented it—eh?/to implement domination/eh? largely" (113/19), thereby unconsciously endorsing both the early synthesis of Marx and Freud achieved by Wilhelm Reich and the present sociological views of Herbert Marcuse.

These efforts of the early communist communities are extolled yet again in Canto 114/22: "These simple men who have fought against jealousy,/as the man of Oneida./Ownership! Ownership!/There was a thoughtful man named Macleod:/To mitigate ownership." And a few lines later Pound's own family link with Oneida is also recollected: "This is not vanity, to have had good guys in the family/or feminine gaiety—quick on the uptake/'all the same in a hundred years'/'Harve was like that' (the old, cat-head re a question of conduct)." The thought underlying this passage is set forth more directly in the author's early autobiographical essay *Indiscretions* wherein he recounts how an old lady (Sarah Loomis) in Oneida had described to him the Loomis side of the Pound family, which had migrated from Vermont to a place in Oneida County in York State, as "charming people, in fact the 'nicest' people in the County, but horse-thieves, very good horse-thieves, never, I think, brought to book." Again we find a measure of doubt thrown upon the sanctity of private property. Grandma Loomis, "the old cat-head," is likewise partially responsible for Pound's striking out for the rights of the individual vis-à-vis the clan. In *Indiscretions* he further records: "from her presumably I derive my respect for the human being as an individual, my dislike of herding, and of the encroachment of one personality upon another in the sty of the family. I can remember no phrase of hers save that once in a discussion of conduct she said: 'Harve was *like* that.' The statement ended the matter."

Although we have now obtained some insight into Pound's dissenting opinions, at the age of 72/73, on the subject of marriage, the family, and proprietary claims over human beings, the full range of his thinking on these matters only becomes apparent when we consider it in relation to the bio- logical or animistic level on which so many of the lyrical assenting passages in *The Cantos* are placed. We already caught a glimpse of this in the references to the anthomedusa. On closer inspection this is seen to be no mere illus- tration of a point that the poet wishes to make, but to have much wider implications. The very definition of Odysseus, the protagonist of *The Cantos*, as "polymetis" (Cantos 9 and 128) should be understood on the biological level, just as the neo-Plotinian principle of "et omniformis omnis intellectus est" (Cantos 5 and 23) posits the unlimited adaptability of man's mind, or, in other words, his non-specialization. This open-ended principle forms the very basis and justification of the poet's venture in writing *The Cantos*, just as it provided him in his early seventies with whatever hope he still retained for humanity and for his poem.

His special way of seeing things may be traced back to the ideas of Remy de Gourmont, whose extremely odd book, *La Physique de l'amour: Essai sur l'instinct sexuel* (1903) Pound translated under the title *The Natural Philosophy of Love* (New York, 1922). The abiding impression that de Gourmont's book made upon his mind is demonstrated by the fact that, whenever the poetry of *The Cantos* runs dry in the course of some detailed critical analysis of past and present evils, Pound time and again turns back to de Gourmont, who represents to his mind the "artist of the nude" *(Literary Essays)*, an artist who "asserts emotional values" that are exempt from the passing fashions of time. With de Gourmont, Pound sees the creative impulse as a variant of the sexual, as an "assertion of a desire"; it is to this that he refers in Canto 7 as his "Passion to breed a form in shimmer of rain-blur." In earlier years he had felt, he records in the introduction to his translation of de Gourmont's book, "a sensation analogous to the male feeling in copulation" when "driving any new idea into the great passive vulva of London." The remarkable thing is that the analogy of the desire to create with sexual desire and its fulfillment has dominated his self-awareness as a poet to such an extent that it became all but impossible for him to accept mere conceptualization as viable by itself, so that throughout *The Cantos* he repeatedly falls back on de Gourmont's way of thinking for the "nutrition of impulse," to the positive and synthetic as against the critical and analytical functions of the mind, to poetry as against prose, to emotion as against intellect, to the timeless phenomena of nature as against the "timekept" events of history.

De Gourmont's lasting fascination for Pound was due to the Frenchman's endeavor to understand various forms of human cohabitation by analogies drawn from biology, zoology, and sometimes even entomology. His *Physique d'amour* is accordingly an at once stimulating and absurd book, a maverick strayed into the field of the exact sciences whose serious limitations it nevertheless exposes by its own broad philosophical scope and the wide range of discourse and speculation. Nor should it be overlooked that the new school of behaviorism which is currently throwing so much new light on human and animal motivations and mental processes follows quite closely the line first taken by de Gourmont, except of course that it is far less speculative and more scientific.

If we accept de Gourmont's view that thinking is simply a mode of feeling, and that thoughts are of little significance in isolation from the sensibility out of which they arise, it does not appear fanciful for Pound to refer back to his own inborn sensibility rather than to his intellectual faculties whenever, in composing *The Cantos*, he came to a mental impasse. His procedure in this respect must be seen as a break with the rationalist tradition of the French Enlightenment which in other respects set his tone. While his mental quest usually starts out positivistically from selected facts, it invariably ends in an effort to determine the soil or biological culture-medium out of which such facts—historical events, ideas, works of art—have evolved. His essential search is for the underlying *forma, paideuma, virtu* or, structuralistically expressed, *epistème*, of which the formulated abstract statement or argument is but a specific instance at the surface level.

This urge to discover the common multiple behind appearances, the *forma* behind concrete realities, the *paideuma* underlying cultures, is in fact one of the dominant structures of his mental processes which is also manifest in the Final Cantos in his turning away from the phenomenon of civilization and towards nature as the substrate of all human life. On the personal level the structure is to be discerned in his falling back upon his sensibility and his personal understanding of it. "Sensibility" indeed becomes the central concept around which these final cantos revolve. This leads him to the threshold of a great insight which, however, he is never to cross. For if conscious ideas are embedded in a sensibility of greater significance than the ideas themselves, then rational thoughts cannot be more than narrow isolated instances of articulation within the broad spectrum of the inarticulate and the irrational, or at least the rational and the irrational or inarticulate must be seen as *coincidentia oppositorum* of interacting factors. In this sense Pound's rigorous exclusion of the irrational and of insanity from his own sensibility has ultimately limited both his poetic scope and his depth of understanding: It is this act of exclusion which concludes his great vision of universal inclusivity, of the realization of an open form, and of the artistic application of the omniformis principle.

There is a terrible conscious irony in Pound's efforts to realize the all-encompassing principle in the image of the great sphere of light that is Dante's crystal paradise. "I have brought the great ball of crystal; / Who can lift it?" (116/25) he asks, remembering once again the easy upward motion of his early Plotinian poem "Phanopoeia" ("Phanopoeia" having been the title originally intended for *The Cantos*), and continues: "Can you enter the great acorn of light? / But the beauty is not the madness." Leaving aside the sexual image here involved, it is of interest to recall that in the Middle Ages and the Renaissance the ball of crystal was the symbol of madness. "Whereas the man of reason and wisdom perceives only fragmentary and all the more disquieting forms [of knowledge]," writes Michel Foucault in his *Histoire de la Folie*, "the madman carries his in an unbroken sphere: that ball of crystal which is, for all other eyes, empty, is in his own mind densely packed with invisible knowledge; Breughel makes fun of the invalid who tries to penetrate this ball of crystal." Pound seems to be aware of the bitter ambiguity of his—and Dante's—image, even though he jumbles its meaning ("I cannot make it cohere"), in that he consistently associates it with the idea of madness as, for instance, in Canto 76: "the sphere moving, crystal fluid, / none therein carrying rancour / Death, insanity / suicide, degeneration." The irony of these four lines is without parallel.

The germ of Pound's ball-of-crystal image can actually be traced back to his early writings in 1910, where we read: "As to his [man's] consciousness, the consciousness of some seems to rest, or to have its center more properly, in what the Greek pychologists called the *phantastikon*. Their minds are, that is, circumvolved about them like soap-bubbles reflecting sundry patches of the macrocosmos. And with certain others their consciousness is 'germinal' . . . In the Trecento the Tuscans were busy with their *phantastikon* . . . After the Trecento we get Humanism . . . Man is concerned with man and forgets the whole and the flowing" (*Spirit of Romance*). His renunciation of man's concern with man in favor of nature is thus from the outset linked with an attempt to restore "the whole and the flowing," to make things "cohere," to find what Foucault in *Les Mots et les choses* defines as a "syntax which holds words and things together."

To this end Pound resorts to the "germinal" method or, more precisely, to holistic invocations such as the quotation from *Enneads* 4, 3, 20 in which Plotinus is recorded as stating that the body is inside the soul, the soul is inside the Nous (mind), and the Nous is inside the One. Pound's brief "That the body is inside the soul" (118/18), a phrase we have already encountered in Cantos 98 and 99, is followed a few lines later by a double allusion to the all-encompassing sensibility which, for de Gourmont, is the nervous system pure and simple:

> And the bull by the force that is in him—
> not lord of it,
> mastered.
>
> (Canto 113/19)

One part of this allusion recalls de Gourmont's assertion that "what drives the fiery beast at his female is not the lure of a pleasure too swift to be deeply felt, but a force exterior to the individual although included in his organism" (*Natural Philosophy of Love*). The other part emerges later in the same book in the observation: "Every organised animal has a master, its nervous system; and there is, doubtless, no real life save where a nervous system exists. Animals bear this tyranny better than man. Their master asks fewer things. Often it asks only one: to create a being in its own likeness. The animal is sane, that is to say, ruled; man is mad, that is to say, out of rule: he has so many orders to execute at once, that he scarcely does any one well."

De Gourmont's words, "a force exterior to the individual although included in his organism," define what has for Pound's *Cantos* been a universal structure, specifically the nature of the individual's participation in the collective, which goes back to and beyond the transient phenomena of history and civilization to reach the dimension of tragedy, whose immutable roots underlie human existence. It is this tragic, Dionysiac element that Western society, despite its own heavy atmosphere of irrationality and madness, perversely strives to reject, to repress to silence.

DANIEL D. PEARLMAN

The Barb of Time

The reading of Cantos 1 through 30 becomes most satisfying if one can discern some sort of thematic development or progression in them. The natural question is, after all, "What is Pound driving at by means of all these mythical, historical, and autobiographical shenanigans?" The answer seems quite clearly to be that Pound is portraying the decay of Western civilization, both moral and spiritual, from its vital, legendary beginnings in ancient myth to the sapless chaos of modern times. The method of "narration" is not chronological, but resembles rather the stream-of-consciousness technique of a Joyce or a Faulkner—especially the technique of Faulkner in *Absalom, Absalom!*, in which certain images are briefly and obscurely introduced at the beginning, then picked up again and expanded, and later retrieved and elaborated ever more explicitly until there is a final merging of the separate strands into coherence. The method is anticipatory and can be graphically represented as an ever-widening spiral which corresponds to the cyclical order of human memory, where the past, the present, and the future "are not serially, progressively, and uniformly ordered but are always inextricably and dynamically associated and mixed up with each other." The logic of the stream-of-consciousness technique is the subjective logic of images whose sequence "is causally determined by *significant associations* rather than by objective causal connections in the outside world."

Pound's technique involved the initial "planting" of certain myths of passion which are then to be elaborated in various ways through the pro-

From *The Barb of Time: On the Unity of Ezra Pound's* Cantos. © 1969 by Daniel D. Pearlman. Oxford University Press, 1969.

gressive introduction of new materials—mythic, literary, historical, autobiographical. The new materials are intended to have *significant associations*
with the initial myths; flashes of history, for example, reveal the timeless
verity of the truths shadowed forth in myth. Cantos 2–7, as [Christine
Brooke-Rose] points out, "deal with passion myths, modes of love and violence in metamorphosis." In the myths Pound chooses, the theme of metamorphosis is obvious not only in the sense of "bodies changed / To different
forms" by the gods, but also, more generally, in the Platonic sense which
implies the recurrence of eternal "ideas," in different forms according to the
accidental differences of time and place in which they emerge. The idea of
eternal beauty, for example, embodies itself in various goddesses like
Aphrodite and Diana, and in various mortal women like Helen of Troy and
Eleanor of Aquitaine. One has to distinguish, however, between two distinct
kinds of metamorphosis, positive and negative. Positive metamorphosis is
characterized by the persistence within change of the untrammeled manifestations of forces such as Love, Beauty, Wisdom: Tiresias recurs as Confucius, for example, to re-embody Wisdom in its undiluted glory. Negative
metamorphosis is Pound's major technique of irony in *The Cantos*, by which
we see in various historical events or characters a garbled or debased version
of the mythic archetype. To take just one instance, Baldy Bacon in Canto
12 is a debased modern version of many-minded Odysseus and functions as
a commentary on modern times.

I shall limit my focus [here] to Cantos 2 through 5, developing especially
an analysis of Canto 5, the first of Pound's obviously intended "time" cantos.
A distant view of Cantos 2 through 5 discovers a broad alternating movement:
two succeeding pairs of cantos in which the first of each pair presents passion
myths and the second concentrates on the ravages of time. Within the broad
movement of alternation there is also a thematic progression, an intensifi-
cation of the conflict between the irrepressible urgency of the natural passions
and man's misdirected attempts to harness his passional self.

Canto 2 has been treated critically many times, and *The Analyst* (no. 18)
devotes a twenty-five page issue to it alone. It is true, of course, that Canto
2 is Pound's first experiment in the poem with the Ovidian theme of metamorphosis, but it seems to me that much of the scholarship has dwelt upon
matters of secondary importance and that the *formal* significance of the canto,
that is, its relationship to *The Cantos* as a whole, has not received adequate
attention. The canto develops at length only three myths, which appear
successively to the mind's eye of Odysseus-Pound, the voyager, as visions
taking form in the sea.

The first vision is from an episode in the third book of the *Iliad*, in which the Trojan elders, admiring the divine beauty of Helen, nevertheless counsel Priam to ship her back whence she came, "Back among Grecian faces," out of fear of the danger she represents to the city. The second vision, occupying most of the canto, is from the third book of Ovid's *Metamorphoses*. Greedy sailors, in defiance of their captain, Acoetes, attempt to kidnap the young god Dionysus "for a little slave money," unaware of the true identity of the drunken lad. The result is their transformation into fish. Acoetes is recounting the story to King Pentheus in obvious warning to the king to respect the power of god. (In Ovid, not in Pound, Pentheus attempts to repress the rites of Dionysus and is in turn torn limb from limb by the female devotees of the god.)

The third vision, which has no classical source but is paralleled by Pound to the myth of Daphne and Apollo, concerns the transformation of the sea-nymph Ileuthyeria into coral. Her metamorphosis saves her from rape by a "band of tritons," lured to her by her great beauty. It is interesting to note that the attempted "rape" of Dionysus results in the punitive metamorphosis of the greed-inspired, would-be rapists, whereas the attempted rape of the nymph brings down no vindictive metamorphosis upon the would-be rapists; it results rather in the transformation of the nymph herself—into the rich permanence of coral. Where love is the motivating force, the transformation appears to be a positive one. The subordinate myth of Tyro, raped by Poseidon, appears immediately after that of the sea-nymph, as though to affirm the devine nature of natural passion and its ultimate creativity.

All three visions, not only the last two, involve metamorphoses. Helen, feared as a destroyer, brings on the destruction of Troy. Dionysus, object of the sailors' greed, turns the irreverent seamen into fish. The nymph, object of the tritons' passion, is transformed by the divine power of love into a coral-tree, which has the permanence and beauty of a work of art. The initial point I have to make in summarizing these myths is that *fear*, *greed*, and *love*, in that order, are suggested by Pound to be the motivating forces of the respective transformations. The major point I have to make is that these myths are an intentional elaboration, in precise order, of the sequence of possible attitudes of the will to the life-force given in Canto 1 as Sirens-Circe-Aphrodite.

The Sirens are a projection of the will's fear of nature and consequent rejection and repression of her. The Sirens symbolize nature regarded by man as a power for destruction only. And so the myth of the Sirens is metamorphosed by Pound in Canto 2 into the myth of Helen feared by the Trojan elders as a force for destruction. Circe represents the possibility of the will's achieving harmony with nature. Acoetes, in the Dionysus myth, achieves a proper relationship to the god, whereas the sailors' greed provokes them to "rape" the god and they are transformed as Circe transforms lust-ridden men into animals. The sailors' love of money is a perversion of natural love, of reverence for nature, and prefigures the usury theme of *The Cantos*. Lastly, the vision of a beautiful sea goddess in the beauty of a coral formation develops the theme of Aphrodite, the form which love takes when man's will is directed toward the creation of order and beauty out of the welter of nature. The mood of the lines describing the sea-nymph is lyrical and imitates the movement of waves:

> If you will lean over the rock,
> the coral face under wave-tinge,
> Rose-paleness under water-shift,
> Ileuthyeria, fair Dafne of sea-bords.
> [*The Cantos of Ezra Pound*, New York,
> New Directions, 1975]

"Aphrodite we glimpse," says Hugh Kenner, "whenever the work breaks through into lyric, or forms half-congeal in the waves, or eyes pierce the mist, or some flux of events locks into an intelligible pattern."

I think that what these myths suggest, fundamentally, is that nature cannot be repressed or perverted for long without serious consequences being visited upon her violators. One is reminded of Emerson's idea of "Compensation," but more pertinent are the Greek concepts of Hubris and Nemesis. The irreverent call down a Nemesis upon themselves for their Hubris in acting contrary to the will of the gods. The inexorable consequence of a denial of the life-force is not only the outrage perpetrated against others but a spiritual impoverishment, a diminution of being, in the wrong-doer himself. The punishment is expressed trenchantly in the fate of the "obstructors of knowledge" in Canto 14, where Episcopus is shown "waving a condom full of black-beetles."

Perhaps the profoundest anticipation of Phase Two of *The Cantos* is discoverable in these concepts of Hubris and Nemesis. It is well enough known that Confucianism is the philosophical underpinning of the *The Cantos* as a whole, but Confuciansim is itself based on the older Chinese myth of the Yang and Yin. The Confucian document *Li Ki*, or *Book of Rites*, a portion of which Pound translates in Canto 52 as introduction to the Chinese history cantos, is thoroughly permeated with the Yin-Yang philosophy. The Greek concept of Hubris and Nemesis finds its Chinese equivalent in the ethical implications of Yin-Yang thought. Professor Yu-Lan states [in his *Short History of Chinese Philosophy*] that

> *yang* originally meant . . . sunshine and light; . . . *yin* meant . . .
> shadow or darkness. In later development, the *Yang* and *Yin* came
> to be regarded as two cosmic principles or forces, respectively
> representing masculinity, activity . . . for the *Yang*, and femi-
> ninity, passivity . . . for the *Yin*.

Everything in the universe arises from the interaction of these two cosmic principles, and if either is repressed, "then there are earthquakes." When violence is done to nature, nature reacts violently in reprisal. In Chinese thought, a kind of poetic justice inheres in the universe, to which the Greek Nemesis corresponds. The myths Pound employs in *The Cantos*, then, seem to have the further function of revealing the *moral* nature of things, intuited by the archaic consciousness but more annd more to be ignored, forgotten, and repressed as Western civilization advances, rudderless, into chaos.

Canto 3 is the first portrait in the poem of the "drear waste" of Western history. Two images of the baffled will, locked out of "home," are developed at length. In an autobiographical passage at the beginning, Pound describes himself as the penniless young poet he was in 1908, sitting on the steps of the gondola platform beside the Venetian customshouse (he lived nearby in a room in San Trovaso). He portrays himself in ironic contrast to Browning, who in the third Canto of *Sordello* sits on Venetian palace steps in a much more romantic setting. Pound stresses his unromantic inability to afford a gondola, apparently the one that still crosses the Grand Canal to St. Mark's Square: to reach San Marco by foot from the Dogana is, of course, possible, but would require a rather long roundabout walk. If "the gondolas cost too much, that year," the poet may not simply be saying that he couldn't afford one, but that the price was in any case unjust. He is economically frustrated from freely moving about the city he loves, the city which is depicted in Canto 17 as a type of the earthly paradise. In contrast to his present circumstances, the poet, looking across the Grand Canal, has a vision of the timeless beauty of Tuscany, of the gods floating "in the azure air" in the unspoiled time before time began, "back before dew was shed." The theme of time is thus beginning to be explored, although it will not become explicit until Canto 5.

We see another type of the baffled will in the Cid, an Odyssean hero who is literally exiled from home. One strongly suspects a subject-rhyme, an intended comparison and contrast, between the young Pound and El Cid. Unjustly deprived of home, money, possessions, El Cid needs "pay for his menie" to break "his way to Valencia." Rather than passively sitting on steps, however, the Cid is shown as resourcefully acting to relieve his distress by tricking the money-lenders Raquel and Vidas into provisioning himself and his entourage so that he may gain the means to improve his condition. Perhaps Pound is intentionally contrasting the will of modern Western man, stymied by economic injustice, with the creative will of the European Middle Ages, which did not allow a perverse economic system to frustrate its creativity. The Cid is an heroic model for modern man to follow.

The cultural decay intervening between the Middle Ages and modern times strikes us in a few brief flashes at the end of the canto. What happened to the constructive will of the Middle Ages before it became baffled in modern times is evidently its perversion to destructive ends: "Ignez da Castro murdered" introduces the Renaissance theme which is to gather resonance in the cantos to come. The Renaissance, for Pound, is generally a time of violent disorder and decay in the spheres of religion, morality, politics, and art. The treacherous political murder of beautiful Ignez de Castro, described in Camoëns's *Lusiads*, reappears in Canto 30. The decay of the Renaissance is most powerfully suggested in the final line of the canto, "Silk tatters, 'Nec Spe Nec Metu,' " in which the stoic motto of the Este family, "With neither hope nor fear," is contrasted with the decay that supervened when the Estes fell away from this noble precept. The decay of the Estes is one of the major historical subjects treated in the first thirty cantos.

In the first thirty cantos, the theme of man exiled from the city that he loves, of natural feeling thwarted by social tyranny, whether political or economic, reaches climactic development in Pound's lengthy treatment of the rise and fall of Venice. This "city" theme, presented in a muted and undramatic way at the beginning of Canto 3, is introduced in Cantos 4 and 5 with an ominous suggestiveness. The beginning of Canto 4 parallels that of Canto 3. The narrator in Canto 4 again looks at a city—now the smoking ruins of Troy—and contrasts it with his paradisal vision of a "Choros nympharum," a vision of Dionysian ecstasies. It is obvious that something has gone wrong, and the myths of violent passion that follow serve to "explain" what has gone wrong. In these myths, the male will is seen as incapable of controlling sexual passion, and the result is tragic violence for the innocent and guilty alike. The muted theme of ideal harmony of the will with nature is expressed in allusions to Catullus's epithalamion praising the bride Aurunculeia, "Hymen, Io Hymenaee!" But the theme of disharmony emerges pointedly in Pound's rendering of "Fu-Fu" ("Wind Song," or "Ode to the Wind"), which he found in the Fenollosa manuscripts.

> And So-Gioku, saying:
> "This wind, sire, is the king's wind,
>   This wind is wind of the palace,"
>   . . . .

> And Ran-ti, opening his collar:
> "This wind roars in the earth's bag,
>   it lays the water with rushes;
> No wind is the king's wind."

The relation of the will to the passions, or of the ruler to his subjects, is in dispute in these lines. The irreverent delusion that a man can have absolute sway over the forces of nature is what Ran-ti attempts to puncture.

The theme expressed by Ran-ti, and the materials with which it combines in the opening lines of the next stanza, serve as a kind of bridge giving direct access to Canto 5. This transitional passage is worth close examination, for a proper explanation of the lines will clarify the time-theme of the following canto:

> The camel drivers sit in the turn of the stairs,
>   Look down on Ecbatan of plotted streets,
> "Danaë! Danaë!
>   What wind is the king's?"

The myth of Danaë is treated less cryptically fourteen lines later, where it is once again associated with the city of Ecbatan: "Ecbatan, upon the gilded tower in Ecbatan/Lay the god's bride, lay ever, waiting the golden rain." Danaë was imprisoned in a brazen tower by her father Acrisius, King of Argos, who feared an oracle predicting that she would bear a son who would kill him. Eventually Zeus visited Danaë in the form of a "golden rain" and she became the mother of Perseus, who grew up and ultimately killed Acrisius by accident with a discus.

Ecbatan (or Agbatana), the great fortress-city of the Medes, was built by King Deioces in the sixth century B.C. in the form of concentric circles of walls. "There are seven circles in all," says Herodotus; "within the innermost circle are the king's dwellings and the treasuries." Each of the walls is of a different color, "and the battlements of the last two circles are coated, these with silver and those with gold." In the first of *The Pisan Cantos* Pound refers to Ecbatan as "the city of Dioce," an image for the earthly paradise. Deioces was chosen by the Medes to be their king because of his reputation for justice. Once enthroned, he established law and order among his people. But the association in Canto 4 of the cruel Acrisius with the just Deioces is contradictory. As a matter of fact, the Ecbatan of Cantos 4 and 5 is a city of *injustice* rather than of justice. The most obvious clue is the line "What wind is the king's?" which implies criticism of Acrisius for his arrogance against nature and the gods in trying to suppress his daughter's sexuality. Less obvious is the disdain of the camel drivers, who "Look down on Ecbatan of plotted streets." The original version of Canto 4 reads "Look down *to* Ecbatan of plotted streets" (my italics), so that the later change implies a change in meaning from neutral observation to observation with superior, detached *disapproval* of the "plotted streets," the *artificial order* that government achieves at the cost of violence to nature, irreverence to man and the gods. The myth of Danaë, in which the oracle speaks the truth in spite of all appearances, suggests that Hubris has encountered Nemesis and that those who attempt to achieve order at the cost of life do so finally at the cost of their own lives as well.

What remains unaccounted for is Pound's association of Ecbatan, presumably the city of Deioces, with the unjust Acrisius' Argos. The explanation emerges, however, upon a further reading of Herodotus. Ecbatan, the capital of Media, had *four* kings, the first of whom was the founder, Deioces, then Phraortes, Cyaxares, and Astyages. It is the Ecbatan that represents the Median kingdom in its last stage of decline, the Ecbatan of Astyages, that Pound couples with the Argos of Acrisius. For Astyages was dethroned by *his* grandson Cyrus the Elder, founder of the Persian empire, in the same mythical manner by which Acrisius met his nemesis in his grandson Perseus. Astyages had a dream which seemed to portend that his grandson would become ruler of all Asia. To eliminate that possibility, he kept his pregnant daughter Mandane well guarded and upon the birth of Cyrus delivered him to his faithful servant Harpagus with orders to kill the child. In the manner of such legends, the child escaped death, grew up, and led the Persians in battle against Astyages, whom Cyrus defeated and imprisoned. The supremacy of the Medes thereby passed to the Persians. Pound is setting up the general thesis that the achievement of order at the expense of Eleusinian energy is the sure sign that a civilization is dying.

Canto 5 begins in the same manner I have described for the two previous cantos. First the narrator presents his composite vision of an evil, unnatural city; then he gives us paradisal images of perfect order in terms of Neoplatonic light imagery. Neoplatonic philosophers have a significant but frequently undifferentiated role to play in *The Cantos*. In the poem, the most important of these philosophers is Plotinus, who serves as Pound's guide through the Hell of Canto 15 and out into the sunlight. Pound employs the light imagery used by a number of Neoplatonists, or philosophers influenced by Neoplatonism (late-classical, non-Christian figures such as Plotinus and his disciple Iamblichus, as well as medieval Christian thinkers such as Scotus Erigena or the humanist Gemistus Plethon) to stand generally for a state of divine ecstasy including total illumination of the mind. In his *Guide to Kulchur* he speaks of "Iamblichus on the fire of the gods [the "Iamblichus' light," apparently, of Canto 5] . . . which comes down into a man and produces superior ecstasies, feelings of regained youth, super youth, and so forth." Of the "two mystic states" that "can be dissociated," Iamblichus, and the Neoplatonists in general (the chapter title is "Neo-Platonicks, Etc.") incline toward "the ecstatic-beneficent-and-benevolent, contemplation of the divine love, the divine splendour with goodwill toward others." The other mysticism Pound characterizes as "the bestial, namely the fanatical, the man on fire with God and anxious to stick his snotty nose into other men's business." Pound feels that the Platonists have always made men aware of transcendent Mind, which he associates with light:

> Plato periodically caused enthusiasm among his disciples. And the Platonists after him have caused man after man to be suddenly conscious of the reality of the *nous*, of mind, apart from any man's individual mind, of the sea crystalline and enduring, of the bright as it were molten glass that envelops us, full of light.

Platonists, in Pound's generalizing view, have tended to affirm the life-force:

> Plato has repeatedly stirred men to a sort of enthusiasm productive of action, and . . . one cannot completely discount this value as life force.

Canto 5 is constructed on an interesting directional metaphor, movement upward contending with movement downward in physical, aesthetic, and moral terms. The first twelve lines begin with an image of stasis that develops into a quick downward tumble into history and time. The first lines carry over the Danaë-Ecbatan theme from Canto 4:

> Great bulk, huge mass, thesaurus;
> Ecbatan, the clock ticks and fades out [,]
>
> The bride awaiting the god's touch; Ecbatan,
> City of patterned streets; again the vision:

The thesaurus or treasury of Ecbatan, which parallels the central citadel in which Danaë-Mandane, the life-force, Aphrodite herself is locked away, is presented unbeautifully as a meaningless and sterile mass of matter corresponding to the static, unimpregnated body of the waiting "bride" of Zeus. Ecbatan is, as we have seen before, an image of *sterile order*, and Pound introduces the theme of clock time, mechanical time, as a symbol of *order* without time-abrogating *significance*, the mere marking of time, the empty succession of equally dead intervals. The clock becomes the symbol, then, of the unhealthy, misdirected will as it manifests itself in social injustice. Clock-time characterizes also the passive "feminine" consciousness of the poet when unimpregnated by the "god's touch" of inspiration or "the vision." This theme will shortly emerge more openly, so that clock-time will have multiple reference to the state of the arts as well as to that of government and of individual moral action. The alternation of clock-tick and vision marks the dilemma of the poet as well as of society, and the two are for Pound intimately related.

The following lines reveal the pattern of downward movement that results necessarily from spiritual stasis:

> Down in the viae stradae, toga'd the crowd, [and arm'd,
> Rushing on populous business,]
> and from parapet looked down
> and North was Egypt,
> > the celestial Nile, blue deep,
> > cutting low barren land,
> Old men and camels
> > > working the water-wheels;

The allusion is again to Herodotus, now to the invasion of Egypt by Cyrus' son Cambyses. If we recall that Cyrus was the nemesis of his grandfather Astyages, whose Ecbatan is the one logically alluded to in this and the previous canto, then we find Pound continuing to relate a family history of disaster. Cambyses, dreaming that his brother Smerdis would replace him as king, proceeded to have his brother killed. Later, however, a pseudo-Smerdis usurped the throne in Ecbatan, and Cambyses, marching back from Egypt to quell the revolution at home, died of an accidentially self-inflicted wound in the genitals, "in the same part where he himself had once smitten the Egyptian god Apis." Although the theme of fratricide is not alluded to by Pound in connection with Cambyses, it crops up later in the canto in the murder of Giovanni Borgia, presumably by his own brother Cesare. Cambyses was not only fratricidal, but incestuous as well, so that he, too, like Acrisius and Astyages, meets an appropriate nemesis for violating nature, in the sense of violating the moral order established by the gods and conceived of as "natural" for man.

Pound alludes only to Cambyses' march against Egypt and emphasizes the *downward* moral and spiritual direction of his activities with the repetition of "down" and the sense of reaching bottom in the "low barren land" along the Nile. The "Old men and camels / working the water-wheels" again symbolize the empty repetition of mechanical time (the Egyptians measured time with water-wheels). It is ironic that Ecbatan, the clock, and the water-wheel are superficially images of circular order but represent, in their barren futility, linear time.

The Neoplatonic imagery of the next lines draws us sharply *upward* in direction:

> [Measureless seas and stars,]
> Iamblichus' light,
>   the souls ascending,
> Sparks like a partridge covey,
>   Like the "ciocco", brand struck in the game.

Integrative ascent of souls toward unity in the One (Plotinus' Absolute) contrasts with the previous imagery of descent into the multiplicity of the togaed "crowd" bent on destruction. Pound draws on Dante's description of the sphere of Jupiter, which is the sphere of justice and world order in the *Paradiso*, for the images of bird and burning brand used for souls arising. In Dante the souls fly up "*come augelli surti di rivera* [as birds risen from the river-bank]" and as innumerable sparks rising "*nel percuoter de' ciocchi arsi* [when burning logs are struck]." These rising souls are lights which form the phrase "DILIGITE JUSTITIAM QUI IUDICATIS TERRAM [Love justice, ye that judge the earth]," the final group of souls forming "the head and neck of the Roman eagle, the divine augury and promise . . . of the world's final order and peace." The merging of a *togaed* crowd with the previous Cambyses material suggests that Pound intends a contrast between Rome in decline, due to injustice, and Rome in its full glory as a symbol of order and justice.

In the following lines the theme of time emerges again, but in relation now to the theme of artistic creativity rather than to the theme of social injustice with which it was connected at the opening of the canto:

> Topaz I manage, and three sorts of blue;
>   but on the barb of time.
> The fire? always, and the vision always,
> Ear dull, perhaps, with the vision, flitting
> And fading at will. Weaving with points of gold,
> Gold-yellow, saffron . . .

Topaz belongs in the range of yellow and golden colors classically associated with Aphrodite. In *The Analyst* (no. 3), John J. Espey identifies "three sorts of blue" as an allusion to Pound's own early poem "Blandula, Tenulla, Vagula," in which the poet addresses his soul and speaks of meeting it, after physical death, in an earthly, sensuous paradise: "Will not our cult be founded on the waves/Clear sapphire, cobalt, cyanine,/On triune azures, the impalpable/Mirrors unstill of the eternal change?" Blue, however, has in any case become associated in previous cantos with the changing colors of sea and sky, so that it is self-sufficient as a symbol of natural beauty. The relative permanence of the topaz as a gem and its golden color suggest that it is the poet's "philosopher's stone" of Love, by which he is enabled to transmute the ever-changing beauty of nature, the flux, into the permanence of poetic form just as the alchemist ideally can change baser metals into gold. "Weaving with points of gold," which represents poetic creation, carries forward this muted alchemical image of turning crude experience into golden art. *The barb of time* is the antithesis to the permanence of topaz and is the intruder which from time to time disrupts the poet's creative accord with nature. This intrusion is nothing else than *time as social evil*, the point of the opening lines of the canto. It would be extremely misleading to give time here the stereotyped meaning of "the flux of experience," which lumps to-gether the flux of nature and the flux of history as if they were much the same thing. I have, I believe, already indicated that Pound's attitudes toward nature and toward history are diametrically opposed, and it is this funda-mental distinction which is indispensable to an understanding of the theme of time and thereby of *The Cantos* as a whole.

The three lines beginning with "The fire? always, and the vision always" are a restatement of the topaz-time antithesis. The fire of passion and the light of vision are permanent possessions of the poet in the potential sense, but "the barb of time" occasionally dulls the melopoeic or music-making ear just as it dulls the phanopoeic or image-making vision. The result is an art that bears witness to this struggle against chaos. The poet pictures himself as "weaving" a tapestry of various hues of gold, culling his golden threads from the poetry of Catullus, Propertius and Sappho, in that order; but "time" punctures the vision and the music; the "Titter of sound about me, always" makes classical perfection extremely difficult to achieve. The result is art as only partially ordered chaos, which Pound considers an effect as satisfactory as that of classical perfection. He said, in an essay of 1928:

> Art very possibly *ought* to be the supreme achievement, the "ac-complished"; but there is the other satisfactory effect, that of a man hurling himself at an indomitable chaos, and yanking and hauling as much of it as possible into some sort of order (or beauty), aware of it both as chaos and as potential.

In addition to representing different types of poetic gold, the series "gold/Gold-yellow, saffron" seems also to have the general function of announcing the theme of love dealt with in the classical poems that are then alluded to. Topaz, gold, and other yellows are associated with Aphrodite, goddess of love, and the color saffron now reintroduces the bride Aurunculeia from Canto 4 ("Saffron sandal so petals the narrow foot").

In the web of allusions to classical poems which follows, Pound gives us images of three types of love shown in a sequence of descent from perfect hymeneal harmony to the barren frustration of unrequited love. First, according to this pattern, is Catullus' epithalamium to Aurunculeia (Carmen 61) which represents the ideal union of lovers in marriage. Secondly, the phase "here Sextus had seen her" suggests the adulterous love relationship, unfaithful on the male's part, between Sextus Propertius and Cynthia. The "Titter of sound" constantly breaking in upon the harmony of the poet's vision suggests the cynicism, skepticism, and faithlessness that undermine the harmony of pure love. Thirdly, Pound presents a kind of montage of Sappho's poems to Atthis, the young girl who deserted the poetess for another woman, Andromeda. The theme of infertility is stressed with the mournful repetition of "the vinestocks lie untended" in association with the phrase "Atthis, unfruitful." Sappho's love is the vinestock blasted by Atthis's betrayal, and perhaps the literal fruitlessness of Lesbian love is also suggested. "Fades the light from the sea," Pound writes in paraphrasing the grief of Sappho. Pound has been weaving a tapestry of types of poetic gold, and at the same time a tapestry of types of love, from ecstatic to mournful.

This downward movement in the spectrum of love seems now to be counterbalanced by a thematic upswing, a movement towards reintegration suggested by two love legends from the troubadour biographies. The first tale ends as mournfully as Sappho's, but on a note of reunion of a sort. (After "Fades the light from the sea," the pathetic fallacy accompanying the Sappho montage, the light seems now dimly to return in the Poicebot episode, which is marked near the end by the parenthetical "Sea change, a grey in the water.") Poicebot, irresponsibly abandoning his wife, succumbs to wanderlust. Sometime after she had been abandoned, his wife is made pregnant by a knight "out of England" who has "put glamour upon her." Poicebot, returning from Spain, footloose and lusty, seeks out a prostitute and finds one—his wife, "changed and familiar face." The "moral" seems to be that the laws of nature, as we saw in Danaë's case, do not suspend themselves for the convenience of men. The second motif, the tale of Pieire de Maensac, suggests that love obeys a law higher than the laws of men, that in the ideal society the laws of the heart are acknowledged as superior to the laws of men, which are frequently short-sighted and tyrannically abusive of the nature of things. The troubadour Pieire de Maensac ran off with the wife of Bernart de Tierci

(who was obviously a failure as a lover) to the castle of the Dauphin of
Auvergne. Tierci tried to gain her back by force but could prevail neither
against love nor the Dauphin, who "stood with de Maensac." The Dauphin's
defense of de Maensac is the peak of the last upward movement in the canto;
it represents the ideal of social order, a united front of love (nature), poetry
(the arts), and politics. (Tierci reappears significantly in Canto 23 in connection with the theme of Christian fanaticism that is developed in the latter
portion of the first thirty cantos.)

At this point the metaphor of *descent* takes sudden hold and dominates
the canto to the end:

> John Borgia is bathed at last. (Clock-tick pierces the vision)
> Tiber, dark with the cloak, wet cat gleaming in patches.
> Click of the hooves, through garbage,
> Clutching the greasy stone.

The first line of this passage is spaced more effectively as two lines in the
first printed version (*Dial*, August 1921), where the theme of time is given
central—and centered—prominence as follows:

> John Borgia is bathed at last.
>   (Clock-tick pierces the vision)

Giovanni Borgia, presumed to have been murdered (in 1497) at the instigation
of his brother Cesare, recalls us to the theme of unnatural violence against
kindred suggested in the legends of Acrisius, Astyages, and Cambyses. The
clock-tick, like the sword that pierced the body of Borgia, is the "barb" of
time that pierces the vision of perfect harmony the poet has just enjoyed.
Mechanical time is the symbol of moral disorder, the violation of nature,
the perversion of natural feeling that reaches a maximum in an act such as
fratricide. The clock-tick reverberates through the quoted passage in "cloak,"
"click of the hooves," and "clutching." The Borgia murder recurs obsessively
in the remainder of the canto. It is presented twice more with added detail,
intruding upon the contemporary historical account of the murder of Alessandro de'Medici by *his* kinsman Lorenzino de'Medici (in 1537), and entwining itself with allusions to the murder of Agamemnon. The clock-tick
echoes again in the last and longest glimpse Pound gives of the Borgia murder:
"Hooves clink and slick on the cobbles. / Schiavoni . . . cloak . . ." [*Schiavoni:*
the church at the place where a watchman saw Borgia's body dumped into
the Tiber.] The emphasis on the clicking hooves of the murderer's horse as
measuring mechanical time seems to stem from the image of time as a "barb,"
one of whose meanings is barbary horse. The image of time as a kind of

horse recurs ironically in another incident described in the canto. For Pound, disorder in the body politic ultimately shows up in a perversion of the arts, so that the poetaster Mozarello receives poetic justice when "smothered beneath a mule." Fittingly, he is destroyed for his artistic sterility by a mule, the sterile offspring of jackass and mare and an ironic version of the *barb* of time.

The ascent to Neoplatonic light has changed into a descent into the darkness of time ("Tiber, dark with the cloak"), and the " fire" of passion is replaced by the "ice" in the lowest circle of Dante's hell, where *"Caina attende. /* The lake of ice there below me"; Caina, one of the four divisions of the lowest circle of Dante's *Inferno*, contains betrayers of their kindred. Mechanical time, bad poetry (meter without meaning), history as a record of moral perversion, and Dante's *Inferno* are all closely associated with one another for the first time in this first of the important "time" cantos.

The insistence on the imagery of *descent* to characterize time or history is carried on in this last half of the canto in climactic fashion. First, the corpse of Borgia is plunged down into the Tiber. The historian Varchi of Florence then relates one of Lorenzo's initial plans to murder Alessandro by having him thrown from a wall, whereupon we are plunged into the "lake of ice" of Caina. Mozarello falls beneath a mule, but then Pound describes his death as "a poet's ending, / down a stale well-hole." The canto ends on the note of death, *"Ma se morisse!"*

Pound views the Renaissance generally as a period of moral, political, and aesthetic disorder in comparison with the golden age of the troubadours, when poetry flourished and "The air was full of women" [Canto 5]. Canto 5 is linked in a number of ways to the second great "time" canto, Canto 7, which is concerned with an examination of *modern* Europe in the light of the time concept. The most important link is the theme of the Florentine tyrant Alessandro's passivity in the face of death foretold to him "thrice over" by his astrologist Del Carmine. Alessandro, like Acrisius, Astyages, and Cambyses, had his doom prophetically revealed to him, but unlike these legendary tyrants, he failed even to *try* to exert his will against destiny. As opposed to the perverted will of Lorenzo, Alessandro's "abuleia," or willlessness, is in Pound's view the particular mark of modern civilization. Renaissance man acted out of misdirected passion; modern man, his natural passions almost totally suppressed (Canto 7 dates back to 1921), does not act.

LOUIS L. MARTZ

Pound's Early Poems

And Malrin beheld the broidery of the stars become as wind-worn tapestries of
ancient wars. And the memory of all old songs swept by him as an host blue-
robèd trailing in dream, Odysseus, and Tristram, and the pale great gods of
storm, the mailed Campeador and Roland and Villon's women and they of
Valhalla; as a cascade of dull sapphires so poured they out of the mist and were
gone.

—"Malrin"

We present [in the *Collected Early Poems of Ezra Pound*] a volume that contains ninety-nine poems that Pound published in his early books but rejected when he made his definitive selection for *Personae* ("Collected Poems") of 1926; and we also include twenty-five poems that appeared only in periodicals or miscellanies, along with thirty-eight previously unpublished poems selected from more than a hundred unpublished early poems known to exist at Yale, Harvard, Texas, Chicago, and perhaps other places as well. What is the effect, one may ask, what is the use, of thus resurrecting so many poems that the author himself called "a collection of stale creampuffs," when some of them were republished in 1965? But then he added, with a wry gesture of affection, echoing his poem "Piccadilly": "Chocolate creams, who hath forgotten you?"

One might attempt to describe the experience of reading all these poems by such phrases as "filling the void," "shattering the mist," "banishing the twilight," or, best of all, "escaping from Swinburne to Cathay." For the first impression one may have from the earliest of these poems has been rightly set forth by T. S. Eliot in his estimate of the poetical situation faced by Pound in the first decade of this century: "The question was still," says

From *Collected Early Poems of Ezra Pound*, edited by Michael John King. © 1976 by Louis L. Martz. New Directions, 1976.

Eliot, "where do we go from Swinburne? and the answer appeared to be, nowhere." It was a problem clearly grasped by Pound himself in a poem . . . entitled "Swinburne: A Critique"—a poem in which Pound, perhaps deliberately, twice spells the name "Swinbourne," as though he were describing some country from whose bourne no traveler returns:

> Blazes of color intermingled,
> Wondrous pattern leading nowhere,
> Music without a name,
> Knights that ride in a dream,
> Blind as all men are blind,
> Why should the music show
>   Whither they go?
> I am Swinburne, ruler in mystery.
>   None know the ending,
>   Blazes a-blending   in splendor
> Of glory none know the meaning on,
> I am he that paints the rainbow of the sunset
> And the end of all dreams,
>   Wherefor would ye know?
>   Honor the glow
> Of the colors   care not wherefore   they gleam
>   All things but seem.

It is a brilliant evocation of Swinburne-land, as Pound himself frequently created it in his own early poems—a land of dreams and sorrows derived not simply from Swinburne, but also from Rossetti and the other pre-Raphaelites with whom Swinburne began his career; and also from the heirs of Swinburne, the "Decadent" poets of the 'Nineties, Dowson, Davidson, Lionel Johnson, and the rest, especially the early Yeats, with his Celtic variations on the Swinburnian dream. These are poems, in Pound's own phrase, "That Pass between the False Dawn and the True"—the title of a discarded poem:

> Blown of the winds whose goal is "No-man-knows"
> As feathered seeds upon the wind are borne,
> To kiss as winds kiss and to melt as snows
> And in our passing taste of all men's scorn,
> Wraiths of a dream that fragrant ever blows
> From out the night we know not to the morn,
> Borne upon winds whose goal is "No-man-knows."

But even as he mastered this melancholy, languid manner of writing, Pound was reaching far beyond the 'Nineties, as in another poem here first published, "The Summons," addressed to a lady who seems to be an image of poetic inspiration (perhaps, literally, "H.D."):

> I cannot bow to woo thee
> With honey words and flower kisses
> And the dew of sweet half-truths
> Fallen on the grass of old quaint love-tales
> Of broidered days foredone.
> Nor in the murmurous twilight
> May I sit below thee,
> Worshiping in whispers
> Tremulous as far-heard bells.

All this faded idiom, he says, "is gone/As the shadow of the wind." The echo of Dowson's most famous phrase shows the immediate ancestry of the foregoing lines, but not of the following Dantesque vision:

> But as I am ever swept upward
> To the centre of all truth
> So must I bear thee with me
> Rapt into this great involving flame,
> Calling ever from the midst thereof,
>   "Follow! Follow!"
> And in the glory of our meeting
> Shall the power be reborn.

Pound knew that the power of the masters, Rossetti and Swinburne, had been diluted and enervated by the languid eroticism, the misty land- scapes, the melancholy dreams, and the pallid archaisms of their followers, and while the mode attracted him, he knew it had no future. Thus he could imitate the "Celtic Twilight" of Yeats in "La Fraisne" (and indeed he planned to make "La Fraisne" the title-poem of his first volume), but he could also ridicule "the impassioned rehash of the mystically beautiful celtic mythology" in his ballad of "P'ti'cru," though, like his "Critique" of Swinburne, the ballad remained unpublished. Thus too in "The Decadence" we find ad- miration for those poets' devotion to the cause of Art, along with an undertone that seems to mock their self-pity and their posture of exhausted heroism:

> Tarnished we! Tarnished! Wastrels all!
> And yet the art goes on, goes on.

> Broken our strength, yea as crushed reeds we fall,
> And yet the art, the *art* goes on. . . .
>
> Broken our manhood for the wrack and strain;
> Drink of our hearts the sunset and the cry
> "Io Triumphe!" Tho our lips be slain
> We see Art vivant, and exult to die.

Pound knew that somehow he must discover a source of imaginative power such as Swinburne himself had found in the Greeks, as Pound shows in his perfervid tribute to Swinburne, written three years before Swinburne's death in 1909, and appropriately published in Pound's first volume, 1908. It bears the title "Salve O Pontifex!" with the subtitle "To Swinburne; an hemichaunt." The last phrase sums up the heavily mannered archaism of the 'Nineties in which this tribute and most of Pound's earliest poems abound:

> One after one do they leave thee,
>   High Priest of Iacchus,
> Toning thy melodies even as winds tone
> The whisper of tree leaves, on sun-lit days . . .

(Iacchus being the deity of the Eleusinian mysteries and a deity assimilated to Bacchus, perhaps through the similarity of name.)

> Wherefor tho thy co-novices bent to the scythe
> Of the magian wind that is voice of Prosephone,
> Leaving thee solitary, master of initating
> Maenads that come thru the
> Vine-entangled ways of the forest
> Seeking, out of all the world
>   Madness of Iacchus,
> That being skilled in the secrets of the double cup
> They might turn the dead of the world
> Into beauteous paeans,
>   O High Priest of Iacchus . . .
>   Breathe!
> Now that evening cometh upon thee,
> Breathe upon us that low-bowed and exultant
> Drink wine of Iacchus . . .
>   O High Priest of Iacchus
> Breathe thou upon us
>   Thy magic in parting!

"Balderdash," Pound added in a note when he reprinted the poem in 1917—"but let it stand for the rhythm," he apologized. Clearly, even as late as that, the spell of Swinburne was upon him, and indeed it never wholly left him, for even in the prison camp at Pisa the Greek gods of Swinburne are present in the great lynx-hymn of Canto 79, with its cries of "Iacchos," "Iacche." What he admired in Swinburne was more than the rhythm. It was Swinburne's power to evoke the gods of the past and thus compensate in some measure for the mercantile and industrial world of Victoria from which the gods had departed in despair, leaving behind the gray world of Matthew Arnold's woman who has forsaken her beloved Merman:

> She steals to the window, and looks at the sand;
> And over the sand at the sea;
> And her eyes are set in a stare;
> And anon there breaks a sigh,
> And anon there drops a tear,
> From a sorrow-clouded eye,
> And a heart sorrow-laden,
> A long, long sigh,
> For the cold strange eyes of a little Mermaiden,
> And the gleam of her golden hair.

This is the sort of thing that drew from Pound's friend T. E. Hulme his violent objection to the weeping ruins of romanticism: "I object," says Hulme, "to the sloppiness which doesn't consider that a poem is a poem unless it is moaning or whining about something or other . . . The thing has got so bad now that a poem which is all dry and hard, a properly classical poem, would not be considered poetry at all . . . Poetry that isn't damp isn't poetry at all . . . There is a general tendency to think that verse means little else than the expression of unsatisfied emotion." Hulme then went on to recommend his famous antidotes to all this dampness: "It is essential to prove that beauty may be in small, dry things . . . The great aim is accurate, precise and definite description . . . the particular verse we are going to get will be cheerful, dry and sophisticated."

Such were the views that Hulme and Pound came to share after their first meeting in 1909, and so it is no wonder that, in 1911, Pound should publish his "Song in the Manner of Housman":

> O woe, woe
> People are born and die,
> We also shall be dead pretty soon

> Therefore let us act as if we were
> > dead already.
>
> The bird sits on the hawthorn tree
> But he dies also, presently.
> Some lads get hung, and some get shot.
> Woeful is this human lot.
> > *Woe! woe, etcetera.*

But Pound's dissatisfaction with this dampness had been manifested earlier, in a poem published near the end of *Personae*: "Revolt: Against the Crepuscular Spirit in Modern Poetry"—a poem that denounces and renounces the mode of many of the poems that precede it in this book:

> I would shake off the lethargy of this our time,
> > and give
> For shadows—shapes of power
> For dreams—men.
>
> "It is better to dream than do"?
> > Aye! and, No!
>
> Aye! if we dream great deeds, strong men,
> Hearts hot, thoughts mighty.
>
> No! if we dream pale flowers,
> Slow-moving pageantry of hours that languidly
> Drop as o'er-ripened fruit from sallow trees . . .
>
> Great God, if men are grown but pale sick phantoms
> That must live only in these mists and tempered lights
> And tremble for dim hours that knock o'er loud
> Or tread too violent in passing them;
> Great God, if these thy sons are grown such thin ephemera,
> I bid thee grapple chaos and beget
> Some new titanic spawn to pile the hills and stir
> This earth again.

But where will the voices be found to scatter the shadows and stir the earth? In Robert Browning, certainly, whose strident voice is humorously imitated in "Mesmerism," and whose bracing impact upon the whole Victorian scene Pound represents in a poem to Elizabeth Barrett Browning, ["To E.B.B."]. The voice of Browning is clear in many of these early monologues, in "Cino," "Marvoil," "Piere Vidal Old," in the long poem here first published, "Capilupus Sends Greeting to Grotus," and in many other places, as late as the bitter parody in Canto 80: "Oh to be in England now that Winston's out." But the impact of Browning is far from dominant in these early poems, far less significant than it appears in the *Personae* of 1926, where Pound retains nine of his most Browningesque poems, while discarding more than sixty that tell of crepuscular times.

The masks that Pound adopts usually derive from other promptings: from Yeats, from Ovid ("An Idyl for Glaucus"), from Rossetti, and from the literally pre-Raphaelite poets that Rossetti revived in his great translations of Dante, Cavalcanti, and the other medieval Tuscan poets. Introducing his own versions of Cavalcanti, published in 1912, Pound says: "In the matter of these translations and of my knowledge of Tuscan poetry, Rossetti is my mother and my father." Pound read all these poets in the Temple Classics edition, where Rossetti's translations were reprinted; Pound's own volumes still exist, heavily annotated. Then there was the Villon that Swinburne praised and translated, and Pound's own discoveries, the medieval troubadours of Provence or the Anglo-Saxon poet of "The Seafarer."

Deeper still, Pound's varied ways of speaking in dramatic monologue seem to be based upon his sense of a prophetic mission, *prophetic* in the basic Greek sense. For a prophet, in Greek, is first of all "one who speaks for another." This may mean "one who interprets the will of a god," or one who speaks through some divine inspiration; thus poets were called prophets (interpreters) of the Muses, and more generally, the word prophet might be applied to an interpreter of scripture or to an inspired teacher. ("I do not teach—I awake," says Pound in a manuscript note to "Histrion.") Pound also takes on the role of a Biblical prophet, as in the manuscript poem of 1913 entitled "From Chebar"—the reference being to the first verse of Ezekiel: "In the thirtieth year, in the fourth month, on the fifth day of the month, as I was among the exiles by the river Chebar, the heavens were opened, and I saw visions of God." It is a poem that mingles a Biblical rhythm with the prophetic strain of Walt Whitman:

> Before you were, America!
>
> I did not begin with you,
> I do not end with you, America. . . .
> Oh I can see you,
> I with the maps to aid me,
> I can see the coast and the forest
> And the corn-yellow plains and the hills,
> The domed sky and the jagged,
> The plainsmen and men of the cities. . . .

> I have seen the dawn mist
> Move in the yellow grain,
> I have seen the daubed purple sunset;
> You may kill me, but I do not accede,
> You may ignore me, you may keep me in exile,
> You may assail me with negations, or you
>   may keep me, a while, well hidden,
> But I am after you and before you,
> And above all, I do not accede.

"There is no use your quoting Whitman against me," he adds, even as he writes in Whitman's cadence: "His time is not our time, his day and hour were different." The whole poem derives from Pound's profound conviction that the arts constitute a moral, civilizing instrument:

> The order does not end in the arts,
> The order shall come and pass through them.
>
> The state is too idle, the decrepit church is too idle,
> The arts alone can transmit this.
> They alone cling fast to the gods.

That is one role of the prophet—a role that grew upon Pound as he grew older, but it is related to the earlier prophetic role that he describes in the discarded poem "Histrion" ("Actor"):

> No man hath dared to write this thing as yet,
> And yet I know, how that the souls of all men great
> At times pass through us,
> And we are melted into them, and are not
> Save reflexions of their souls.
> Thus am I Dante for a space and am
> One François Villon, ballad-lord and thief
> Or am such holy ones I may not write,
> Lest blasphemy be writ against my name;
> This for an instant and the flame is gone.
>
> 'Tis as in midmost us there glows a sphere
> Translucent, molten gold, that is the "I"
> And into this some form projects itself:
> Christus, or John, or eke the Florentine;
> And as the clear space is not if a form's
> Imposed thereon,

> So cease we from all being for the time,
> And these, the Masters of the Soul, live on.

What Pound seems to be describing here (beneath the histrionic claptrap) is his own sense of his remarkable mimetic genius, his ability to absorb the style, manner, and meaning of another poet, and then to interpret and recreate that role, in translation, in creative adaptation, or in original poems in a particular kind of writing. His masks, his personae, are modes of poetry: masks through which the modern poet transmits his apprehension of the past and makes it available to the present, as a civilizing force. This is truly to be a prophet of the Muses. Hence the motto that concludes *A Lume Spento* and begins *Personae:* "Make-strong old dreams lest this our world lose heart."

All this is related to Pound's belief in a principle that runs throughout his early poetry and underlies *The Cantos:* the belief that the poetic power breaks through the crust of daily life and apprehends a transcendent flow of spirit, or energy, or divine power, which Pound calls "the gods." His poetic imagination attempts to live in an animate universe, where things of nature and beyond nature can be merged with inner man, as he explains in a note in the San Trovaso Notebook:

> All art begins in the physical discontent (or torture) of loneliness
> and partiality [i.e. being only a separate part of existence].
>   It is to fill this lack that man first spun shapes out of the void.
> And with the intensity of this longing gradually came unto him
> power, power over the essences of the dawn, over the filaments
> of light and the warp of melody . . .
>   Of such perceptions rise the ancient myths of the origin of
> demi-gods. Even as the ancient myths of metamorphosis rise out
> of flashes of cosmic consciousness.

Thus, as he seems to say in the discarded poem "Plotinus," such perceptions grow from within man and reach outward toward the eternal.

This is what happens in his many poems of love for woman, where he adopts the image of an ideal woman as his inspiration, after the manner of Dante and Cavalcanti and the troubadours of Provence. An apt example of how these readings in the medieval poets showed him a way of escaping from the Swinburnian twilight is found in the curious history of the poem which appeared in 1908 under the title "Vana"—"empty things," "fruitless things." But the title holds a certain irony, for the "vain" thing in the end proves to be the effort to deny the creative desire for "song": the magical, fertile words are within the lonely speaker, crying for a song that has not yet been created:

> In vain I have striven
>   to each my heart to bow;
> In vain have I said to him
> "There be many singers   greater than thou."
> But his answer cometh,   as winds and as lutany,
> As a vague crying upon the night
> That leaveth me no rest,   saying ever,
>   "Song,   a song."
>
> Their echoes play upon each other in the twilight
> Seeking ever a song.
> Lo, I am worn with travail
> And the wandering of many roads hath made my eyes
> As dark red circles filled with dust.
> Yet there is a trembling upon me in the twilight,
>   And little red elf words   crying "A song,"
>   Little grey elf words   crying for a song,
>   Little brown leaf words   crying "A song,"
>   Little green leaf words   crying for a song.
> The words are as leaves, old brown leaves in the spring time
> Blowing they know not whither, seeking a song.

That is a perfect expression of the twilight of the 'Nineties, the poetic imagination seeking expression, but finding no voice, no poetical way out of the gloom. Then in 1909 the poem reappears in *Personae* under the title "Praise of Ysolt"—but here it forms the first twenty lines of a poem that runs to fifty-eight lines. Whether the first part was written separately or whether this was all written as one piece and only the first part published in 1908, we do not know; in any case the important point is that the sequel of 1909 tells how the speaker's *soul* (seat of the intellect), as distinguished from his *heart* (seat of the feelings), has escaped from its empty state by responding, like Dante, to the memory of a woman of transcendent power:

> But my soul sent a woman, a woman of the wonderfolk,
> A woman as fire upon the pine woods
>   crying "Song, a song."
> As the flame crieth unto the sap.
> My song was ablaze with her and she went from me
> As flame leaveth the embers so went she unto new
>   forests
> And the words were with me
>   crying ever "Song, a song."

And I "I have no song,"
Till my soul sent a woman as the sun:
Yea as the sun calleth to the seed,
As the spring upon the bough
So is she that cometh the song-drawer
She that holdeth the wonder words within her eyes.

In poems such as these one has the sense of a tormented, lonely genius crying for release from a faded idiom, seeking a way in which his song can emerge into a sort of naked clarity, free of archaic diction and dead poetical properties. Even in these early days, his natural manner of writing seems to have been much simpler and more direct than his published manner, as the manuscript version of "Idyl for Glaucus" seems to suggest; but the idiom of the 'Nineties called for the imposition of stilted inversions and archaisms. Nevertheless Pound is everywhere seeking a song that he can call his own, and here and there, perfectly, he finds it, as in "Francesca," where the Dantesque name presides over a poem of our own immediate world and language:

You came in out of the night
And there were flowers in your hands,
Now you will come out of a confusion of people,
Out of a turmoil of speech about you.

I who have seen you amid the primal things
Was angry when they spoke your name
In ordinary places.
I would that the cool waves might flow over
        my mind,
And that the world should dry as a dead leaf,
Or as a dandelion seed-pod and be swept away,
So that I might find you again,
Alone.

There is the free verse, the supple language, the clear imagery that marks most of the poems in *Ripostes* (1912), but it is a poem published in 1909.

Everywhere, throughout these early volumes, one feels the unsteady oscillation between the dream world of the Swinburnians and another world in which moments of human experience are caught in a modern language and a modern movement. Thus in *Exultations* (1909), only two pages before "Francesca," we come upon the discarded sequence "Laudantes Decem Pulchritudinis Johannae Templi." Mary de Rachewiltz has suggested a con-

vincing explanation of that enigmatic title: "Joan of the Temple" is the
Giovanna ("Joan" in Rossetti's version) of Dante's *Vita Nuova* and Cavalcanti's
sonnets—which Pound read in the Temple edition, making especially heavy
annotations upon Cavalcanti's sonnets to this lady. It is a characteristic
Poundian twist, with the Tuscan lady (also called "Primavera") working
within a predominantly Yeatsian sequence: "When your beauty is grown old
in all men's songs . . . O Rose of the sharpest thorn! / O Rose of the crimson
beauty . . . The unappeasable loveliness / is calling to me out of the
wind . . ." And then, with a typical Yeatsian subheading:

> *He speaks to the moonlight concerning the Beloved.*
> Pale hair that the moon has shaken
> Down over the dark breast of the sea,
> O magic her beauty has shaken
> About the heart of me;
> Out of you have I woven a dream
> That shall walk in the lonely vale
> Betwixt the high hill and the low hill;
> Until the pale stream
> Of the souls of men quench and grow still.

Yet in the midst of all this tapestry of echoes, one comes upon the eighth
section with surprise, for here, suddenly, the rose imagery is drawn into the
mind of the speaker who ponders the problem of memory in a delicate and
subtle way, as the movements of the verse mirror the hesitations and nuances
of the mind in action:

> If the rose-petals which have fallen upon my eyes
> And if the perfect faces which I see at times
> When my eyes are closed—
> Faces fragile, pale, yet flushed a little, like petals
>   of roses:
> If these things have confused my memories of her
> So that I could not draw her face
> Even if I had skill and the colours,
> Yet because her face is so like these things
> They but draw me nearer unto her in my thought
> And thoughts of her come upon my mind gently,
> As dew upon the petals of roses.

This is no dream: the motion of thought re-enacts the effort of memory so
often represented in Dante or Cavalcanti: *dove sta memoria*. Here is verse with

an intellectual base, a rational element working its way out of the dream and the lethargy and the twilight of depleted feelings.

In another partly discarded sequence, "Und Drang," the twelve poems concluding *Canzoni* (1911) move through a series of masks that seem to reflect the various aspects of Pound's early poetical experience. The opening voice here seems to be that of a lost follower of Nietzsche:

> I am worn faint,
> The winds of good and evil
> Blind me with dust
> And burn me with the cold,
> There is no comfort being over-man;
> Yet are we come more near
> The great oblivions and the labouring night,
> Inchoate truth and the sepulchral forces.

The poem then moves through memories of bitterness and pain, changing from belief to a state where "The will to live goes from me," and from there to a Yeatsian memory when "I was Aengus for a thousand years." Section 4 is an elegy for the Decadents, a recreation of their sombre hedonism:

> All things in season and no thing o'er long!
> Love and desire and gain and good forgetting,
> Thou canst not stay the wheel, hold none too long!

In section 5 the voice of a critical commentator enters, clearing away the crépuscule:

> How our modernity,
> Nerve-wracked and broken, turns
> Against time's way and all the way of things,
> Crying with weak and egoistic cries!

This speaker knows that "the restless will / Surges amid the stars / Seeking new moods of life, / New permutations." And soon the new moods come. Section 6 brings us into a theater where, between the acts, the speaker catches a glimpse of a beloved face in something very close to the kind of intense moment exalted by Walter Pater:

> A little light,
> The gold, and half the profile!
> The whole face
> Was nothing like you, yet that image cut
> Sheer through the moment.

He goes on seeking the face "in the flurry of Fifth Avenue," and then in Section 7 we emerge into "The House of Splendour," a perfect poem in its kind—a vision out of Cavalcanti and his peers, through Rossetti:

> And I have seen my Lady in the sun,
> Her hair was spread about, a sheaf of wings,
> And red the sunlight was, behind it all.

Section 8, "The Flame," pursues a transcendent vision through allusions to Provence and "Oisin":

> There *is* the subtler music, the clear light
> Where time burns back about th' eternal embers.
> We are not shut from all the thousand heavens:
> Lo, there are many gods whom we have seen,
> Folk of unearthly fashion, places splendid,
> Bulwarks of beryl and of chrysoprase.

Then, after two four-line "inscriptions" commemorating the past, the poem moves forward into the present, with a language, wit, and attitude that T. E. Hulme must have relished:

> I suppose, when poetry comes down to facts,
> When our souls are returned to the gods
>   and the spheres they belong in,
> Here in the every-day where our acts
> Rise up and judge us;
>
> I suppose there are a few dozen verities
> That no shift of mood can shake from us:
>
> One place where we'd rather have tea
> (Thus far hath modernity brought us)
> "Tea" (Damn you!)
>   Have tea, damn the Caesars,
> Talk of the latest success, give wing to some scandal,
> Garble a name we detest, and for prejudice?
> Set loose the whole consummate pack
>   to bay like Sir Roger de Coverley's.

And the sequence ends, appropriately, with a poem that teases a famous, very fragile poem by Yeats, "The Cap and Bells."

The sequence "Und Drang" deserves to be read entire as a self-conscious version of Pound's efforts to imitate and then to disengage his muse from nineteenth-century trappings and move into his own world. Yet even in *Ripostes* (1912) the oscillations are evident, as within the poem "N.Y.," where his prophetic voice speaks to the city with love and hope, while the murmur of the realist tells the prophet that his efforts are in vain:

> My City, my beloved, my white! Ah, slender,
> Listen! Listen to me, and I will breathe into thee a soul.
> Delicately upon the reed, attend me!
>
> *Now do I know that I am mad.*
> *For here are a million people surly with traffic;*
> *This is no maid.*
> *Neither could I play upon any reed if I had one.*
>
> My City, my beloved,
> Thou art a maid with no breasts,
> Thou art slender as a silver reed.
> Listen to me, attend me!
> And I will breathe into thee a soul,
> And thou shalt live for ever.

Or we may contrast the Swinburnian sapphics of "Apparuit" (another complex union of Dante and the 'Nineties) with the London salon world of "Portrait d'une Femme." As in "The Needle," Pound's career stands at the turn of a tide. He has beat the 'Nineties at their own game (indeed, except for Yeats, Pound might be called the best poet of the 'Nineties!). He has matched the intricate stanza-forms of Provence or Tuscany in *Canzoni*, has seen the Greek gods making their tentative return, has even begun to make his peace with Whitman, as he says in an essay of 1909:

> Mentally I am a Walt Whitman who has learned to wear a collar and a dress shirt (although at times inimical to both). Personally I might be very glad to conceal my relationship to my spiritual father and brag about my more congenial ancestry—Dante, Shakespeare, Theocritus, Villon, but the descent is a bit difficult to establish. And, to be frank, Whitman is to my fatherland . . . what Dante is to Italy and I at my best can only be a strife for a renaissance in America of all the lost or temporarily mislaid beauty, truth, valor, glory of Greece, Italy, England and all the rest of it.

But how does one deliberately start a Renaissance? Pound knew. As he wrote in 1915: "The first step of a renaissance, or awakening, is the importation

of models for painting, sculpture or writing . . . We must learn what we
can from the past, we must learn what other nations have done successfully
under similar circumstances, we must think how they did it." The first step,
then, is what he calls the preparation of the "palette": we must find in foreign
literature the "pure colors" out of which a new poetry, created by America
for all the world, will arise.

Now, in 1912, Pound felt that the palette had been prepared, for in
that year Pound sent to Harriet Monroe, for publication in her new magazine,
a poem entitled "Epilogue," in which he offered to America his versions and
studies of medieval poetry, as spoils brought from Europe to enrich his own
beloved country. He could not know that one more "pure color," perhaps
the most important of all, remained for him to receive; a pigment indispensable to the development of his poetical future, indispensable to the structure,
movement, and meaning of his Cantos. In the very next year the gift arrived,
from an unexpected quarter.

In 1913 Ernest Fenollosa's widow, in an act of inspired intuition, saw
in Pound the poet who would understand her husband's studies in Chinese
poetry and the Japanese drama, and she gave Fenollosa's papers to Pound
to work with as he would. In those papers Pound discovered the fulfillment
of his deepest poetical needs: another country, another kingdom, as different
from Swinburneland as one could ever wish. Here was an ancient, established
civilization, preserved in poetry of local realism, touched with sadness, aware
of mortality, but never overcome with melancholy. Here was poetry of live,
precise detail, mingling a love of nature with a love of man. And best of all,
the materials were free for him to recreate within the matrix of his own
developed craft. For Fenollosa's notes gave him English equivalents for
Chinese characters, but no ancient forms of meter or rime to be followed.
The lonely void was suddenly filled with the riches of an entire civilization,
ready to be transmitted by his highly prepared and adaptable muse. So
Cathay, that ideal kingdom, came into being: Pound's first perfect book, or
rather booklet, and one that presented Pound's mature voice through a new
mask, colloquial in language, precise in imagery, free and flexible in its
movement, as in the opening words of *Cathay* ("Song of the Bowmen of
Shu"), where the calendar of hardship and sorrow is revealed and controlled
by the changing imagery of fern-shoots:

> Here we are, picking the first fern-shoots
> And saying: When shall we get back to our country?
> Here we are because we have the Ken-nin for our foemen,
> We have no comfort because of these Mongols.
> We grub the soft fern-shoots,

When anyone says "Return," the others are full of sorrow.
Sorrowful minds, sorrow is strong, we are hungry and thirsty.
Our defence is not yet made sure, no one can let his friend
    return.
We grub the old fern-stalks.

This is hardly the cheerful verse that Hulme foresaw; the coming of war
had dashed that hope. But now Pound's experience in working with Chinese
poetry enables him to "abbreviate" Hulme's conversation about trench war-
fare into a powerful poem of accurate, precise, and definite description.

"The last century rediscovered the middle ages," Pound wrote in February 1915, already casting his medieval studies into the past. "It is possible,"
he added, looking forward, "that this century may find a new Greece in
China . . . Undoubtedly pure color is to be found in Chinese poetry, when
we begin to know enough about it; indeed, a shadow of this perfection is
already at hand in translations." Close at hand—for only two months later,
Cathay appeared.

MAX NÄNNY

Context, Contiguity and Contact in Ezra Pound's Personae

The aim of this article is to explore some of the characteristic ways in which Ezra Pound's early poetry collected in his *Personae*, especially the poetry written after 1910, *works*. To do this, I shall have recourse to Roman Jakobson's seminal analysis of the bipolar nature of language, his distinction between the "metaphoric" and the "metonymic" modes of discourse [*Fundamentals of Language* (The Hague, 1956), part 2, pp. 55–82; and *Selected Writings*, 2 (The Hague, 1971), passim]. By these two somewhat problematic terms Jakobson describes two basic functions of the mind that also govern our language behavior.

The metaphoric mode of a discourse thus connects one topic or verbal unit with another, though from a different context, on the basis of some internal similarity (likeness, similitude, equivalence, resemblance, analogy). The chief mental operations demanded by the metaphoric mode are the selection and substitution of similars.

The metonymic mode of discourse, on the other hand, connects topics and verbal entities by means of external contiguities in space and time. Hence, relationships no longer derive from patterns of similarity but from temporal or spatial associations due to neighborhood, proximity, subordination, and coordination. Here the chief mental operations consist in combination and contexture, that is, in a rearrangement or deletion of contiguous entities.

Now Jakobson discovered that these two distinct functions or "poles" of language, namely metaphor and metonymy, are related to two types of

From *ELH* 47, no. 2 (1980). © 1980 by The Johns Hopkins University Press.

aphasia (loss or impairment of the power to understand and use language). Depending on whether the faculty for perceiving and establishing similarity-relations or whether the faculty in control of contiguity-associations is impaired or entirely lost, we get in the first case a similarity-disorder and in the second case a contiguity-disorder (which reverses the features of the similarity-disorder).

Aphasics suffering from a similarity-disorder (and this is the only disorder that will interest us in the following) are heavily dependent on context, i.e. on contiguity-associations, in their speech: "The sentence 'it rains' cannot be produced unless the utterer sees that it is actually raining." Hence, this kind of aphasic speech tends to define objects by reference to their specific context rather than by abstract generic terms ("black" being defined by such an aphasic as "what you do for the dead"); it also tends to be reactive in that sentences are conceived as "elliptical sequels to be supplied from antecedent sentences uttered"; and while it omits the grammatical subject, it prefers words with an inherent reference to the context such as pronouns and pronominal adverbs. Furthermore, aphasics of this type are incapable of finding synonyms, they cannot perform metalinguistic operations or code-switching (e.g., translation from one language into another); they tend to prefer metonymies and synecdoches to similarity-tropes such as metaphors, similes, or analogies; and, in semiotic terms, they give preference to icons and indices rather than to verbal symbols.

While the two types of aphasic disturbance mark the two pathological extremes or "poles" of verbal behavior, all normal language use is bipolar, is both metaphoric and metonymic. But according to Jakobson any individual use of language, any verbal style, any trend in literature displays a clear predilection either for the metonymic or metaphoric function.

Now apart from the offering criteria for the definition of the styles of individual writers, literary periods and fashions, Jakobson's general theory of the bipolar nature of language and his supporting evidence from the clinical study of aphasia is especially relevant to the study of modern literature and its notorious "obscurity." As David Lodge rightly points out: "If much modern literature is exceptionally difficult to understand, this can only be because of some dislocation or distortion of either the selection or the combination axes of language; and of some modern writing . . . it is not an exaggeration to say that it aspires to the condition of aphasia."

For two decades critics like Richard Ohmann, Taylor Stoehr, [J.] Hillis Miller and others have demonstrated the critical fruitfulness of Jakobson's concepts when applied to writers like Shaw and Dickens. It was at a relatively late stage, in 1976, that Herbert Schneidau was the first to approach Pound's poetics (with some references to *The Cantos*) in terms of Jakobson's bipolar view of language.

What Schneidau discovers in his fine essay is that Pound seems to show symptoms of a "similarity disorder" or "selection deficiency," for there seems to be "an uncanny correspondence between the Pound-Fenollosa poetics and the aphasic who cannot perform similarity functions, and who grasps words literally but not metaphorically." According to Schneidau, it was Pound's extreme, well-nigh pathological bias towards combination and total contexture, which brought about "a revolutionary break-away from metaphorical habits in composing poems."

As proofs of Pound's quasi-aphasic "escape from sameness to contiguity" (Jakobson) Schneidau mentions his general irritable attitude towards the similarity functions of analogy and metaphor; his contempt for poetic similarity devices such as regular metre, rhyme, regular stanzas; his "crossing" verse with the prose tradition of realism which is "forwarded essentially by contiguity" (Jakobson); his belief in discontinuity and in the juxtapository process of the ideogrammatic method; and, last but not least, his tendency towards ellipsis and elliptical sequels that leads his poetry to the brink of aphasia and explains his fascination with all forms of concision, the epigram, the Japanese *haiku*.

As Schneidau's highly perceptive remarks mainly restrict themselves to a general discussion of Pound's poetics, I shall now make a new departure by analysing his early poetry in the light of Jakobson's concepts. But before I do so, I should like to state clearly that despite the "uncanny correspondences between the Pound-Fenollosa poetics and the aphasic who cannot perform similarity functions," I do not maintain, nor does Schneidau, that Pound actually suffered from an aphasia of the similarity-disorder kind.

What I suggest, however, is that Pound's mental make-up and predilections as well as his innovative strategies of reforming an excessively metaphorical poetic tradition pushed him close to the metonymic pole. Be this as it may, the characteristics of similarity-disorder, which is merely an extreme manifestation of metonymic behavior in general, offer concepts and criteria that seem to me of great help for an understanding of Pound's early poetry, too.

I shall, therefore, approach his *Personae*-poems on the three semiotic levels of pragmatics, syntactics, and semantics, that is, in terms of verbal or non-verbalized context, in terms of syntactical contiguity, and in terms of physical and spatio-temporal contact.

CONTEXT

One of the most striking facts about Pound's early poetry is its derivative
nature. I do not know any other poet whose poetry is so dependent on
existing texts as Pound's is. One may even say that he is at his best and
most original when his talents are controlled by an existing text; and often
he is at his worst and, in the pejorative sense, most conventional, when there
is no text to stimulate him into poetry. "Where there is actually an original
to control him," R.P. Blackmur has said, "he will do his freest, best, and
also his most personal work."

In Jakobson's terms, Pound's verbal behavior seems very strongly *reactive*, as is the behavior of an aphasic suffering from a similarity-disorder.
Hence, what Jakobson says of this type of aphasia may also be applied to
Pound's early poetry: "The more his utterances are dependent on the context,
the better he copes with his verbal task. He feels unable to utter a sentence
which responds neither to the cue of his interlocutor nor to the actual situation." In fact, most of Pound's early poetry is cued to, or responds to,
poetic "interlocutors" of the past and present. In the form of allusion, translation, paraphrase, or quotation his poetry is embedded in the poetic context
of the fin-de-siècle, Renaissance Italy, Provence, ancient Greece and Rome,
Japan and China.

But Pound not only cued his work to various poetic interlocutors—
"Mesmerism" and "A Pact" show him in conversation with Browning and
Whitman, for instance—but also to what Jakobson calls "the actual situation." For Pound made a cult of the contemporary. He wrote two series of
poems with the telling titles of "Moeurs Contemporaines" and "Contem-
porania." Furthermore, declaring that "all ages are contemporaneous," he
saw all the relevant cultures and poets "as contemporary with himself "
(Eliot), as present contexts. In short, Pound had the true metonymist's preference for external phenomena *in praesentia*, a preference that also accounts
for his stress on "presentation" in his poetics and poetry. It is in line with
this stress on "presentational immediacy" (Schneidau) that Pound, like a man
suffering from a similarity-disorder, tends to prefer *icons* and *indices* to verbal
symbols. To some extent, this explains his fascination with the Chinese
ideogram, which, like Fenollosa before him, interprets iconically by sup-
pressing its symbolic (phonetic) components, and whose iconic nature he
favorably contrasts with the "merely" symbolic code of the alphabet:
"Chinese ideogram does not try to be a picture of a sound, or to be a written
sign recalling a sound, but is still the picture of a thing; of a thing in a given
position or relation, or of a combination of things."

In connection with Pound's "reactive poetry" let me say a word or two on his *translations* which are so basic to his early poems. Unlike the true aphasic with a similarity-disorder Pound had not lost his polyglot abilities. But one may still say that his switching to heteronyms, i.e., to equivalent expressions in another language demanded by the act of translation, seems to have been affected to some degree. For it is due to his deficient or negligent switching of linguistic codes, which normally consists in a selective and substitutive word-for-word translation governed by principles of equivalence, that his "translucencies" (Eliot), his version of the Anglo-Saxon "Seafarer," his paraphrases from the Chinese, and his *Homage to Sextus Propertius* have come in for so much criticism. For, as T. S. Eliot says of the latter, a classical scholar wonders "why this does not conform to his notions of what translation should be. It is not a translation, it is a paraphrase, or still more truly (for the instructed) a *persona*. It is also a criticism of Propertius . . ." In other words, Pound once more escapes from sameness to contiguity by providing contextually oriented paraphrases instead of verbally equivalent texts, paraphrases that concentrate "less on finding the words than in bringing the emotion into focus."

Translations by Pound, therefore, are less subject to the internal similarity relations of textual fidelity than to such external contiguity relations as functioning as "windows into new worlds, as acts of homage or as personae of Pound's." Hugh Kenner makes the contextual nature of Pound's translations as personae quite clear when he writes:

> A persona crystallizes a modus of sensibility in its *context*. It derives from an attempt to enter an unfamiliar world, develop in oneself the thoughts and feelings indigenous to that world, and articulate them in English. A translation, by extension, is a rendering of a modus of thought or feeling in its *context* after it has already been crystallized, by a Cavalcanti or a Rihaku . . . the English poet must absorb the *ambience* of the text into his blood before he can render it with authority; and when he has done that, what he writes is a poem following the *contours* of the poem before him. *He does not translate words.* The words have led him into the thing he expresses: desolate seafaring, or the cult of the plum-blossoms, or the structure of sensibility that attended the Tuscan anatomy of love.

I do not think a more telling commentary on Pound's method of translation can be found, a method that operates by means of contexture rather than by a selection and substitution of words. I would further suggest that

Pound's later habit of quoting passages in their original language and not in English translation may not be due only to an orally inspired belief in the authenticity of words, but perhaps also to a growing unwillingness or inability to code-switch so typical for aphasics with a similarity disorder.

A further sign of the importance of contexture in Pound's work is his method of composition by means of compression, contraction, or deletion. "The craftmark of Pound's work," Schneidau comments, "is not expansion but contraction." To write with an eraser, "dichten" as "condensare," to create poetry of gists and piths was his poetic ideal and practice. Or as Hugh Kenner puts it: "Pound omits, omits." I do not think I have to offer examples here, for his reduction of a thirty-line poem to the Metro-*haiku*, his compression of the Sappho-poem to the "Papyrus"-fragment, to mention only these instances, are too well known to need further commentary.

Now deletion is basic to the metonymic process. For in it deletion is to combination what substitution is to selection in metaphoric processes: all metonymies and synecdoches are relics or condensations of deleted contexts. They are produced "by deleting one or more items from a natural combination, but not the items it would be most natural to omit: this illogicality is equivalent to the coexistence of similarity and dissimilarity in metaphor." Deletion, then, is the operation by which metonymic devices are generated, be it the "selective detail" of realistic prose or be it Pound's "luminous detail." Unlike the average man, Pound seemed to have had, and to have expected on the reader's part, the similarity-disorder aphasic's perfect sense of "transitional probabilities," his great ability of building contexts from fragments.

Let me now point out some further poetic devices that are context-oriented, that depend on a recreative contexture by the reader.

Pound's adoption of the *dramatic monologue* in his early poetry is an important index to his metonymic dependence on the context. "To me the short so-called dramatic lyric," he comments in a letter to W. C. Williams, "is the poetric part of a drama the rest of which (to me the prose part) is left to the reader's imagination or implied or set in a short note."

In other words, the text of the dramatic monologue is embedded in a suppressed or deleted but assumed context ("the prose part") which by means of implication, textual cues (e.g., "Take your hands off me": "Piere Vidal Old," or footnotes must be reestablished by the reader.

But Pound uses other contextualizing devices (i.e., devices presupposing a deleted context) that have not been given the proper attention so far.

An analysis of the *titles* of many of the poems in *Personae* shows that they rarely stand in a similarity-relation with the text of the poems (e.g., as summaries of content or indications of subject). However, they often allude to contextual phenomena contiguous to the subject matter. Titles like "The Garret," "The Garden," "In a Station of the Metro," "Women before a Shop," "Black Slippers: Bellotti," "The Tea Shop," etc., refer to the physical or spatial context, whereas "The Spring," "April," "Alba," "L'Art, 1910," etc. are an indication of the temporal context with all its additional connotations. Such titles as "After Ch'u Yuan," "Liu Ch'e," (possibly "Ts'ai Chi'h") refer to an implied verbal context, be it to the manner of execution or to the authors of the original texts. Many foreign language titles are cannibalized quotations (synecdochic clues) from the texts Pound paraphrases, alludes to, or finds contextually relevant to what he himself is saying.

A title that is especially deeply embedded in the nonverbalized context is "Papyrus." For it not only refers to the actual material substratum on which Sappho's poems are preserved and with which their texts are physically contiguous, but by a further contextual implication of the general fact that papyri are mostly fragments it accounts for the fragmentary nature of the poem.

But one of the most frequent devices of contextualization in *Personae* is Pound's use of "anaphoric" *determiners*, that is, of the definite article and of demonstrative pronouns (this, that, these, those), without providing the relevant antecedent referent. This contextualizing use of determiners, which automatically implies the reader's familiarity with a context the poet does not bother to mention, is found in both titles and at the beginnings of poems.

Here is a selective list of titles: "*The* Tree" (but the more normal "*A* Girl"), "*The* Eyes," "*The* Cloak," "*The* Needle," "*The* Plunge," "*The* Picture," "*The* Encounter," "*The* Social Order," "*The* Tea Shop," "*The* Gypsy," "*The* Garret," "*The* Garden," "*The* Spring," "*The* Bath-Tub," etc.

Similarly, Pound frequently starts his poems off with the definite article or with a demonstrative adjective. To give a few examples: "*The* tree has entered my hands" ("A Girl"), "*This* thing that has a code and not a core" ("Quies"), *The* apparition of *these* faces in *the* crowd" ("In a Station of the Metro"), "*This* government official" ("The Social Order"), "*The* girl in *the* tea shop" ("The Tea Shop"). "*That* was *the* top of *the* walk, when he said" ("The Gypsy").

An equivalent contextualizing effect is achieved by Pound's introduction of his characters or subjects by means of third person pronouns (he, she, it, they), that is, parts of speech with "an inherent reference to the context." For instance: " '*Tis* not a game that plays at mates and mating" ("The Flame"), "See *they* return" ("The Return"), "Like a skein of loose silk blown against the wall / *She* walks by the railing" ("The Garden"), "*She* passed and left no quiver in the veins" ("Gentildonna"), "As cool as the pale wet leaves of lily-of-the-valley / *She* lay beside me" ("Alba"), "All the while *they* were talking the new morality / *Her* eyes explored me" ("The Encounter"), etc.

It is the cumulative use of all these contextualizing devices, demanding a reader able to reconstitute the intended context from them, which makes many of Pound's early poems very difficult and elusive indeed, especially when they are approached with the traditional metaphoric expectation of a symbolical meaning. But one may also say that these poems are among his greatest successes. This may be due to the fact that Pound did the right thing when gravitating towards the metonymic pole of language, even risking symptoms of similarity-disorder. For what Jakobson says of this disorder also seems to apply to Pound's poetry: "The deeper the utterance is embedded in the verbal or non-verbalized context, the higher are the chances of its successful performance."

CONTIGUITY

Semantic or syntactical contiguity in Pound's poetry and poetics is so well known and has been dealt with so often that relatively little needs to be added under this head. Poundian notions like the image as an emotional and intellectual complex or vortex, the image as superposition, the ideogrammatic method as radical juxtaposition, the *phantastikon* as a filmy shell reflecting "sundry patches of the macrocosmos" are all too familiar and their structural affiliation with "planes in relation" in the visual arts or with "any chord may be followed by any other" of Pound's harmonic theory fairly obvious.

Such poems as "Sestina: Altaforte" and "The Game of Chess" as well as Pound's insistent use of "against" (e.g., in "Commission," "Salvationists" and "The Rest") even show that he seemed to have delighted in contiguous clashes and oppositions.

Thus, the radical contiguities of meaning and syntax used, for instance, in "In a Station of the Metro" and "Liu Ch'e"—in both of which, symptomatically, the connective of similarity ("like") is suppressed—in "Coitus," "Shop Girl," "Papyrus," etc. need no further quotation. But it is noteworthy that contiguities do not stop at the sentence-boundaries, as the ellipses, anacolutha or aposiopeses in "Papyrus," "L'Art, 1910," "Women before a Shop," and other poems demonstrate.

On the purely semantic level the two chief tropes of contiguity, namely *metonymy* and *synecdoche*, that is, the two tropes which are "widely employed by aphasics whose selective capacities have been affected," are pervasive in *Personae* and will become the dominant tropes in *The Cantos*. A few illustrations shall suffice. Thus synecdoches or concrete particulars or parts may stand for more abstract wholes: "faces" for "women" or "girls," and "petals" for "blossoms" or "spring" in the Metro-poem; "eyes" and "fingers" for an erotic contact in "The Encounter"; "the rustling of the silk" in "Liu Ch'e" for "a woman's garment," for "upper class," for "life."

Similarly, metonymies are present in Pound's best poems, for instance when he puts concrete effects for more abstract causes. "Wet" in "Petals on a wet, black bough" ("In a Station of the Metro") is either the effect of morning dew at dawn, or of spring showers; and the "blackness" of the bough may indicate early spring when blossoms sprout before the leaves, again an effect standing for a cause. In "Liu Ch'e," "The rustling of the silk is discontinued" as well as "There is no sound of footfall" are both the result of absence or death while "Dust drifts over the courtyard . . . and the leaves / Scurry into heaps" describes the effects of November storms. In both poems the seasons are implied metonymically by means of contextual deletion.

It is in his note to "The Jewel Stairs' Grievance" that Pound reverses this process of deletion by making the contextual implications of the poem's synecdoches and metonymies explicit: "Jewel stairs, therefore a palace. Grievance, therefore there is something to complain of. Gauze stockings, therefore a court lady, not a servant who complains. Clear autumn, therefore he has no excuse on account of weather. Also she has come early, for the dew has not merely whitened the stairs, but has soaked her stockings. The poem is especially prized because she utters no direct reproach." (Pound does not mention that "white," and not black, metonymically suggests mourning in Chinese culture and hence accounts for the grievance in the title).

Like the *mot juste*, which as a "bound form" (Jakobson) is syntagmatically embedded in the verbal context to such a degree that any substitution by any other word from a paradigm of equivalents is impossible, Pound's propensity to avoid metaphors and analogies also reinforces the contiguous or syntagmatic axis of his poems.

However, when he does want to establish a similarity relation, Pound tends to make use of a simile (by means of "like," "as—as") rather than a metaphor. In other words, he uses a more syntagmatic form than metaphor, a form in which the similarity-relation is made explicit, lifted to the verbal surface, subjected to an external contiguity relation.

But Pound's irritability with similarity is sometimes so strong that he suppresses the connective of similarity ("like") altogether, as in "Liu Ch'e" and "In a Station of the Metro." For it seems that as with his famous ideogram for "red" (rose, cherry, iron dust, flamingo), Pound tends to hide or smother

similarities under contiguities, not stopping short of "metonymic overkill"
(David Lodge) in *The Cantos*. As with an aphasic with impaired substitution
and intact contexture, "operations involving similarity yield to those based
on contiguity" in Pound's poetry.

CONTACT

Reading through Pound's *Personae* one is struck by the frequency and seeming
importance of physical, spatio-temporal contacts. This confirms the impression that Pound, almost like an aphasic with a similarity-disorder, was also
"guided by spatial or temporal contiguities rather than similarity."

Pound's constructions with "among," "amid," "about" and "round" are
too many to be merely accidental. And it is interesting to note that being
contiguously surrounded by, in contact with, people, trees, objects, etc., is
an important if not privileged form of knowledge to him, a knowledge in
the etymological sense of "understanding" as "standing among."

Correspondingly, other words of contact or spatial location such as
"upon," "on," "over," "above," "beneath," "under," "against," etc. abound
in *Personae*. Furthermore, in about a dozen poems immersion is of great
significance, and a great number of poems deals with palpable effects on the
contiguous environment by the movement, walking, passing of a person, by
the action of wind and water. In addition, verbs expressing material or bodily
contact are also pervasive in *Personae*, such as mingling, edging, piling, smear-
ing, binding, entwining, crushing, touching, engulfing, caressing, sheathing,
etc. No wonder, then, that clothing and metaphoric extensions of it play an
important part in the poems.

In some poems, for example, in "The Encounter" and "Shop Girl,"
direct physical contact is also favorably contrasted to metaphorical verbali-
zations and evocations of literary equivalences:

Shop Girl

For a moment she rested against me
Like a swallow half blown to the wall,
And they talk of Swinburne's women,
And the shepherdess meeting with Guido.
And the harlots of Baudelaire.

But let me tackle a final problem now: What is the appropriate critical
response to Pound's kind of extremely metonymic poetry, a poetry that banks
on context, contiguity and contact and, as all literature written in the metonymic mode, tends to disguise itself as non-literature?

   As this poetry primarily offers mere surfaces, "a disconcerting literal-
ism" (D. S. Carne-Ross), such critics as R. P. Blackmur have felt uneasy
about the fact that "it is unnecessary to pierce the verse to understand it."
Demystifying the vertical, paradigmatic world of depth, spirituality, and
metaphor by proclaiming the natural object as the adequate symbol, Pound's
horizontal, syntagmatic world of surfaces, "things" and metonymy must, of
course, be dealt with by restoring the deleted details and by putting the texts
back into their original verbal or nonverbalized context from which they
derive. This is what most traditional Pound-criticism has been about. My
suggestion, however, is that Jakobson's model of metaphor and metonymy,
although it is derived from speech pathology, offers helpful new tools for
retracing and analyzing Pound's often elusive *procedures* of contexture and
deletion themselves.

DANIEL D. PEARLMAN

Ezra Pound: America's Wandering Jew

The recent publication of *"Ezra Pound Speaking": Radio Speeches of World War II* [Leonard W. Doob, ed.], in as complete and accurate an edition as we are ever likely to have of these 120 controversial broadcasts from fascist Italy, gives us the chance to see in their entirety what has till now been published in highly selective fragments or in samples purporting to be representative. The author of the Series Foreword applauds "the respect for a complete historic record which has allowed the Pound Literary Trustees to overcome an understandable reluctance toward seeing these scripts in print," and I suppose that if they had continued to be withheld from publication, the general public might justifiably assume that the "absolute worst" there is to know about Pound was still being kept a dark secret. In fact, some of the absolute best and absolute worst of these speeches have been available in one book or another for years (not usually, however, the two extremes together), and their publication in full does not add very much of significance to the knowledge we already have of Ezra Pound's opinions. Their value must be largely of another sort. I think this hefty volume—465 pages, including scholarly apparatus—forces us, for the first time, to take a good long accurate and unexpurgated look at Pound during the ugliest period of his career and to face again that old issue so many of us would rather avoid: the seeming incompatibility between Pound the poet and Pound the man, between the servant of the Muse and the champion of Mussolini, between the creative genius and the ideological fanatic. We ask again how, in the service

From *Paideuma: A Journal Devoted to Ezra Pound Scholarship* 9, no. 3 (Winter 1980).
© 1980 by the National Poetry Foundation.

of truth, he could espouse so many lies, and how he could out of love of
humanity preach the most virulent form of racial hatred.

The poet's daughter can offer "no other explanation for some of his
violent expressions" during these war years than to say that Pound was
"losing grip on what most specifically he should have been able to control,
his own *words*," that "his own tongue was tricking him, running away with
him, leading him into excess, away from his pivot, into blind spots" [Mary
de Rachewiltz, *Discretions*]. This is not an explanation, of course, but rather
a *description* of her father's loss of self-control, and so much is admitted by
Pound himself in his last cantos: "That I lost my center / fighting the world"
[*Drafts & Fragments of Cantos CX-CXVII*]. The reader unacquainted with
these broadcasts should be reminded that their content caused the United
States government to charge Pound with treason and that, declared mentally
unfit to stand trial, Pound spent thirteen years imprisoned in a federal mental
hospital until a group of his friends finally convinced the government to
release him in 1958. I think that no serious student of Pound believes him
to have been clinically insane, and therefore without moral responsibility
for his words, either before, during, or after World War II. We would have
to discount a good deal of his literary output, including some of his best
poetry, as the incoherent ravings of a lunatic if we were to adhere to that
medical hypothesis, and I am afraid that many literary mediocrities would
prefer to dismiss an "insane" Pound from serious critical consideration not
so much because of moral crudeness of his opinions as because of his extremely difficult and highly original poetic style. We must take seriously,
then, these radio speeches of World War II, in all their intemperateness,
and try to find some meaningful link between the evil and ugly Pound so
abundantly represented in them and the good and beautiful Pound so over-
whelmingly present in the poetry.

I have no idea whether a jury would have convicted Pound of treason
on the basis of these broadcasts. I find no direct incitement to American
troops to mutiny, but again and again Pound exhorts the citizen to show
loyalty to the Constitution by eliminating the usurers and their puppets, the
Roosevelt administration, who have undermined the Constitutional basis of
U.S. government through the practice of economic policies and dictatorial
stratagems that have led directly to American involvement in the war.
Pound's vehemence in urging the removal of Roosevelt is at times a thinly
veiled call for his assassination:

> Don't shoot him. Don't shoot him. Don't shoot the President. I
> dare say he deserves worse, but don't shoot him. Assassination
> only makes more mess . . . Di/ag/nose him. Diagnose him.

In a speech made to the United Kingdom at some indeterminate time in 1941 before the United States joined the war, Pound exhibits similarly but more overtly violent wishes against Churchill, who was attempting to involve America in the war against the Axis powers:

> Months ago I typed the draft of a radio talk, and destroyed it. I advised you to bump off Churchill before he bumped off all the rest of you.
>
> That appeared to be out of order. It was not my place to advise civic violence in a foreign country, especially as it might cost some clean and decent young lad his life.

As we can see clearly in both these cases, the crude mentality of the lynch-mob dangles contemptuously over its nakedness a sort of legal figleaf. (We shall see much the same later, and with barely a figleaf at all, in the case of Pound's most violent anti-Semitic outbursts.) As to the treasonability of such barely disguised incitements to lawlessness, I am unable to guess what a court of law would conclude on the matter.

Fortunately, there is very little of such a directly provocative and demagogic nature in the speeches. Most of Pound's anger finds vent rather in abusive language, a small stock of epithets repeated with little variation throughout the whole course of these talks, so that their initial shock value wears thin and their predictability becomes embarrassing. "Repetition was the device most frequently employed both within a broadcast and from broadcast to broadcast," says the editor, and "Name-calling was his favored form of repetition, especially in connection with usurers, Communists, and Jews." Apart from the repetitious manner is the repetitious matter, and the subject that almost never fails to be brought up in all these broadcasts is the putative conspiracy of a small clique of vile international and anti-national banker-usurer-kikes (these terms are almost always synonymous) who are shrewdly engineering the downfall of Western civilization by exercising control over the world's currency operations. The subject of this "conspiracy" becomes dear to Pound's heart right after the end of World War I and increasingly occupied his attention through the thirties until, by the outbreak of World War II, it totally obsessed him.

His obsession was so obtrusive that it kept on breaking the bounds of rhetorical control:

> Don't know which, what to put down, can't write two scripts at once. NECESSARY facts, ideas, come in pell-mell. I try to get too much into ten minutes . . . Mebbe if I had more sense of form, legal training . . . could get the matter across.

But Pound is almost never interested in true expository form, either in these talks or in his preceding prose of the thirties in general, for true exposition requires not only his stringing of "one bit of evidence after another," as he assumes he is doing, but their persuasive presentation by means of some satisfying logical pattern. His answer to this objection would very bluntly be, "I am not arguing, I am just telling you." This is his "favorite stance," says [William M. Chace] in examining the prose style of Pound's *Guide to Kulchur* of 1938:

> Disagreement is out of the question. His manner is not only informal, abrupt, and at times strangely avuncular; it is also the manner of a man who confidently assumes that his answers to the problems of the world will have a validity denied to mere experts.

Ultimately, Pound's authoritarian manner is telling us that his personality alone is guarantor of the truth of his opinions, both fact and reason be damned! This is an unconscious parody of the style of the fascist "Leader," whose power in the final analysis rests on nothing more than the spellbinding force of his personality. I do not believe that one single British or American listener not already inclined to fascism was ideologically swayed by these broadcasts. Even the Italian government, although persuaded that Pound was a supporter of the Duce, was perplexed by these talks and had at one time to be convinced that they were not some sort of secret code. Not only are they clumsy as Axis propaganda, but their shrieking, unreasoning fanaticism besmirches the few valuable ideas they do have to offer. Speeches 70 and 71, for example, are very clear, emotionally restrained summations of Pound's idea of the place of money in history; they have decent expository form and they do not break down into impatient rantings about "usurer-kikes"; but their little light is lost in the surrounding darkness. As Pound himself says in these talks, "Ideas are colored by what they are dipped in."

The most detestable element in all these broadcasts, and that most in need of some sort of "explanation," is their almost unremitting anti-Semitism. If not for this relentless "Jew-baiting," these speeches would hardly seem so notorious now that World War II with the merely political issues it aroused is long over. If Pound's most sustained passion through the whole period of these broadcasts was anti-Semitism, we should try to determine what lay behind that passion and transformed it into an overriding obsession. The obvious answer that Pound was a fascist sympathizer and therefore predictably anti-Semitic will not do, especially because anti-Semitism was not essential to the fascist social and economic program in Italy as it was, *ab initio,* in Germany. The answer that Pound's hatred of usury necessitated his anti-Semitism is logically absurd and had in fact been denounced as a non sequitur by Pound himself, who entertained the theory, even as late as 1935, "that organized anti-Semitism might be the hidden war of Swiss Protestant dynasties against the Rothschilds, whom they had never forgiven for breaking into their banking monopoly" [Noel Stock, *Life of Ezra Pound*].

Attempts have been made by embarrassed critics to exonerate Pound of real dyed-in-the-wool anti-Semitism, even in the case of a passage such as the following, surely one of the blackest in all these broadcasts:

> Don't start a pogrom. That is, not an old style killing of small Jews. That system is no good whatsoever. Of course if some man had a stroke of genius and could start pogrom UP AT THE top, there might be something to say for it.
>
> But on the whole legal measures are preferable. The sixty Kikes who started this war might be sent to St. Helena as a measure of world prophylaxis. And some hyper-kike, or non-Jewish kikes along with 'em.

Or take a later outburst:

> I think it might be a good thing to hang Roosevelt and a few hundred yidds IF you can do it by due legal process, NOT otherwise. I know this may sound tame, but so is it. . . . Sometimes one feels that it would be better to get the job done somehow, ANYhow, than to delay execution.

Is the incitement to kill Jews any the less "anti-Semitic" simply because small Jews are to be exempted (as certain critics have pointed out) or because the number suggested is limited? Does the aroused mob ever heed such nice distinctions? In any case, we saw earlier with reference to Churchill (and, again, Roosevelt) Pound's scarcely restrained tendency toward rabble-rousing during this period.

We have already seen that Pound's position against the Jews, by his own earlier admission, has no necessary foundation in fact or logic. What, then, do we make of the monotonous insistence in these broadcasts that a group of the most powerful Jews in the world have for some indeterminately long period been conspiring to gain world dominion in order, out of revenge, to reduce all gentiles to slavery? Unfortunately, we are sometimes forced to remember that, as Sartre writes just after World War II, "Anti-Semitic passion . . . precedes the facts that are supposed to call it forth; it seeks them out to nourish itself upon them; it must even interpret them in a special way so that they may become truly offensive" [*Anti-Semite and Jew*]. For years before the United States entered the war, Pound had been receiving anti-Semitic literature in English from overseas that he would routinely put aside unread; now, isolated by the war, he read with amazing credulity all this material formerly rejected by his better judgment. His obsession nourished itself on whatever inferior matter was at hand.

The great mass of anti-Semitic literature between the wars battened on a notorious forgery and fiction called *The Protocols of the Elders of Zion*, whose every absurdity Pound now took as sound evidence of an international Jewish plot against Christendom. His mind was fertile soil for seeding by the *Protocols*. It is worth noting that Pound's formative years coincided with the first major period of anti-Semitism in America, 1880 to 1900. The stereotype of the Jew that developed during this period, [according to Morton Rosenstock], included the following elements:

> the attribution of distinctive, unpleasant physical traits; a pervasive concern with money (Shylock); the wielding of power through control of gold and banks (Rothschild); the existence of an invisible, financial oligarchy ruling the world; anti-nationalism; and an identification with trade and the hated, feared city. . . .
> With the rise of racialist anti-Semitism, popularized by Houston Stewart Chamberlain and soon imported to the United States, the stereotype was almost complete and remained effective, with additions, well into the twentieth century.

One of the chief "additions" to this stereotype, emerging after the Russian Revolution of October 1917, was the logically contradictory image of the Jew as both international banker and Bolshevik subversive. Since fact and logic are not deterrents to the mind predisposed to believe, Hitler effectively used this stereotype in a speech as early as 1922, in which he pictured Moses Kohn the capitalist holding out against the demands of the workers while his brother Isaac in the factory urges them to strike. Further, "that most ingenious of Hitler's publicity stunts, the cry of a secret alliance between the Jewish capitalist and Jewish socialist" [Hannah Arendt, *The Origins of Totalitarianism*], is echoed by a totally credulous Pound in his own speeches:

> As to Bolshevism two things are established everywhere. . . .
> First, that Bolshevism pretended to be an attack on capital, that it was financed by New York Jew millionaires, and that it, in effect, attacked private ownership of land and of living space (. . . YOUR kitchen and bathroom).

The most insidious addition to the foregoing stereotype, however, was the idea of the global conspiracy against the gentiles—to be achieved, with the help of "Freemasons, certain political parties, atheists, speculators, and corrupt politicians," by means of economic crises, and monopoly over gold and the press—as elaborated in the *Protocols*. These were forged about 1900, most probably by the Russian secret police, and published "by a group of reactionary extremists who wished to discredit progressive influences on the Czar by associating new ideas with a Judeo-Masonic plot to overthrow the established government." The *Protocols* were first published in English (in England) in early 1920 as *The Jewish Peril*, but shortly thereafter, in a series of articles in the London *Times* during 1921, they were revealed to be pla-giarisms of little-known French and German works of the 1860s. Meanwhile, in America, the anti-Semitic [Henry] Ford gave them great publicity and further embroidered their dangerous absurdities through a series of articles he commissioned and had published through a newspaper he owned. Be-ginning in 1920, his newspaper reprinted many of its articles in several low-priced pamphlets entitled *The International Jew* that circulated in the hundreds of thousands in America alone and soon made its way to Europe, where it sold widely in all the leading languages.

The fact that the *Protocols* had been proved fraudulent did not temper the credulity of those millions already predisposed to believe all imaginable slanders against the Jews. Hitler is reported [in Vamberto Morais's *A Short History of Anti-Semitism* (New York: W. W. Norton, 1976)] to have had the following conversation about the *Protocols*, years before he achieved power, with one of the financial backers of his party, Hermann Rauschning:

> "I have read the *Protocols of the Elders of Zion*—it simply appalled me [Hitler says]. The stealthiness of the enemy, and his ubiquity! I saw at once that we must copy it—in our own way, of course. . . ."
>
> "But," I said, "the *Protocols* are a manifest forgery. . . . It is evident to me that they can't possibly be genuine."
>
> "Why not?" grunted Hitler.
>
> He did not care two straws, he said, whether the story was historically true. If it was not, its intrinsic truth was all the more convincing to him.

The measure of Pound's loss of intellectual integrity during the war years is discovered in his identical reaction to the fact that the *Protocols* were a forgery:

Certainly they are a forgery, and that is the one proof we have
of their authenticity. The Jews have worked with forged documents for the past 24 hundred years. . . . And no one can qualify
as a historian of this half century without having examined the
Protocols. Alleged, if you like, to have been translated from the
Russian, from a manuscript to be consulted in the British Museum, where some such document may or may not exist.

The interest in them does not lie in [the] question of their
having been, or NOT been concocted by a legislative assembly
of Rabbis. . . . Their interest lies in the type of mind, or the
state of mind of their author. That was their interest for the
psychologist the day they first appeared. And for the historian
two decades later, when the program contained in them has so
crushingly gone into effect up to a point.

Our own interest in such confused rhetoric lies, of course, in Pound's
own state of mind at this time. [Stock], the poet's chief biographer, says that
by the late thirties Pound had become "absorbed in a world of make-believe
over which he ruled according to laws of his own devising." Pound's
megalomaniacal confidence in his power to diagnose and cure the world of
its ills emerges not only from these broadcasts but also in most of his prose
of the thirties and, even more dramatically, in his trip in the spring of 1939
to the United States in order to keep his country out of the approaching
war. He went to Washington, D.C., "personally to see American leaders,
to point out to them the road to economic sanity, and if necessary to accept
an advisory post and to spend some months at least each year in his own
country." It seems that Pound, for many years in self-imposed exile in
England, France, and Italy, had become too long isolated from the salutary,
chastening give-and-take of a "normal" social context—especially the rapidly
changing social context of his home country. In Rapallo one of his chief
social pleasures for many years was to conduct his "Ezuversity," to sound
off on his opinions to an ever-changing group of visitors from abroad, mostly
admirers, who would not tend to pester him with objections to his increasingly dogmatic assertions. In other words, he acted every bit the cultural
mandarin, and in his flattering sketch of Mussolini as "Artifex" (in his *Jefferson
and/or Mussolini* of the early thirties) he is in fact portraying himself as The
Artist under the mask of the fascist dictator. Even more strangely, by 1940
he seems to have imagined that "Italian proposals for money based on work"
followed so closely his own suggestions that his ideas must be indirectly
influencing the government's economic policy. There is no doubt that wishful

thinking had become his major intellectual solace, for visitors now were few, and he may well have indulged the fantasy that he, Ezra Pound, was in truth the unacknowledged "Brain Trust" of Mussolini's government.

The poet's power-fantasy is crucial to our understanding of the parallel development of his all-consuming anti-Semitism during this period. A recent writer on Pound's anti-Semitism makes a point of the "relationship of aestheticism to the rise of Fascism and Nazism [Hyam Maccoby]." The aesthetes could view "Hitler as the Artist in Power, a grotesque caricature of Shelley's 'unacknowledged legislators of the world,' " for it was axiomatic with them to subordinate the sphere of morality to the sphere of art. Further that Paterian program which impressed the young Pound so indelibly not only devalued morality, but in exalting art for art's sake and experience for experience's sake, it fatefully devalued the intellectual—the whole realm of discursive reason. As Pater says in the famous conclusion to *The Renaissance*, "The theory or idea or system which requires of us the sacrifice of any part of this experience . . . has no real claim upon us." Pound short-changed the discursive intellect—and the responsibility to the rules of logic and evidence therein implied—all his career long. In Pateresque fashion, he had no patience except for the sort of truth he could instantly recognize by means of *intuition*. Hence his scorn of mere scholars or experts, slaves to discursive reason; and his "ideogrammic" method of writing both poetry and prose, by which particulars are juxtoposed without explanatory links, "became a means to instant polymathy." "Pound's lack of attention to essential detail and his inability to reason closely from point to point," deplored by [Stock], was not a native by a carefully cultivated trait, and that anti-intellectual intuitionism of his, although it served him extremely well as imagist/vorticist poet, helps to explain in part his gullibility to fascist propaganda.

If Pound had employed more systematically and responsibly the neglected tool of his intellect, he might not have fallen prey so easily to the rampant anti-Semitism of the twenties, thirties, and forties. But he would have had also to develop that parallel discipline that his aestheticism taught him to despise: the moral and psychological discipline of *introspection*. Pound's life-long ingorance and distrust of modern psychology—particularly psychoanalysis—can easily be documented. In 1918 Freud is nothing more than a "sex crank," and in the 1950s Freud and Marx are coupled in "their kikery" as enemies of "holiness" (Canto 91). This ignorance, of course, owes a good deal to the superiority pose of the aesthete. Then again, on a more practical level, the artist has good reason to distrust the sort of psychological reductivism that threatens to tear down his imaginative constructs into their presumed elements. But we have also to do with a highly extroverted personality—the type of optimist so common at the turn of the century in an expansionist America almost incapable of self-doubt, the self-confident instrumentalist who became this century's most renowned cultural salesman. For Pound, this whole matter of introspection, this Greek business about knowing thyself, is mere "ANALYSIS, . . . dissection," whereas life is a proccess that moves like the sprouting of a seed in just the contrary direction, i.e., out from a center that lies within. This distrust of introspection and its consequence, a naive lack of psychological and moral self-awareness, is the great weakness in Pound that his friend Eliot hits on in *After Strange Gods* when he criticizes Pound's version of Hell in *The Cantos* as "a Hell for the *other people* . . . not for oneself and one's friends." Pound, like many another who is unable or unwilling to look into himself, sees in "other people" the failings he refuses to recognize as his own.

It seems to me that this incapacity for introspection, leading to the most unwitting and dangerous sort of *projection*, is the one factor that weighs more heavily than any other in helping us to understand Pound's succumbing to fascism's particularly vicious brand of anti-Semitic rhetoric. As Sartre put it, what the anti-Semitic most flees "is his intimate awareness of himself." Psychoanalytical studies of anti-Semitism made in the years following World War II give clinical support to Sartre's perception. "The mechanism of projection," by which inner conflicts are externalized upon an objective scapegoat, "permeates the entire personality of the anti-Semite," declares one important study [Ackerman and Jahoda, *Anti-Semitism and Emotional Disease: A Psychoanalytical Interpretation* (New York: Harper & Bros., 1950)]. "The need to attribute to other persons or groups qualities and emotions belonging to the self arises when one cannot face in oneself the conflict created by the existence of these very same qualities and emotions." As I hope to demonstrate in Pound's case, "the anti-Semite projects onto the Jew the aggressions diverted from his own ego, thereby sparing himself the perception of guilt" [in *Anti-Semitism: A Social Disease*, ed. Ernst Simmel]. The specific content of what Pound projects upon the Jews, which will occupy the rest of this paper, is outlined with precision and clarity in Otto Fenichel's definition of anti-Semitism [in Simmel] as

> a condensation of the most contradictory tendencies: instinctual rebellion directed against the authorities, and the cruel suppression and punishment of this instinctual rebellion, directed against oneself. Unconsciously for the anti-Semite, the Jew is simultaneously the one against whom he would like to rebel, and the rebellious tendencies within himself.

Sartre, writing at about the same time as Fenichel but from an entirely different intellectual framework, comes to exactly the same conclusion with respect to one of Fenichel's main points: "Anti-Semitism is . . . a covert form of what is called the struggle of the citizen against authority." The anti-Semite, he perceptively adds, "demands rigorous order for others, and for himself disorder without responsibility. He wishes to place himself above the law."

Aestheticism, Pound's ideological cradle, despising the norms of morality and the rules of discursive reason, despised equally the democratic political organization of that bourgeois society with which morality and reason were nearly synonymous. [John R. Harrison], a recent student of the "anti-democratic intelligentsia," writes:

> When the aesthete enters the sphere of politics, he tends . . . to reject democracy and prefer a hierarchic system where the opinion and judgement of the mass should have no effect on the rulers, whom, by virtue of their moral superiority, he would prefer to be creative artists. Thus is produced the concept of the artist-hero in modern politics.

Hannah Arendt has discussed the ironic result, after World War I, whereby the crowd-despising intellectual elite sang in strident chorus with the growing ranks of the dispossed "mob" a nihilistic song of hatred against the bourgeois social and political order. In France, Barrès, Maurras, and Daudet constituted "a kind of elite of the younger intellectuals. These men, who despised the people and who had themselves but recently emerged from a ruinous and decadent cult of estheticism, saw in the mob a living expression of virile and primitive 'strength.' " The intellectual elite shared with the heroes of the mob, the leaders of the post-World War totalitarian movements, "the fact that both had been outside the class and national system of respectable European society even before this system broke down."

Increasingly projected into Jew-hatred was the fear coupled with the sheer envy, common to both the intellectuals and the mob, of the social and political power of a bourgeois establishment that was in fact spiritually bankrupt and on the point of collapse after World War I. The enormous propaganda associating the Jews with an international conspiracy to undermine the existing social order provided both mob and elite with an easy, socially acceptable whipping-boy, the Jew, for their own anti-social envy and rage. Neither the mob nor this intellectual elite could understand the complex workings of modern industrial society, but their deep insecurity and dissatisfaction were real enough and required a concrete symbol—

answering to the source of all current evils—for their rebellious passions to become externalized. Hannah Arendt notes that, after World War I, "the masses' furious interest in the so-called 'suprastate powers' . . . *i.e.*, the Jesuits, the Jews, and the Freemasons [eventually focussing almost exclusively upon the Jews]—did not spring from nation or state worship but, on the contrary, from envy and the desire also to become a 'suprastate power.' "

Pound's identification with the anti-Semitic mob, like that of so many other ex-aesthetes, springs from precisely this same combination of impotent rage against—and unconscious envy of—Authority. It is easy to document his fuming iconoclasm throughout his whole career; it is equally easy to observe his failure to understand the complexities of modern social organization (who does understand them?) and his consequent tendency to espouse simplistic solutions to the problem of social evil; but it is far less easy, in the case of a person so sincerely and unstintingly generous to so many individuals as was Pound, to discern in him a pattern of repressed envy of authority projected in his fulminations against the "international Jewish conspiracy." Envy is such a shameful emotion! To the generous and proud it seems infinitely despicable. And yet, I believe, if we come to perceive the peculiar component of hidden "envy" in Pound—based on his unconscious identification with both real and imagined seats of Power, and projected in his own career-long urge to exercise total control—we can arrive at a true appreciation of the psychological dynamics that led one of the greatest artistic sensibilities of our century into the vicious Jew-baiting recorded so blatantly in his wartime broadcasts and less obtrusively in some of his other writings.

The ironical portrait I wish to sketch here is that of Pound as Wandering Jew, Pound as expatriate poet identifying (largely unconsciously) with the main features of that archetype, exhibiting those features to an extreme throughout his whole career, and engaging in an ever more desperate subliminal struggle to deny his increasing resemblance to that Eternal Wanderer. In its more popular form, the myth of the Wandering Jew developed in Germany. He was pictured as "a very tall and gaunt old man, with a long beard and white hair," who had at the time of Christ denied that Jesus was the Messiah and was among the crowd chanting for His crucifixion. After the trial he returned to his house and stood outside with his family to watch Jesus pass by, under the burden of His cross, toward Golgotha. When Jesus stopped for a moment to rest in front of the Jew's house, Ahasuerus (as the Wandering Jew came to be called) shouted rudely, "Go on, Jesus, go on! Why do you tarry?" Jesus replied, "I shall go and rest, but you shall know no rest—tarry till I come back." Ahasuerus then left his house to watch the Crucifixion and has wandered everywhere since then without finding rest.

The Wandering Jew is represented as "the typical repentant sinner," everywhere "treated with respect and even reverence. In a way he is sacred because he lies under a curse or taboo." Like Oedipus or the Ancient Mariner, he has achieved wisdom through suffering. His inability to find peace until the return of the Messiah is an aspect of the legend that may link it to early Jewish Messianism. The Jews expected that after the spread of the Diaspora through the whole world the Messiah would finally come and "lead his people back to the Holy Land: it would be a repetition, on a much larger scale, of the traditional forty years of wandering in the wilderness after the Exodus," [Morais].

Pound, too, was a rootless wanderer who nursed the Messianic hope of a paradise on earth, "the city of Dioce whose terraces are the colour of stars" (Canto 74), and he came to regard Mussolini as the political saviour who would transform this vision into a reality. As is well known, during the early years of Pound's career as an expatriate poet, the chief bone of contention between him and his friend William Carlos Williams was precisely Pound's rootlessness, his estrangement from American soil. Although London was the center of the arts, prolonged absence from one's native land might have some unforeseeable desiccatory effect upon a poet, and it appears to me quite probable that Pound's transatlantic twitting of Williams for his "provincialism" concealed a good deal of self-doubt and the primitive fear of Nemesis. His self-exile must in some sense have appeared to the young Pound as a betrayal of his mother country, and from one point of view his whole subsequent career is a compensatory assertion of his Americanness. A major theme of *The Cantos*, of course, is the wanderings of Odysseus and his struggle to return to his native land. Pound's Odysseus persona as a type of the Wandering Jew is, of course, an image-complex borrowed fairly directly from Joyce's Bloom.

Pound's own wanderings were not only geographical—including prolonged stays in England, France, and Italy—but also spiritual, and involve his rejection of Christianity (which accentuates his resemblance to the Wandering Jew), his championing of a highly idiosyncratic pantheon of pagan deities, and his progressive conversion to a sort of custom-tailored Confucianism. Pound seems to have been conscious, from the very beginning of his career, of the parallel between the life he projected for himself as poet and the desert wanderings of Moses, who anticipates the figure of the Wandering Jew. His earliest allusion to the envisioned *Cantos* occurs in his first published volume, *A Lume Spento*, in which the poem "Scriptor Ignotus" mentions "that great forty-year epic / . . . yet unwrit." The parallel between the post-Exodus wanderings of Moses and the time-frame conceived for *The*

Cantos stayed with Pound at least through World War II. We see it in a letter of 1915: "I am also at work on a cryselephantine poem of immeasurable length which will occupy me for the next four decades unless it becomes a bore." And in 1944 he writes, in *An Introduction to the Economic Nature of the United States:* "For forty years I have schooled myself . . . to write an epic poem."

If more direct evidence were required, however, for the thesis that Pound identified himself with the figure of the Wandering Jew, we find it strikingly available in the crucial year 1938 when, in *Guide to Kulchur* he writes:

> It is nonsense for the anglo-saxon to revile the jew for beating him at his own game. The nomad in search of cattle, the romantic tradition. Happy is the man who inherits a rich field and a strong house and can take up a classic "Anschauung" with no inconvenience (to himself). . . .
>
> Frobenius' lists of characteristics of races leave one with inability to accept, for oneself unconditionally, either a patriarchal or a matriarchal disposition. I prefer a lex Germanica to a lex Salica. *My predisposition (at least in youth) being nomadic. It is not for me to rebuke brother semite for similar disposition.* Happy the man born to rich acres, a saecular vine bearing good grapes, olive trees spreading with years. [My italics]

Pound exhibits here a complex, ambivalent attitude toward the Jew, regarding him on the one hand as the clever outsider and identifying with his foxy intelligence, but preferring, on the other hand, the "happy," "classic" state of secure citizenship, of Establishment rootedness. The image of the clever nomad, the Wandering Jew, emerges in more generalized form a little later on in *Guide to Kulchur:* "A conspiracy of intelligence outlasted the hash of the political map." The idea that intelligence should have to be in "conspiracy" against society is one that never sat easy with Pound.

The Jew (whether wandering or not) and the artist are willy-nilly alike in that both are perceived by the average member of society around them as strange and even dangerous outsiders. It was the condition of being an outsider, however, that Pound appears never to have accepted. In fact, his whole career exhibits an unflagging effort to deny the separation of the artist from society and, on the personal level, to reverse his status of an outsider to that of an insider. The outsider, no matter how he may inspire awe, is in a position of weakness, and Pound was not the sort of man to admit to weakness in any sphere.

Throughout his entire career Pound did not cease from attempts to form around himself as nucleus "a conspiracy of intelligence," a cell of like-minded individuals capable of exerting enormous influence for positive change upon a surrounding society considered passive, spiritually sclerotic, but redeemable. The dynamic image of the vortex, one of his own favorite images for center of creative force, describes this ceaseless activity of his precisely. The formation of these power-centers, or germs of potential renascence, was always accompanied by a good deal of promotional noise advertising some simply and dogmatically stated doctrine. The most influential such vortex, as far as the history of modern culture is concerned, was the imagist movement, with its still meaningful doctrine of the Image and its still helpful principles of poetic technique. Ditching imagism when the movement fell under the financial sway of Amy Lowell and degenerated into what he called "Amygism," Pound fell in (rather uncomfortably) with Wyndham Lewis and others at the beginning of World War I to found Vorticism, one of many competing isms in the art-world of the time and equally short-lived, except for its profound effect on all of Pound's own subsequent poetry, which it endowed with the dimension of social satire and criticism. Pound's efforts to influence the arts during his residence in London are not limited only to the aforementioned movements, but include his pseudonymous activities as a reviewer, particularly the extensive body of music criticism he printed in the *New Age*, and his successful promotion of the careers of individual writers such as Eliot and Joyce.

His attempts to influence the world of music continued in the early twenties in France through his work as impresario for a small group of artists including Olga Rudge and George Antheil. He was unable to dominate the Parisian world of Anglo-American letters or the visual arts, for those were the suzerainties of Gertrude Stein, who was not likely to share her dominion with a man she regarded as a mere "village explainer." Moving on to Rapallo, then, Pound discovered virgin soil—no Wyndham Lewises or Gertrude Steins cluttering the landscape—for founding a new cultural center that had its short-lived literary arm (his journal *The Exile*) but eventually concentrated on the organization of a series of concerts according to artistic principles which Pound hoped would be imitated throughout the rest of the world.

In Rapallo he also found the "village" where he could comfortably ensconce himself as chief "explainer" on matters political and economic, and his correspondence and other writings became increasingly obsessed with the latter concerns. In particular, he began to trumpet Mussolini as herald of a New Era for Western civilization, and he hoped to export fascistic and Douglasite economic doctrines to the United States by conducting an ag-gressive correspondence throughout the thirties with a select group of American Congressmen (e.g., Senators Borah and Cutting), who, he felt, could form a powerful nucleus for translating these economic obsessions into political action. Ironically, failing to penetrate the inner sanctum of power in Washington, D.C., before World War II, he was at last to find lodgement in the Capitol after the war, but in a federal mental ward.

This sketch of Pound's attempts to create select groups of cultural revolutionaries leads, however, to a more meanignful irony. Can we not see the exact resemblance of this life-long activity of his to the conspiratorial workings of his hated inner circle of powerful Jewish usurers? They, too, strove ceaselessly for power in order to impose upon the world their own set of economic principles and cultural values. Not only was Pound able to project his own cell-forming proclivities upon the Jewish capitalist, but also upon the readily available myth of the scheming international Jew in his flip-side identity as Bolshevik subversive. In fact, as his own attempts to influence the world around him (more insane than he ever was, to be sure!) grew more frantic, his anti-Semitism grew more irrational and uninhibited. The more futile appeared his efforts at political puppeteering, and the more inevitably the world seemed to plummet toward war, the more single-mindedly anti-Jewish became his fulminations against the "usurocracy." Whereas in 1935 he could say, "Usurers have no race," and in 1938 he could still remark that "international usury contains more Calvinism, Protestant sectarianism than Judaism," by 1939 his published references to Jews were becoming cruder (e.g., "Jewspapers"), and by the time of the radio speeches, having uncritically swallowed the Nazi version of anti-Semitic propaganda, he had become totally convinced that the "usury racket" was the foundation stone of a specifically Jewish plot to enslave the world.

The envy and hatred of Authority that shows through all of Pound's movement-forming activities is deflected and narrowly, safely focussed on an assumed group of exploitative usurer-Jews, with whom he unconsciously identifies through *their* presumed hatred of a gentile civilization that rejects *them* as outsiders. He can not help but envy what he can imagine as their total economic freedom and lack of responsiblity to anyone but themselves. Oddly parallel to his view that society is kept under unjust obligation to the usurer is his feeling that "society has obligations to the artist," and one of the various ways in which Pound has expressed this idea "is that artists should receive state subsidies. One thousand dollars per year should be settled on an artist of creative ability, and he should nominate his successor when he no longer has need of the money." It is not difficult to see in this elitist suggestion the substitution of the artistic for the economic drone upon society—for it is the artist himself, not bourgeois society, who is to have the power to select fellow-artists "of creative ability." In the same manner, society has no regulatory power over the dynastic successions of usurers who are supposed to be milking it.

As great as is Pound's consciously inadmissible envy of the Jews' imagined power, so great is his moral indignation at such power in such hands. The lower the ebb of Pound's literary reputation, and the greater his personal isolation and insecurity as the thirties collapse into war, the more thoroughgoing is his compensatory anti-Semitism. Through that fashionable prejudice he gained a false sense of solidarity with the economically devastated masses and felt himself the champion of those whom he had always, in fact, despised. By the beginning of the war, Pound, the rootless poet, cut off and vulnerable in a foreign land, came so much to incarnate the archetype of the pitiable but unassimilable Wandering Jew that for him the mysterious international Jew became the reviled symbol of his own powerlessness as well as of his conscious hatred and unconscious envy of the powerful.

For Pound—particularly during these war years—as for the anti-Semite in general, the Jew became "the symbol of what man fears: his own weakness, his own dark impulses, and his own conscience." The unreasoning fanaticism with which Pound attempted to convert others (through his radio speeches, contemporary news articles, etc.) to his anti-Semitic views is further evidence of the degree to which he violently rejected conscious admission of his extraordinary embodiment of that sad figure of the Eternal Wanderer. Speaking of "the fanaticism with which some anti-Semites try to convert others to their point of view," Ackerman and Jahoda provide an explanation I regard as completely applicable to the Pound of World War II:

> They are afflicted with the compulsion to convert lest they themselves be converted; that is, admit to themselves their submissive position, their passivity which entails danger, their fundamental identification with the Jew. For such conversion would expose their weakness, leaving them defenseless and open to attack.

I have attempted to show that a situation of extreme personal vulnerability, involving repressed envy of the secure and the powerful, was a determining factor in the dynamics of Pound's World War II anti-Semitism. It would make an interesting psychological study, for which there is no space here, to trace the origins of the sort of envy I have suggested, but I will mention one or two facts which a more thorough investigation should take into account. The poet's grandfather, Thaddeus Coleman Pound, at one time Wisconsin's Lietuenant-Governor and elected to three terms as a U.S. Congressman, took on legendary importance for Pound, as we see in *The Cantos* and elsewhere. The poet's father, Homer, became no more than an assayer at the U.S. Mint and already represents a decline in the family fortunes compared to Thaddeus, who occupied major seats of power. Ezra himself, an expatriate poet enjoying neither social nor financial security for most of his career, symbolizes the "end of the line" in a certain sense that he must surely have been aware of. Even as a child in Philadelphia he lived in a neighborhood that "generally became richer and more pretentious" while "the Pounds continued to make do on Homer's salary as assistant assayer. . . . [T]here was no money to spare and Ezra was sometimes conscious of the fact that some of his friends and acquaintances were better off than he was" [Stock]. In view of this background, Pound's career-long, obsessive concern to achieve power and wield influence in the cultural sphere is so much the more understandable. Indeed, his desire for political influence as well—amply demonstrated in his highly propagandistic correspondence with a group of American Congressmen, and in his personal visit to the Capitol in 1939 to lay his presumed expertise in foreign affairs at the service of the U.S. government—now becomes equally comprehensible.

Although this investigation into the psychodynamics of Pound's anti-Semitism is admittedly sketchy, my aim has been neither to mitigate the ugliness of his unfortunate obsession nor to put him on trial once again for the error of his ways. I have tried, rather, to understand how Pound's otherwise remarkable intelligence could have harbored at all seriously the shabby vice of anti-Semitism, and I believe that a close study of the interplay between psychological and historical factors will enable us to approach such an understanding.

FRED C. ROBINSON

"The Might of the North":
Pound's Anglo-Saxon Studies and "The Seafarer"

Pound's translation of "The Seafarer" together with Canto 1, *which has been largely influenced by Pound's Old English studies, are, in terms of themes and structures, an anticipation, a nucleus, and a technical synthesis right from the start. . . . It is Pound's poetics in a nutshell.*
—GEORG M. GUGELBERGER, *Ezra Pound's Medievalism*

This emphatic statement of the centrality of "The Seafarer" in Pound's poetic development faithfully represents recent assessments of the poem's importance. But this growing consensus that "The Seafarer" is a key document in the Pound oeuvre carries with it a paradox of literary biography and, ultimately, of literary interpretation, for while there is general agreement that the translation had major consequences for his subsequent career, there is also agreement that this astonishing performance is to a considerable extent the result of schoolboy howlers and naïve butchering of the original text by a man who had dabbled only superficially in Anglo-Saxon and who produced no other translations from early English poetry. Preceded apparently by no apprenticeship in such translation and by little serious study of the language, "it is very surprising indeed," says Donald Davie, "coming as it did in *Ripostes* (1912) from the poet who had seemed wedded to the Romance languages of Southern Europe" *(Ezra Pound: Poet as Sculptor)*. And others have echoed his surprise. A momentary aberration in Pound's poetic development, we are to understand, is at the same time "an anticipation, a nucleus, and a technical synthesis," and Dr. Gugelberger even adds that it is "the

From *The Yale Review* 71, no. 2 (January 1982). © 1982 by Yale University.

thematic link" between all the diverse literary cultures on which Pound drew throughout his career.

The present essay will argue that this puzzling quality of "The Seafarer" is in fact an illusion resulting from our hitherto incomplete knowledge of Pound's early development and our inattention to the philological methods which he applied when he composed his crucial poem. My good fortune in having access to the extraordinary riches of Yale University's Pound Archive and to the equally extraordinary generosity of the curator of the Archive, Mrs. Mary de Rachewiltz, enables me to draw attention to earlier poetic translations from Anglo-Saxon by Pound (previously unpublished) and to other materials which document his serious and continuing interest in the subject. It is also possible now to identify the immediate source of the Anglo-Saxon poems which he translated, and this identification requires a new assessment of his methods and intentions in the "Seafarer" translation and of his often derided claim that it is "as nearly literal, I think, as any translation can be."

It is possible that Pound had a taste of Anglo-Saxon as early as his freshman year at the University of Pennsylvania, where he took a course in "English Language and Analysis." A piece of college verse dated 1902 in the Pound Archive registers a hebetic nostalgia for the Germanic world as a whole:

> The Gods of the North are fallen
> Thor's laid his hammer down
> Men fear not the wrath of Odin
> Nor the dark Valkyries frown.

His serious study of the subject, however, began only after he transferred to Hamilton College in Clinton, New York, and became, as a college yearbook tells us, "Bib's pride"—the favorite student, apparently, of Professor Joseph D. Ibbotson, who taught him Anglo-Saxon. Pound took three terms of work with Ibbotson, spanning the academic year 1904–05 and his letters to his parents at this time frequently report on his progress in the subject. To his mother he says that he is translating "Alfred's account of the voyages of Ohthere & Wulfstan" (a prose text usually taken up early in the first term of Anglo-Saxon), and adds that "Anglo-Saxon is for the literature and if you will pay expressage, I'll send you a list of a few of the things in Ang.-Sax. worth reading." He mentions Cynewulf, *Beowulf*, and King Alfred among others. "Find Anglo-Saxon very fascinating," says a subsequent letter, and another adds, "The old French & Saxon are the chief matters of interest just now." A terse jotting in one letter to his mother says simply, "Account of

Caedmon in Ang.Sax.," from which one would not deduce that he was moved by the old tale of an illiterate neatherd's miraculously acquiring the power of poetic composition and inaugurating the entire tradition of recorded English poetry. But apparently he was moved, for he sketched out a poem on the subject (hitherto unpublished), probably his first experiment with verse based on Anglo-Saxon subject matter:

> Caedmon:
> Clear eyed draming [sic] above the sun   [1]
> Child man to father God
>   With heaven for his heart begun
> While yet earths green ways he trod.
>   Vates and seer stand forth   [5]
> Singing with all the might of the North
>   behind thee
> Singing the strong Lord God
>   Thru the seven kingdoms broad
> Master in visions makeing the cross' high tree   [10]
> Stand in skys visibly speaking to thee.
>   Maker of that higher state God's kingdom for Gods
>   earthly sons
> Serious tho he ever smiled.

Although an original poem and not a translation like "The Seafarer," this exercise echoes words and motifs that Pound had been reading in his Anglo-Saxon course with Ibbotson. Line 12, for example, alludes to Caedmon's *Hymn*, in which we are told that the Maker *(Scyppend)*, the Lord of the heavenly kingdom *(heofonrices Weard)*, created Heaven for earth's sons *(gesceop eorthan bearnum heofon)*. (Throughout this essay I have used *th* in place of the two Anglo-Saxon characters for this sound, following Pound's usual practice in his own quotations from Anglo-Saxon.) Lines 10-11 credit Caedmon with authorship of "The Dream of the Rood," a poem of disputed authorship which has always been included in standard textbooks of Anglo-Saxon. The "seven kingdoms" in line 9 are the Anglo-Saxon Heptarchy, about which Pound would have learned in his background reading or in Ibbotson's lectures.

"We begin Beowulf pretty soon," he says in a letter of February 13, 1905, and a subsequent letter adds that he has "begun Beowulf. . . . If Dad can find a copy of Beowulf edited by A. J. Wyatt, published by Cambridge Press, please send right away. . . . No other edition wanted." Pound got his copy of Wyatt's *Beowulf,* and over the ensuing years he came back to it again and again. Since Pound scholars persist in the assumption that the poet knew little about Anglo-Saxon literature outside of "The Seafarer"— even Dr. Gugelberger, who is concerned to emphasize Pound's knowledge of Old English, insists that "he probably never read [*Beowulf*] in its entirety"—it will be well to glance ahead at the references he makes to the poem after his school years. Among his papers, three blank cablegram forms which he used for jottings in the late 1920s contain on one sheet the words "Beowulf—Wyatt Cambridge U.P. 1894" followed on the next two sheets by an accurate transcription of lines 1 through 14 of the poem as it appears in Wyatt's edition. On the cover of a pad containing notes toward *Confucius to Cummings* "Wyatt" appears once again; this item dates from the late 1950s. A set of metrical scansions of uncertain date are accompanied by a scribble at the bottom of one page: *Hwaet weh gar dena in gear dagum / eraforth while oft throwade.* This is line 1 of *Beowulf* and line 3 of "The Seafarer." Both are precisely accurate as to the words, but the spelling deviates several times from the Old English text: evidently Pound was writing the lines out from memory in order to check his scansions against actual Anglo-Saxon verses. Finally, an unpublished, eight-page, typewritten essay called "The Music of Beowulf" which Pound produced around 1920 develops a hypothesis that the music to which Anglo-Saxon epic was chanted survives in the " 'heroic chant' of the Gael" as represented by the Aillte Pound heard performed in London. After hearing the concert, he says, he searched through the text of *Beowulf* until he found lines that fit the tune of the Gaelic song.

The evidence of the unpublished letters and papers suggests strongly, then, that Pound knew *Beowulf* and knew it in the original language. Critics who, unaware of this evidence, have insisted that he never read the poem, have made the poet out to be something of a charlatan, for in his published writings he repeatedly implies that he had read the epic and had evaluated it. "We may count the *Seafarer*, the *Beowulf*, and the remaining Anglo-Saxon fragments as indigenous art; at least they dealt with a native subject, and by an art not newly borrowed," he says in one of his *Literary Essays*, and in *The ABC of Reading* he recommends *Beowulf* more than once, although judging it, by implication, to be inferior to "The Seafarer" when considered as a "whole poem": "There are passages of Anglo-Saxon as good as paragraphs of *The Seafarer*, but I have not found any whole poem of the same value." Elsewhere in the *Literary Essays* he recommends "the Anglo-Saxon *Seafarer*, and some more cursory notice of some medieval narrative . . . possibly the *Beowulf*," and again, "some knowledge of the Anglo-Saxon fragments—not particularly the *Beowulf* . . . " His reaction to the poem is what we might expect: *Beowulf* has grand passages, but judged by the standards of other

West European epics it would appear digressive and its architectonics somewhat baffling. But certainly we have no basis whatever for assuming that
Pound was passing judgment on a poem he had never read. He quoted the
poem from memory, he wrote a small treatise on how it was performed, and
years after he had called for Wyatt's edition of the poem during his college
days he returned to that edition to refresh his memory of its contents.

Assuming Pound's ignorance of another well-known Anglo-Saxon poem
impugns even more directly his integrity as a man of letters. Donald Davie,
usually a skillful and sympathetic interpreter of the poet, makes the surprising
observation that in translating "The Seafarer" Pound chose to work with a
poem generally rated inferior to another Anglo-Saxon elegy, "The Wanderer," "which one suspects that Pound has never read." If Davie's suspicion
is correct, then we must concede that the poet was indeed a humbug, for in
one of his *Literary Essays* he ranks "one passage out of *The Wanderer*" along
with Dante, "The Seafarer," and *The Cid* as essential medieval texts, and
elsewhere he has praised "The Wanderer" with equal enthusiasm. Was he
pretending to knowledge of a poem he had never read? A review of Pound's
references to "The Wanderer" in published and unpublished writings shows
that he was not. In Canto 27, line 6, and [*Canto*] 77, line 45, he quotes *sumne
fugel othbaer* ("a bird bore one away") from line 81 of "The Wanderer," and
the first of these quotations was inexact in the first edition (*ouitbaer* for
othbaer), suggesting that he was quoting from memory. He also quotes from
memory line 29 of the poem, *Wat se the cunnath* ("He who experiences knows")
in *The ABC of Reading*, where he misremembers *cunnath* as *kennath*. In his
essay "The Constant Preaching to the Mob," he quotes lines 15–18 so accurately that he must have had the text before him, while in *Mauberley*, 5,
6 ("There died a myriad, . . . / Quick eye gone under earth's lid") he is
recalling in modern English line 23 of "The Wanderer," which speaks of
earth's lid covering a dead comrade. So taken was Pound with "The Wanderer" that he even toyed with making a verse translation of it. Among his
unpublished remains are renderings of lines 47–48 and 111:

> seafoul bathing foist [?] forth their feathers
> brawl rime and hail falling with snow mingled
>
> . . . .
>
> So saith the plausible in mind, sat him apart at $\begin{cases} \text{rune} \\ \text{counsel} \\ \text{mystery} \end{cases}$

The efforts are tentative, and Pound's full "Wanderer" translation never
came into being, but there can be no doubt that he knew the poem well and

spoke of it with genuine authority. After "The Seafarer" it is probably the
Anglo-Saxon poem that he knew best.

But these are not the only poems that haunted his memory. In "The
Music of Beowulf" he says, "For twenty years thereabouts I have had in
my head a few fragments of Anglo-Saxon:

> Hlude waeron hy la hlude
> Tha hy ofer thon lond rydon
> Waeron anmode, tha hy ofer thon lond rydon

That the verses were indeed "in his head" and not in a text before him is
shown by the slight inaccuracies in spelling and phrase. Following are the
actual lines from the poem he was remembering—a verse charm of incan-
tation which attempts, through word-magic, to remove from a suffering
rheumatic the spearlike pains caused by powerful witches.

> Hlude wæran hy, la hlude,
> tha hy ofer thone hlæw ridan,
> wæran anmode, tha hy ofer land ridan

That he should remember the poem so well is not surprising when we
consider his college papers, wherein we find not only a romantic allusion to
this poem, or poetry of its kind, in some youthful verses—

> Words of subtle might and terrible
> As some word wizzards woven spell
> That none may grasp—

but also a full-dress verse translation of the Anglo-Saxon charm in a metrical
form imitative of the verse of the original. This is Pound's first sustained
effort at "making new" an Anglo-Saxon poem; it is a dress rehearsal for "The
Seafarer." As in his "Seafarer" translation, he deletes parts of the charm
poem which he suspects are not genuine, leaving off a brief prose introduction
and omitting ten lines at the end which break the rhythm of the previous
verses and veer off on a prosier tangent. Scholars and editors of Anglo-Saxon
frequently dissected poems in this manner, and Pound was following their
lead. In the case of the Anglo-Saxon charms, this seems a reasonable procedure, for many of them seem to have originated as pagan incantations
which gradually took on an accretion of Christian elements as Christian
scribes copied the texts in monastic scriptoria. The metrical form of Pound's
translation differs from that of his "Seafarer." This is not simply because
the charm poem is a verse experiment while "The Seafarer" is authentic
poetry. The original verse of the Anglo-Saxon charm is looser than that of

the Anglo-Saxon "Seafarer" and the poem as a whole is more plosive and exclamatory—qualities which Pound retains in his translation. The charm translation survives in two typewritten copies, one obviously a revised draft of the other. I reproduce the second draft, with Pound's title, supplying editorially only the second and third commas and a period at the end of line 9.

Fragment

From an ANGLO-SAXON CHARM

Loud were they, loud, as over the hill they rode
Were resolute, as they rode over the land.
Shield thee now! that thou escape this malice.
Out little spear if ye herein be!
Stood under linden wood under the light shield   [5]
While all the witch women—mihtigan wif—gathered
       their power
Sent spears a-yelling.
I will send again to them, flying arrows
           To ward their advances.
Out little spear if ye herein be!   [10]
There sate the smith,
Struck the little sword
Struck with hammer, mightily.
Out little spear if ye herein be!
Six smiths sate wrighting war spears.   [15]
Out spear lie not in spear.
If herein be any iron at all
By witch work it to melting shall.

The translation is very close, and yet Pound has managed to render the original in a metrical idiom that establishes its own tone and rhythm while suggesting that of the Anglo-Saxon. By way of preparation for our close look at Pound's translational licenses in his "Seafarer" later in this essay, we might usefully note here the few liberties he takes with the original charm text. First, the refrain "Out little spear if ye herein be" ought to be ". . . if it herein be" in the second. But even an Anglo-Saxon teacher red-pencilling student translations would hesitate to carp at the obviously smoother rendering in Pound's translation. That the women referred to in line 6 are witches is made clear in the latter part of the Anglo-Saxon poem, where they are called *hægtessan*, "witches," but in line 6 they are described only as *mihtigan wif*, "mighty women." Pound has anticipated the later "witch" in order to provide the alliteration on *w*, which he completes, arrestingly, by preserving the original Anglo-Saxon phrase untranslated in the second half of the line—a presage of his strategem in "The Seafarer" of retaining some of the Anglo-Saxon words unchanged in order to communicate the flavor of the original poem. (As the poems quoted earlier have shown, "might(y)" was Pound's operative word in describing Anglo-Saxon: "Might of the north," "words of subtle might," and here the "mighty women" are designated in the original language.) Lines 8 and 9 of Pound's poem would be awkward and obscure if they had translated the Anglo-Saxon word for word ("I will send again another flying arrow opposite them"), and he has supplemented the original to bring out the sense more clearly. Similar clarification occurs in line 16 where Pound supplies a verb that is only implied in the Anglo-Saxon, which, if literally rendered, would be "Out spear, not in, spear!" The greatest license is to be found in line 13. The original Anglo-Saxon would yield in modern English "wounded powerfully with iron." Both "struck" and "hammer" have no basis in the Anglo-Saxon text. We shall return to this apparent translational error later when we examine the licenses in "The Seafarer."

Elsewhere in Pound's early writings we find further experiments with the verse-form that he describes in one youthfully exuberant poem as

> the rumbling line
> That runic letters twine
> In Saxon minstrelsy.

The least impressive of these is "At the Heart of Me: A.D. 751," in which some scholars have perceived a foreshadowing of "The Seafarer." The poem is spoken by a wayfaring Anglo-Saxon who has attained wealth and security on his voyages but insists that his achievements will be meaningless if he cannot rejoin his beloved across the sea. This subject was probably suggested by the wandering-lover theme in Anglo-Saxon poems like "The Husband's Message," "The Wife's Lament," and "Wulf and Eadwacer." Indeed, Stopford Brooke's *History of Early English Literature*, which Pound appears to have used during his years at Hamilton, summarizes "The Husband's Message" in terms which could almost as well serve as a summary of Pound's poem: "Treasure of gold the Lover has won and a fair land, and many warriors serve him. He has overcome all trouble; but nothing is worth anything unless he have her with him." Brooke dates the poem roughly near the middle of the eighth century, which probably explains Pound's date "A.D. 751" in the title of his poem. But, faithful though it is to the subject matter of the period, in execution Pound's limp, sentimentalized treatment of the theme is more like late Victorian verse than early English. About the only suggestions of Anglo-Saxon diction are a compound word "Whale-ways" and an untranslated Anglo-Saxon word "Middangeard," which Pound footnotes, "Anglo-Saxon, 'Earth.' " For all its youthful pedantry, this gesture is significant: the trick of retaining untranslated words from the original in order to suggest the flavor of Anglo-Saxon is taking hold.

The "Seafarer" theme of the exilic wanderer recurs in many of the schoolboy drafts preserved among the unpublished papers, and sometimes alliterative patterns suggest that Pound was unconsciously associating this theme with Anglo-Saxon verse, even when he was writing in conventional meters. Thus the lines

> There cometh wafting of some witched bazar
> And soundeth calling of an unsailed main

crop up in a sonnet about the sailor who rejects the easy life of landlubbers and embraces the rigors of the sea. Vaguer reminiscences of "Saxon minstrelsy" occur in the first part of the sonnet along with one very distinct one if the curious word *raeds* is to be understood as the Anglo-Saxon noun *ræd*, "plan, reading lesson":

> I am sore weary of the raeds they tell
> These loafers mumbling at the wonder door
> The wisdom of the schools it urks me sore
> My tongue is keen for winds and wander lore
> My pulse is hot . . .
> I hear the breakers whining at the oar.

Another on the same theme begins, "There is an unrest in me for the road / And I would be amid the bales of cargo." These groping sketches of poems that never came alive seem repeatedly to strain after the combined persona and perspective which Pound was to discover finally in "The Seafarer," and the recurrence of alliterative-accentual lines like

> The blaze upon the hearth all baleful strives
> To be but mock'ry of warm merriment.
> Blood is the blaze, the brothers three low bent

amid incongruous pentameters hints that he could not get out of his head the Anglo-Saxon rhythms he would eventually make his own.

Many of the verse exercises among Pound's papers are imitations of the styles of various earlier English poets, and a number are Chaucerian exper-

iments written in a form of Middle English which is linguistically the equal
of Chatterton's efforts. But there is a persistent underdrumming of the Anglo-
Saxon measure, and at times this ancestral voice becomes dominant and
achieves control and assurance of tone even when the subject matter fails to
come into focus, as in the following curious lines reminiscent of elegiac
passages in "The Wanderer" and "The Seafarer." (I have silently corrected
typographical errors, and where alternate versions of a word or phrase are
given, I have printed only the last.)

> Age full of grudges, you hold up the end,
> Sit late in a weary corpse, why, why,
> Let the life out of this dungeon,
> Death is a rest already, life an aching.
> I am not what I was, the great part is perished
> And the relictions full of languor and horror,
> Light heavy in sorrow, grievous amid all glad things.
> Worse than all burials is the desire for death,
> While youths adornment, while mind and senses were left me
> World wide orator a mouth for all worlds' ears,
> Oft amid poets formed I fair feignings,
> Oft having spoken took I the crown of contention,
> Took I my tongues worth, many a treasure,
> What stays undead now, in dying members,
> What is for an old man, out of life's portions.

Here the thumping alliterations of the earliest efforts are overcome and
something subtler is emerging, although the firm prosody of "The Seafarer"
remains unachieved. But there are suggestions here of both the early poem
on Caedmon and of the *nekuia* of Canto 1. The long experimentation with
Old English rhythms has tuned his sense of versification, and the themes
and attitudes of the old poets have found a place in Pound's well-stocked
mind. At a period in his development when we have heretofore assumed
that the poet was becoming imbued exclusively with "the spirit of Romance,"
he was in fact absorbing with comparable avidity "the might of the North."

   "What text Pound used, how it was punctuated, what glosses accompanied it, remains an unsolved problem," observes Hugh Kenner of the
"Seafarer" translation. The questions he raises are important, since all the
debates over Pound's intentions, his competence in reading Anglo-Saxon,
and indeed the very nature of his poem (translation? metaphrase? phanopoeia?) must be inconclusive so long as we are unable to say exactly what
text of the Anglo-Saxon poem he was translating. Kenner rules out one

possibility, namely that Pound used the text of the poem included in Henry Sweet's *An Anglo-Saxon Reader in Prose and Verse*, a popular and reliable course book then used in many Anglo-Saxon classes. Kenner points out that Pound, in his "philological Note" to the first printing of the poem in *The New Age*, specifically describes and quotes from the concluding section of the Old English poem, which Sweet did not print in his text of "The Seafarer" in his *Reader*. Pound must have used an edition, Kenner reasons, in which the complete text of "The Seafarer" was available. Bernetta Quinn, on the other hand, confidently identifies the source text: "His text was *Bright's Anglo-Saxon Reader*, as familiar to specialists as *Poor Richard's Almanac* is to Americans at large and still in use in some of today's graduate schools." She quotes extensively from Bright and suggests that the reason Pound did not translate all of the Anglo-Saxon poem is that Bright printed only the first part of it. (She apparently ignores Pound's "Philological Note" and the implications Kenner drew from it.) But Bright's *Reader*, though first published in 1891, did not include "The Seafarer" among its readings until the book was revised and enlarged by James R. Hulbert in 1935—twenty-four years after Pound had published his translation. When Hulbert did print the poem, moreover, he printed only the first sixty-four lines, whereas Pound translated ninety-nine lines. Whatever his source text may have been, it was certainly not *Bright's Anglo-Saxon Reader*. K. K. Ruthven, on the other hand, thinks Pound drew on "various scholars," including the Germans Gustav Ehrismann and Friedrich Kluge and the Dutchman R. C. Boer—dry and dreary reading for a vibrant poet eager to master all the primary sources of Western culture. Surely Pound would have availed himself of one of the many reading editions that synthesized pertinent theories of scholars such as these rather than repeat that task of synthesis himself.

But hypotheses about Pound's source task are now, happily, superfluous, since the book he used for his translation survives and is available for scholars' inspection. Long among the poet's books at Brunenburg, it was for a brief period on deposit in Yale's Beinecke Library and is now at the University of Texas. It is *An Anglo-Saxon Reader in Prose and Verse* by Henry Sweet, seventh edition (Oxford, 1898). This volume is inscribed on both flyleaf and endpaper, and several pages are annotated in Pound's hand. Some of these annotations have direct connection with his remarks on Anglo-Saxon literature in other writings. Lines 15–18 of "The Wanderer," for example, are carefully bracketed in the left-hand margin for special attention. These are the four lines quoted and translated in his 1916 essay "The Constant Preaching to the Mob" alluded to above. The text of the Anglo-Saxon charm which Pound translated is among the poems printed in this volume, as is

Caedmon's "Hymn," on which he based his poem "Caedmon." "The Sea-farer" has several telltale annotations, including a gloss by Pound identifying *byrig* in line 48 as "mulberry" ("cometh beauty of berries" in Pound's trans-lation) rather than as "cities," which scholars have noted to be the correct translation. Most significant, perhaps, is Pound's annotation stating where he thinks the poem should end. In the middle of line 99 he draws heavy vertical lines and in the margin he writes "End" and underscores the word twice, while cancelling the remaining ten lines on the page. This is precisely where Pound's translation of "The Seafarer" ends.

But what of Hugh Kenner's point about Pound's "Philological Note" referring to lines of the poem which are not printed in Sweet's *Reader?* Doesn't this at least prove that Pound must have consulted another text of the poem besides the one in Sweet? It does not, because Sweet in fact prints the full text of the poem, only in two different parts of the *Reader*. In his collection of readings, Sweet prints lines 1 through 108. This is the text that Kenner saw. But if Kenner had turned back to the explanatory notes on the poem on pages 222–24 of the book, he would have seen that there Sweet printed the remaining sixteen lines of the poem, from which Pound quotes in his "Philological Note." Sweet removed this portion of "The Seafarer" from the text proper because he thinks these verses "could not have formed part of the original poem" but must have been tacked on by a latter-day meddlesome scribe. This was a common opinion in Sweet's day, one strongly supported, for example, by Stopford Brooke's *History of Early English Literature*, which is cited by Pound in his copy of Sweet's *Reader* at the beginning of the poem "The Wanderer." Pound evidently studied Sweet's and Brooke's discussions and accepted the prevailing scholarly rationale for dissecting the poem, but with characteristic independence of mind, he made his own judgment as to where the cut-off should come, indicating this judgment in his emphatic annotation "End."

It is important to note that in cutting off the last part of the Anglo-Saxon poem Pound was simply following through on the assumptions that Sweet and other Anglo-Saxonists of his day made about the genesis of poems like "The Seafarer." The prevailing view was that these texts were originally pagan poems and that Christianizing scribes had revised them by inserting a Christian reference here and there and then adding a pious homiletic conclusion. The job of the serious student of Anglo-Saxon, they felt, was to disengage the original pre-Christian poem from the monkish adulterations and, by excising the latter, to recover the "real poem." This is what they did in their editions, and this is what Pound sought to do in his translation. It is therefore misleading when Hugh Witemeyer says (with the approval, apparently, of Alexander, Davie, Kenner, Knapp, and virtually every other Pound critic), "The changes he made in the original text subtly modify its spirit and bring it into line with his own preoccupations. . . . The major change is in Pound's systematic elimination of all Christian elements from the poem. . . . Pound's translation paganizes the poem." But Pound's changes and his justification for them in his "Philological Note" are simply accurate reflections of the standard scholarly doctrine he read in Sweet's *Reader*. It is Sweet who discards the Christian conclusion of the poem, saying, "It is evident that the majority of these verses could not have formed part of the original poem." Pound is again adhering to the scholarly dictates of his day when he eliminates a reference to the devil in line 76 of the Anglo-Saxon poem and when he translates *englum* in line 78 as "English" rather than "angels" (a perfectly legitimate translation of the word and not, as some Pound scholars have mistaken it to be, a confusion or a translational error). Anyone who has read E. G. Stanley's *The Search for Anglo-Saxon Paganism*, which details the way in which nineteenth-century scholars and editors revised and dissected their texts in order to recover "the original poem" (i.e., the supposed pre-Christian poem), will realize that Pound was rather conservative for his day and respected the integrity of the transmitted text more than many of Sweet's contemporaries. He does not, for example, substitute names of pagan Germanic deities for references to the Christian God, as did some Teutonizing scholars. What is most important, however, is to understand that what little adapting he did do in his "Seafarer" was *not* done to "subtly modify its spirit and bring it into line with his own preoccupations" but rather was done for precisely the opposite reason, to recover the real, original Anglo-Saxon poem, as that process of recovery was understood by scholars in his day. He was probing for "the English national chemical," just as he claimed, and was not overlaying the ancient text with Poundian prejudices and a modern "spirit."

Critics have also suspected that Pound reconceived the essential genre of his Anglo-Saxon text. "In his note he calls the poem a 'lyric,' distinguishing it from some larger narrative which may have contained it," says James F. Knapp, and Michael Alexander seems to agree: "He detected what he calls a 'lyric' behind the more dramatic and meditative poem that has survived . . . he does not make it clear that he is extensively modernizing his original, perhaps because he did not realize how far he was doing so." But here again what the critics have taken for Pound's revisionary handling of the poem is really an alert adherence to the best scholarly opinion of his day. In the Preface to his *Reader* Sweet introduces "The Seafarer" as "the finest of the Old-English lyrics," and his explanatory note begins by saying "The Seafarer

. . . is by common consent the finest of the Old-English lyric—or rather half-lyric—poems." And at yet another point, Sweet emphasizes that "The Seafarer," "The Wanderer," and a few like poems "show lyric poetry in its earliest stage." It was received opinion recorded in Pound's copy of the poem that proclaimed "The Seafarer" to be a lyric, not some modernizing impulse of Pound's.

The aspect of Pound's "Seafarer" that has received most extensive attention and debate is the "howlers"—those points in his translation where he seems to have misunderstood the Anglo-Saxon words completely and supplied meanings utterly different from the ones intended in the Anglo-Saxon text. Here too some Poundians have argued that he was substituting his own personal feelings and opinions for those of the Anglo-Saxon poet, silently abandoning his stated pledge to render the original literally. "Despite the scholarly rationale," says Witemeyer, dismissing Pound's explanation of his philological method, "the changes mesh too perfectly with Pound's own poetic biases to be motivated by sheerly textual considerations." Yet other critics have tried to excuse the list of translational errors by calling them "deliberate jokes" or by suggesting that Pound was simply imitating the sounds of the original Anglo-Saxon words without regard for their meaning. But most commentators have conceded that the departures from the received text are the result of Pound's ignorance pure and simple, and his admirers no less than his detractors have hooted at his claim to having produced a translation "as nearly literal, I think, as any translation can be." "A great pity," "regrettable," "unfortunate," say his defenders about the mistranslations, and his adversaries respond that the errors are "deplorable marks of the literary fake."

In reassessing the oft-rehearsed list of translational errors we might begin by returning to Pound's earliest poetic translation from Anglo-Saxon, the verse charm printed above. There we noted consistent, faithful adherence to the meanings of words in the original poem, with but one notable exception—the translation of *iserne wund swithe* as "struck with hammer mightily" rather than with the more literal "wounded with iron exceedingly." Before we look too far into Pound's modern biases and linguistic limitations for an explanation of his license here, we should look first at the book from which he was making his translation. On page 215 of Sweet's *Reader,* we find among the explanatory notes to this poem the following annotation to the words in question: "*iserne wund swithe* . . . 'wounded with iron'; that is, 'beaten with an iron hammer.' " His apparent departure from his text was in fact the result of his working conscientiously within the terms of the scholarly apparatus at his disposal. What that apparatus teaches in comment after comment is that attaining the true meaning of the Anglo-Saxon texts requires much more than simply reading the literal meanings of the words preserved in the Anglo-Saxon manuscripts. Sometimes, as in this instance, the rather general meanings of the words in a passage must be interpreted and specified in the light of the overall context. At other times, Sweet's annotations suggest that the Anglo-Saxon words have several meanings and that the reader must make a considered choice among alternative meanings. Quite frequently Sweet indicates that the words preserved in the old manuscripts simply do not make sense in the context of the given poem and so must be changed ("emended") by the editor in order to achieve an acceptable sense for the passage as a whole. In not a few cases Sweet suggests several different emendations for a problematic word or passage, implying that none is wholly satisfactory and so the reader will have to judge for himself which is to be preferred.

An example of the latter kind occurs at line 56 of the Anglo-Saxon "Seafarer." The original manuscript here reads *efteadig secg*, "re-blessed man," which makes little sense in context. Sweet's explanatory note points out that some scholars, in an effort to make the two words meaningful (and metrical), have emended the manuscript reading to *sefteadig secg*, "man in easy circumstances," while yet others have thought more likely the reading *esteadig secg*, "prosperous man." Sweet actually adopts (for metrical reasons) yet another emendation in the text as he has printed it: *secg esteadig*, "man prosperous." But his note implies that all these proposals deserve consideration, and Pound in his translation chose from these alternatives the rendering "prosperous man." A thoughtful reader of the texts in Sweet's book would go through this kind of exercise repeatedly every time he read one of the poems or prose selections. That is, he would be forced to review several possible interpretations of the meaning or structure of a word or phrase and then, in the light of the overall meaning of the work or the immediate context, would have to select the most probable meaning for that occurrence. And frequently he would notice that the scholar who edited the book had decided that the range of meanings offered by the word preserved in the ancient manuscript was altogether unsuitable for the context and so had altered the manuscript reading to some more appropriate word. Most students of Anglo-Saxon manage to get through the course without worrying much about these editorial matters. They simply accept whatever the editor prints and follow his glossary for the meanings of the words. They ignore the explanatory notes which discuss the process of philological review and choice by which the editor arrived at the reading he finally commits himself to in his text. Pound could never bring himself to accept passively a text which was the product of another man's decisions as to what the author had intended. As his "Phil-ological Note" to "The Seafarer" clearly shows, he involved himself in the establishment of the text before he translated it. Indeed, he often indulged in philological speculation. A remarkable note at the end of his verse trans-lation of Arnaut Daniel's "Canzon: of the Trades and Love" offers a solution involving paleography, Latin syntax, Latin accidence, and the possible in-fluence of Virgil's ninth eclogue on Provencal canzon. Moreover, in Pound's copy of Sweet's *Reader* we can see marginalia that show his mind working in this philological vein, as when he marks off part of "The Wanderer" as being "not by original author" and another part as being an addition "of scribe" and not by the author of the poem. At line 44 of "The Seafarer" he appears to question whether *hyge*, "thought" might not be a scribe's error for *hyht*, "pleasure." We must remember this activist, philological dimension of his reading as we reexamine the list of supposed translational errors critics have long deplored in his "Seafarer."

The main reason Pound's admirers conceded so meekly that he was a slapdash translator or a willful betrayer of his Anglo-Saxon text is that they were overawed by the intimidating authority of Kenneth Sisam, the eminent Oxford Philologist who first pilloried the poet for his translational errors in *Times Literary Supplement*, June 25, 1954. But upon examination it will become apparent that Sisam was not altogether fair and accurate in his representation of Pound's translational procedure. Consider, for example, the following three "blunders" cited by Sisam. (The first line number given is that of the Anglo-Saxon poem, the second, in parentheses, that of Pound's translation.)

- line 88 (90): Pound confuses the preposition *thurh* "through" with the word *thruh* "coffin, tomb"
- line 48 (49): Pound translates *byrig* "towns" as "berries"
- line 23 (23): Pound translates *stearn* "tern, sea-bird" as "stern (of a ship)"

Sisam asserts that in each of these instances the poet simply blundered, guessing wildly and wrongly at the meanings of words in his text. In the case of the first instance Sisam even reconstructs for us how Pound came to make his embarrassing error: "Here he looked up the preposition *thurh* ('through,' 'in'), came upon *thruh*, 'coffin,' 'tomb,' and thought it near enough. The method is very old and uncritical." Indeed, as Sisam has described it, it is the method of dim-witted undergraduates. But let us trace Pound's steps through the procedure described by Sisam. If Pound had looked up *thurh* in Clark Hall's *Concise Anglo-Saxon Dictionary* (as he almost certainly would have done), he would have encountered entries for two different words spelled *thurh*. The first is the preposition. The second entry says simply *"thurh = thruh"*: that is, *thurh* occurs as an alternate spelling for the word *thruh*. If Pound then turned to *thruh* to find out what it meant, he would have found the definition "chest, tomb, coffin." The *Dictionary*'s information is precisely right: *thurh* occurs repeatedly in Anglo-Saxon texts as a noun translating Latin *sarcophagus* or in other contexts with the meaning "casket." What Pound found in the dictionary, then, would have placed him in precisely that position he had found himself in so often as he read Sweet's notes. He had to make a choice between two possible meanings of the word before him, basing his choice upon the context and upon his understanding of the poem as a whole. Of the two possible meanings of the word, he chose one while Sisam chose the other. I must add that in this particular case I find Sisam's interpretation more attractive than Pound's, because my reading of the meter of the line does not permit *thurh* to have noun stress, because *thurh* "tomb" is statistically rare compared with *thurh* "through," and because the traditional interpretation of *thurh* as the preposition (which is the one Sisam is defending) accords better with my sense of the spirit and meaning of the poem as a whole. But I respect the process by which Pound arrived at his interpretation, and I do not think that process should be misrepresented as a schoolboy blunder by someone so slow-witted as to be incapable of detecting the difference between the forms *thurh* and *thruh*.

Turning to the second example, we might well ask how Pound ever came to translate *byrig* "towns" as "berries." The answer is very much like that in the case of *thurh*, only this time one might well prefer Pound's interpretation to Sisam's. The Anglo-Saxon dictionaries record two separate words spelled *byrig*. One is the plural noun meaning "towns"; the other is a noun meaning "mulberry tree" or, since the singular and plural of this noun have the same form, "mulberry trees." In his copy of Sweet's *Reader* Pound has underlined *byrig* in line 48 and written out in the margin alongside it the meaning "mulberry." In the poem, *byrig* is the subject of a plural verb *fægriath*, which means "become beautiful." If one chooses to read the word as Sisam does, it would mean "the towns become beautiful"; if one prefers Pound's interpretation, it would mean "the mulberry trees become beautiful" or, as Pound has rendered it in his poetic translation, "Cometh beauty of berries." Considering the immediate context of his phrase in the Anglo-Saxon poem, which may be translated literally as "the groves sprout blossoms, the mulberry trees become beautiful, the fields become fair," one might well conclude that there is at least as much to be said for Pound's reading as for Sisam's. In any case, we must acknowledge that the two interpretations of *byrig*—"towns" and "mulberry"—are equally defensible linguistically. There has been no inept blunder of translation.

Pound's reading of *stearn* as "stern" is more complicated. Detractors like

Sisam have in the past assumed that Pound came upon the Anglo-Saxon word, fancied that it looked something like modern English "stern" and, without bothering to check further, simply translated the word "stern." But let us assume that he began by looking the word up in the *Concise Anglo-Saxon Dictionary*, as he had looked up *byrig*. This is what he would have found:

> STEARN (æ, e) m. sea-swallow? tern? *Gl, Seaf.* ['stern']

What this entry tells us is that *stearn* is a masculine noun, sometimes spelled *stærn* or *stern* rather than *stearn*, that it occurs in Anglo-Saxon glosses and in "The Seafarer," and that its meaning is doubtful, although scholars have guessed that it might mean either "sea-swallow" or "tern." The bracketed 'stern' at the end of the entry means that in modern English the Anglo-Saxon word has taken the form "stern," and such a word does indeed occur in modern English dialects as the name of a variety of bird. Having seen how uncertain the meaning of *stearn* is, Pound might well have returned to his copy of Sweet's *Reader* to examine the word there in context. Doing so, he would find the word printed not as *stearn* but as *stear*[*n*]. The brackets are the editor's device for indicating that the Anglo-Saxon word actually transmitted in the manuscript is *stear* but that he had added the *n* in order to change the scribe's form into a word that he, the editor, finds more suitable. (In fact the word *stearn* is legible in the manuscript and Sweet's *stear[n]* is an editorial error, but Pound could not have known this.) All this conjecture about the word would very likely have suggested to Pound that philologically the status of this word was an open question rather than a solved problem, and he would have felt free to do some conjecturing on his own. If he tried to look up *stear* in the Anglo-Saxon dictionaries, he would not have found such a word, but he would have found the very similar *steor*, which means "rudder, helm." Perhaps he decided that since *stearn* is spelled variously *stern* and *stærn*, *stear* could very likely be a variant spelling of *steor*, and this is the source of his rendering ("stern" being not too far from "helm"). Or conceivably, when he examined the entry for *stearn* his eye fell on "['stern']" and he decided to use this dialect word in his poem, intending the meaning "snow fell on the sea-swallow." Or he may have misunderstood the word as the "stern" (part of a ship). My concern here is not to determine with certainty what Pound meant in line 23 of his poem but to point out that if his interpretation of *stearn* (or rather *stear*[*n*]) differs from that which Sisam and other Anglo-Saxon scholars have been accustomed to assume, it is probable, in view of his usual philological bent, that he was deliberately making an independent guess as to the word's meaning rather than just failing to understand received opinion on the passage. Considering the highly conjectural nature of the word as he encountered it in his text and in the dictionary, one can hardly say that his hazarding an original interpretation would be either unlikely or unwarranted. It should be noted that Pound's entire sentence in lines 23–24 is a rather loose rendering, and this may well be because he detected the uncertainty in Sweet's *stear*[*n*] and so chose to improvise verses around the general images of the original without trying to pin down a literal sense that was seemingly no longer accessible.

I do not propose to reconstruct Pound's rationale for each of his departures from the letter of the received text of the Anglo-Saxon "Seafarer," and I am certainly not suggesting that each of his philological innovations is superior to the traditional readings established by scholars in the field (although I think some of them may be superior). What is important is that we acknowledge that Pound's version is the product of a serious engagement with the Anglo-Saxon text, not of casual guessing at Anglo-Saxon words and of passing off personal prejudices as Anglo-Saxon poetry. Further examination of the most commonly cited "blunders" may help to establish more clearly his seriousness of purpose.

In line 89 of his poem Pound has translated the Anglo-Saxon *wuniath tha wacran* ("the weaker [ones] remain") as "waneth the watch," confusing the word *wuniath* "remain" with the word *waniath* "wane" and confusing *wacran* "weaker" with heaven knows what—or so the critics have said. But it is helpful once again to return to Pound's copy of Sweet's *Reader*. There, twenty pages before he came to *wuniath tha wacran* in the "Seafarer," he would have read the word *waniath* "wane" in line 72 of the Old-English poem "The Phoenix." But there is a footnote attached to *waniath* explaining that the actual word in the original Anglo-Saxon poem is *wuniath*. Assuming that the ancient scribe might easily confuse these two words, the editor has changed *wuniath* to *waniath* in order to give smoother sense. Now when Pound then came upon *wuniath* in the "Seafarer," he simply repeated the same editorial operation, assuming for himself the scholar's right to emend a word for sense. Professional scholars like Sisam might well regard it as presumptuous for a young poet-translator to thus encroach on the scholar's domain, but they should not dismiss such textual decisions as "careless ignorance or misunderstanding." As for *wacran*, this form could well be interpreted as a nominalized form of the adjective *wacor*, "watchful," and Pound evidently chose to read it that way. *Waniath tha wacran* would then mean "waneth the watchful [ones]," and this would be the interpretation that lies behind Pound's "waneth the watch." Although this rendering works very well in Pound's poem, I would not be tempted to incorporate his reading into a scholarly interpretation of the Anglo-Saxon poem. His bold emendation of *wuniath* seems to me unnecessary, and his reading of *wacran* seems strained. But considering his known source (Sweet's *Reader*) and his demonstrated method of translating, one would be reckless to dismiss his rendering as nothing more than a naïf's wild guessing at the meaning of the verse.

In line 81 the Anglo-Saxon poem has *ealle onmedlan eorthan rices*, which is usually taken to mean "all arrogance of the domain of the earth." Pound renders it "all arrogance of earthen riches," and the critics pounce with glee, explaining that he mistook the genitive singular noun *eorthan* "of earth" for a word meaning "earthen" and has misunderstood the noun *rice* "domain, kingdom, power, authority" as meaning "rich." But the genitive singular noun *eorthan* occurs twice elsewhere in "The Seafarer," and Pound has accurately translated it "earth's" (line 62) and "earthly" (line 91), showing that he understood exactly what *eorthan* means. "Earthen" is a reasonable translation of the attributive genitive in any case. We also know from his poem "Caedmon," printed above, that he knew perfectly well what *rice* meant, for that poem is mainly built around the world *rice* "kingdom, domain" as it occurs in Caedmon's "Hymn" (*heofon-rices Weard* "Lord of the heavenly kingdom"): Caedmon sings throughout the seven kingdoms of the Anglo-Saxon Heptarchy about the Kingdom God has prepared for men in Heaven. In the "Seafarer," however, Pound wants to emphasize wealth rather than just kingdom, apparently because he felt this is a more likely concomitant of "arrogance." His "riches" probably is based upon the entry for the word *rice* in Clark Hall's *Concise Anglo-Saxon Dictionary*, where the adjective "rich" appears along with the nouns "power, authority, kingdom," in the definition of the word.

An interesting example of a Poundian rendering which has been construed as the translator's taking liberties in order to project his personal attitudes onto his text is

> Nathless there knocketh now
> The heart's thought that I on high streams
> The salt-wavy tumult traverse alone.

This is generally quite faithful to the original Anglo-Saxon, but Georg Gugelberger detects one word here which "emphasizes the solitary nature of that passage over the sea" and emphasizes it, moreover, "even more than does the original text." The word in question is "alone," which translates the Anglo-Saxon *sylf*, usually taken to mean "myself." Anglo-Saxon dictionaries do record a rather rare usage of *sylf* meaning "alone," but apparently

Dr. Gugelberger (and scholars at large) feel that this rare sense of the word is sufficiently improbable in the "Seafarer" passage that its invocation here can only be the result of Pound's wanting to stress the theme of solitude "more than does the original text." Most people would probably have agreed with this view at the time Pound made his translation and for many years afterward. As it happens, however, one eminent Anglo-Saxon scholar recently subjected this passage to intensive scrutiny and came to the conclusion that *sylf* here could only mean "alone," and he credited Pound with having anticipated this discovery through "his poet's intuition": see John C. Pope's "Second Thoughts on the Interpretation of 'The Seafarer,' " *Anglo-Saxon England*, volume 3 (1974). In the judgment of one modern scholar, then, Pound's inclination to stress the theme of solitude in this passage is an inclination shared with the Anglo-Saxon poet.

Interesting as such moments of Poundian prescience may be, my concern here is not to argue that Pound's "Seafarer" is a close, scholarly rendering of the Anglo-Saxon text or that he was himself an Anglo-Saxon scholar. He often insisted that he was not a scholar (although he took scholarship seriously and used it himself to open doors to new literary cultures), and his poem "The Seafarer" is often loose and inventive (although inventive within the limits of what he took to be faithful, philological translation). My concern here is to show that Anglo-Saxon literature, the heroic literature of the English, had a larger part in Pound's early development than has been realized. Those who have repeated condescendingly the litany of supposed mistranslations in "The Seafarer" have impeded understanding of Pound's Anglo-Saxon interests by implying that his knowledge of Anglo-Saxon was superficial and trifling. And this, in turn, leads to the improbable paradoxes in the usual interpretations of Pound's poetic development: through his "Seafarer" Pound achieved the only poetic idiom adequate for the *nekuia* in English, but the achievement is the result of "ignorance and misunderstanding." *The Cantos* had their inception in Pound's conversations with his Anglo-Saxon teacher ("*The Cantos* started in a talk with 'Bib,' " said Pound), but the only Anglo-Saxon legacy in his oeuvre is a single slapdash paraphrase. In "The Age Demanded" Pound included "emendation, conservation of 'the better tradition' " among his highest aims as a poet, but in "The Seafarer" he leaves us a crude parody of "emendation, conservation of 'the better tradition.' " Pound judges "The Seafarer" as "fit to compare with Homer," but his translation of the poem is a tissue of hasty guesses and linguistic boners. Considered in light of the facts, these paradoxes yield to a more probable pattern of poetic development. Scrutiny of Pound's unpublished as well as published writings shows that his engagement with Anglo-Saxon was longer and more serious than our preoccupation with "The Spirit of Romance" has allowed us to see. Examination of the "howlers" in the light of Pound's source text and of the scholarly tradition within which he was operating reveals that his inaccuracies, or seeming inaccuracies, are more often serious applications of the philological techniques which he had learned from the books and teachers at his disposal. Indeed, his claim to "literalness" and to philological dedication to his text is not an embarrassing pretension but a defensible position, and in his method we can recognize the philological basis of his stated aim in reading all literature—"to see through to the original." Contrary to the misconceptions shared by his admirers and his critics heretofore, Pound's procedures in his "Seafarer" are neither empty pretensions nor jokes and blunders. Empty pretensions would not enable a poet to discover in his Saxon past both "the English national chemical" and the exilic wanderer who, in one guise or another, speaks his sentiments throughout his poetic career. Jokes and blunders would not enable him to gather from the past a live tradition.

DONALD DAVIE

Res *and* Verba
in Rock-Drill *and After*

Pound's preference for *res* over *verba* is so notorious, and has been reiterated so insistently by the master himself (from the resounding Thomist declaration, "Nomina sunt consequentia rerum," in the Gaudier memoir of 1917, through to his preferring on just these grounds in *The Pisan Cantos* Ford's conversation to Yeats's) that, when it comes to a choice or a show-down between a mimetic view of how language relates to reality and a structuralist view, it seems clear that Pound must stand with the conservative and nowadays somewhat embattled champions of *mimesis*. And yet, as people are beginning to notice, Pound's own practice in *The Cantos* (throughout, but more markedly in the later sequences, *Rock-Drill* and *Thrones*) lends itself more readily to explanation in structuralist than in mimetic terms—to the extent that there is at least *prima facie* justification for Massimo Bacigalupo's charge that Pound was culpably naïve in not realizing how his own practice went beyond his own mimetic theory. To be blunt about it, Pound's transitions seem to be frequently from *verbum* to *verbum* (by way of often translingual puns, fanciful etymologies, echoings of sound) with no appeal over long stretches to the *res* supposedly under discussion; Pound moves often from signifier to signifier, leaving the signified to take care of itself. The most obvious example, first appearing very early in *The Cantos* and thereafter insistent enough to be a sort of structural principle, is Pound's taking over from Aeschylus the pun on the name of Helen (*helandros, helenaus, heleptolis*) and extending it to apply to other Helens or Eleanors, principally Eleanor

From *Paideuma: A Journal Devoted to Ezra Pound Scholarship* 11, no. 3 (Winter 1982). © 1982 by the National Poetry Foundation.

of Aquitaine, but also Eleanor of Castile, Eleanor of Provence, and others. This is obviously, and has duly been called, "word-play"; and I incline to think that the most pressing dilemma facing Pound's admirers today is whether such "play" can be considered responsible (as most structuralist theories would agree that it can be), or else must be declared irresponsible (as most mimetic theories have regularly judged it).

If this seems to suggest that, whatever Pound's own asseverations to the contrary, structuralist assumptions give us more access to *The Cantos* than a mimetic approach, there are nevertheless difficulties in the way of the structuralist. First of these is the assumption, made by most structuralists though not all, that there is a radical breach between "the modern" and all previous centuries of verse-writing. Typical is John Steven Childs [*Paideuma* 9,2]: "it is not the interactions of characters which afford meaning in Modernist literature; it is the mental character of the writer/narrator himself which orders events and feelings." Or again, "Modern poetry, eschewing directly social or didactic functions, is based on the exploitation of non-referential discourse." Both of these *dicta* plainly go against the bent of Pound's temperament, so embued with *pietas* towards the recorded and inherited past, so ready to risk the didactic, and so vowed—until the Pisan experience in some degree compelled otherwise—to avoid the overtly and unashamedly "subjective." Moreover, in the one case we have so far considered, Pound might vindicate his word-play by appeal to a precedent so far from modern as Aeschylus. Or else, if this should seem only a debating-point, consider another of Pound's ancient masters, Ovid, who as Edgar M. Glenn points out [*Paideuma* 10,3] indulged just the same word-play in the *Metamorphoses* with the name of the nymph Coronis, a pun on the names for raven (*corvus*) and for crow (*cornix*). Structuralist criticism, it seems, must be ready to offer revisionist readings of Ovid, no less than of a "modern" like Pound. And indeed it's entirely possible that through the many centuries when Ovid has been admired, a mimetic or pre-structuralist understanding of language, and of how language traffics with reality, has failed to do justice to the power and vitality of Ovid's mind; though poets like Dryden have delighted in Ovid's *logopoeia* (his "turns"), one is familiar with apologetic scholarly comments to the effect that this regrettable proclivity in Ovid is a price we must pay for his more solid virtues.

In any case *The Cantos* pose some real difficulties for that traditional criticism which I shall continue to call, somewhat loosely, "mimetic." A very bold and clear example is what Michael Alexander makes of some lines from Canto 95:

I suppose St. Hilary looked at an oak-leaf.
(vine-leaf? San Denys
    (spelled Dionisio)
Dionisio et Eleutherio.
Dionisio et Eleutherio
    "the brace of 'em
that Calvin never blacked out
             en l'Isle.)

To Michael Alexander it is quite clear that this is "not . . . serious."
And he remarks sharply:

> The suppositiousness here is pretty marked. Though it may well
> be true that free love is commoner in Paris than in Geneva, this
> is not a consequence of the etymology of the names of Saints
> Hilary and Denis; nor is it easy to see how Calvin could have
> been able to black it out. . . . In this mood, Pound might have
> been just as happy to play with the names of Calvin and Charles
> le Chauve. The passage is a harmless example of playful free
> association yet suggests a weakness for seeing historical signifi-
> cance in convenient verbal coincidence. There is no reason to
> suppose St. Hilary of Poitiers was particularly cheerful or par-
> ticularly sensitive to nature, pleasant though it is to think that
> he was.

The bluff common sense of this is refreshing. Yet the difficulties it runs
us into are surely obvious; the transition or glissade from Hilary to *hilaritas*,
or from Denys to Dionysus (for which Pound has a pre-modern precedent,
Walter Pater's "Apollo in Picardy") is not at first sight any different from
the "convenient verbal coincidence" that has many times in earlier cantos
linked Helen, or various Helens, with various Eleanors. If a difference is to
be found, it can be found only by appealing in all these cases from *verbum*
to *res*—and pointing out for instance that as a matter of historical record
Eleanor of Aquitaine did destroy men and ships and cities, just as did
Aeschylus' legendary Helen; whereas, as Alexander points out, the historical
record concerning St. Hilaire is just not full enough for us to predicate about
him so certainly. And it's notable that Edgar Glenn, when he discusses
Ovid's glissades among Coronis and *corvus* and *cornix*, seems in the end to
justify them by a similar appeal to *res:* "although this is word play, the
identifications are operative in the tale because all three are betrayers and

all three are punished." The *res* here, however, is much more dubious, for there is no question of appeal to any historical record other than the fabulous history that Ovid chooses to tell, and so the *res* turns out to be nothing other than the internal necessities and structural principles of Ovid's verbal artifact. The *res* in fact *is* structure; which is just what structuralism claims. In precisely the same way the necessities and principles of Pound's poem require that Denys and Hilary and Calvin be given the significances that in this passage he demands for them. It seems, therefore, that to be consistent Michael Alexander would have to deny the plea that Edgar Glenn enters for Ovid.

Alexander says that this passage, though it "suggests a weakness," is all the same "harmless." It is hard to see how this can be true; for anything that diminishes a reader's confidence in this poet cannot help but be harmful to that poet and his poem. And one need not go all the way with Michael Shuldiner in his ambitiously schematic treatment of *hilaritas* in relation to *sinceritas*, *caritas* and *humanitas* [*Paideuma* 4,1] to feel uneasily sure that from *The Pisan Cantos* onwards hilarity, or *hilaritas*, is being asked to carry a lot of weight, in a way that demonstrably irresponsible play with St. Hilary cannot help but weaken. The point at issue is surely much more crucial than Michael Alexander wants to admit, and it follows that if Pound's word-play in this passage *can* be vindicated, that vindication should be spelled out.

To that end we may consider a passage from Canto 92 that is superficially dissimilar:

> But in the great love, bewildered
>   farfalla in tempesta
> under rain in the dark:
>   many wings fragile
> Nymphalidae, basilarch, and lycaena,
> Ausonides, euchloe, and erynnis

I dare say many readers have been content to suppose (hazardously however, for we should know by now that Pound is a tricky poet who for instance neologizes) that the six splendidly resonant nouns in the last two lines name species or families of butterflies; but there may have been others like me who only lately, after knowing the lines for many years, chose to check that hunch against Alexander B. Klots's *Field Guide to the Butterflies of North America, East of the Great Plains* (1951). Klots's Index does indeed list five of these six names, along with others (e.g., "Dryas" and "Dione") which have cropped up in *The Cantos* in contexts where butterflies seemed not to be in question. Having thus linked these *verba* with the *res*, butterfly, one has perhaps achieved something; but certainly one has not achieved meaning, significance, where before there was none. On the contrary, a range of significance has been rather grievously contracted from the time when, in ignorance of Alexander Klots, one mused happily over etymologies, linking "euchloe" with the Greek *euchloos*, with its sense of "making fresh and green"; or recognizing in "erynnis" one form of the Latin word for the furies, the Greek Eumenides; discovering too from the Latin dictionary that the one name missing from Klots, "Ausonides," is poetical for *Ausonii*, Italians. As for "basilarch," that thunderous compound of the Greek roots for "king" (basileus) and for "ruler" (arkhon), one feels positively let down by the discovery in Klots that it names the Viceroy butterfly, so named because for protective puposes it seems to mimic in colors and markings the inedible Monarch butterfly. Further, I can recall from rather long ago the almost mutinous disappointment with which I discovered that "farfalla" is common Italian for "butterfly," thus not ruling out, but certainly muting, a translingual pun that I thought I detected, between "farfalla" ("in tempesta") and an English expression: "far fallen." Do I stand convicted of having been a frivolous, an irresponsible reader? Or was it my poet who was frivolous when he exploited an apparently unearned resonance from the word "basilarch," applied to a *res* that seemed not to merit such a trumpet-note? Or is it not the case, rather, that neither Pound nor I was being frivolous when we refused to let the multivalent potencies of the *verba* be channeled into the narrow duct of a single and highly specialized "meaning"? Supposing that, I am forced to suppose that structuralist criticism has indeed much to offer readers of *The Cantos*, being in this case the only way to let both Pound and me off the hook. "I suppose," says Pound in the passage from Canto 95, "I suppose St. Hilary looked at an oak-leaf." And Michael Alexander rejoins smartly: "The suppositiousness . . . is pretty marked." But surely "I suppose" functions quite precisely in poetic discourse just as does in discourse of another kind, "I propose" or "I postulate"; stated or unstated (and here it is stated), it reiterates what Philip Sidney declared when he said that as for the poet "he nothing affirmes, and therefore never lyeth." This declares that the business of the poet is serious play—play between signifiers, letting the signified for the nonce go hang.

Accordingly, as the first earnest attempt to read *The Cantos* from a structuralist standpoint, John Steven Childs's "Larvatus Prodeo: Semiotic Aspects of the Ideogram in Pound's *Cantos*" has considerable importance, though it is limited, as the title makes clear, from being focused on the special case of how the Chinese ideograms function. The structuralist authority that Childs most often cites is, not surprisingly, Roland Barthes. And some of

the passages cited from Barthes are as usual vitiated by declaring or assuming
an absolute discontinuity between the poetry that can be called "modern"
and that to be called "classique." One of them, however, has peculiar per-
tinence in that it links up with what Barthes could not have known about
and Childs does not notice: the work that has been done on how *forma*, a
concept that originated apparently with Allen Upward, figures alike in
Pound's theory and his practice:

> Dans la Poétique moderne . . . les mots produisent une sorte de
> continu formel dont émane peu à peu une densité intellectuelle
> ou sentimentale impossible sans eux; la parole est alors le temps
> épais d'une gestation plus spirituelle, pendant laquelle la 'pensée'
> est preparée, installée, peu et peu par le hasard des mots [*Pai-
> deuma*,9,2]. [In modern poetics, on the contrary, words produce
> a kind of formal continuum from which there gradually emanates
> an intellectual or emotional density which would have been im-
> possible without them; speech is then the solidified time of a more
> spiritual gestation, during which the 'thought' is prepared, in-
> stalled little by little by the contingency of words (tr. by Susan
> Sontag).]

What Barthes with characteristic incautiousness predicates of all modern
poetry is certainly true of one body of that poetry, the *Rock-Drill* cantos; in
those cantos at any rate (in others less insistently) the *res* to which Pound's
verba point is ultimately not this or that *thing*, still less this or that proposition.
What is pointed to, and earnestly invoked, is a disposition of mind and
feeling, a disposition which *precedes* the framing of propositions or the making
of distinctions, which precedes, and in the event of course may make unnecessary, the distinguishing between medieval Church history (St. Denys,
St. Hilaire) on the one hand, and on the other pagan and perennial morality
(*hilaritas*, the Dionysian); which refuses the demand to know whether
"Druas" and "Dione" and "Erynnis" belong in entomology or in classical
mythology. (The names belong in both realms; and it is just their dual
belonging which, it may be argued, makes them sanative and harmonizing.)
This realm of thought and feeling *before* the crystallizing out and the making
of distinctions is precisely what Upward and Pound alike seem to have
understood by the realm of "the *forma*"; and so that apparently so reasonable plea, "But come, distinguish," is just what they are vowed not to
satisfy.

Nevertheless, Michael Alexander must have some right on his side.
There must be some point at which we feel (and can vindicate the feeling)

that Pound's word-play ceases to be serious and becomes frivolous. For me, and I think for some others, the point comes by and large between the conclusion of *Rock-Drill* and the beginning of *Thrones*. From this point of view nothing is so disappointing in John Steven Childs's discussion as his assumption that *Rock-Drill* and *Thrones* are much of a muchness. I will return to the beginning of this article, and at the same time cite a case that I have used elsewhere, by recalling that in the *Rock-Drill* Canto 94, and thereafter in the *Thrones* cantos, we are required to extend the "Helen" identification to other Eleanors than Eleanor of Aquitaine; and that in the *Thrones* Canto 107 one of these other Eleanors appears, Eleanor of Provence, consort of Henry III of England:

> & this Helianor was of the daughters, heirs
> of Raymond Berengar
> and sister of Arch.   Cantaur

We must note that the case of this Eleanor is not on a par with that of St. Hilaire of Poitiers: the historical records tell us enough of this Eleanor, tell us in particular that she fiddled her kinsman into the see of Canterbury ("Arch. Cantaur"). What baffles and in the end exasperates us is not that we do not have this *res* to which to attach the *verba* about her, but that, the *res* thus established, we do not know what to do with it. Where does Eleanor's maneuvring her relative into Canterbury fit into the still developing structure of Pound's poem? Are we to applaud her for the maneuvre, or deplore it? In neither of these ways, nor in any other, does this *res* rhyme with, or hook on to, anything else in the poem. In other words, the identifying of this Eleanor with the older and greater Eleanor, and through her with Helen of Troy, offends us because it has no *structural* significance, not because it has no meaning in terms of the historical record. This suggests—I may dare to say, it *shows*—that, whereas few structuralists care to stoop to value-judgments, nevertheless their own procedures permit of such judgments being made. They would disarm the prejudices of some of us if they showed more interest in pursuing that possibility. There is *logopoeia* that is legitimate (St. Denys identified with Dionysus), and other *logopoeia* that is not (Eleanor of Provence identified with Helen of Troy); and the test of legitimacy is not any appeal to authorities outside the poem, but on the contrary appeal to the poem's own structural requirements.

I shall assume (for I have argued the case elsewhere) that what goes on in these lines about Eleanor of Provence is fairly typical of the *Thrones* sequence as a whole; that among the rather many things wrong with these cantos is word-play of this tired and pointless sort, *logopoeia* pursued at the expense of *phanopoeia* and *melopoeia*, and also of common sense. This is still a minority opinion, but one that I think is gaining ground—a great deal of *Thrones* is simply a bore. However, some *Thrones* cantos are better than others; and in the better ones one encounters *logopoeia* that is, to put it grudgingly, at least a borderline case. A rather crucial instance is Canto 106:

> Help me to neede
> By Circeo, the stone eyes looking seaward
>   Nor could you enter her eyes by probing.
>   The temple shook with Apollo
> As with leopards by mount's edge,
>   light blazed behind her;
>   trees open, their minds stand before them
> As in Carrara is whiteness:
>   Xoroi. At Sulmona are lion heads.
>   Gold light, in veined phylotaxis.
> By hundred blue-gray over their rock-pool,
>   Or the king-wings in migration
>   And in thy mind beauty, O Artemis
> Over asphodel, over broom-plant,
>   faun's ear a-level that blossom.
>   Yao and Shun ruled by jade.
> Whuder ich maei lidhan
>   helpe me to neede
> the flowers are blessed against thunder bolt
>   helpe me to neede.
> That great acorn of light bulging outward,
>   Aquileia, caffaris, caltha palistris,
>   ulex, that is gorse, herys arachnites;
> Scrub oak climbs against cloud-wall—
>   three years peace, they had to get rid of him,
>   —violet, sea green, and no name.
> Circe's were not, having fire behind them.
>   Buck stands under ash grove,
>   jasmine twines over capitols
>   Selena Arsinoe
> So late did queens rise into heaven.
>   At Zephyrium, July that was, at Zephyrium
>   The high admiral built there;
>   Aedificavit

TO APHRODITE EUPLOIA
            "an Aeolian gave it, ex voto
            Arsinoe Kupris.
                At Miwo the moon's axe is renewed
                HREZEIN
    Selena, foam on the wave-swirl
            Out of gold light flooding the peristyle
            Trees open in Paros,
                White feet as Carrara's whiteness

This passage is a sort of tie-beam. Considered as a structural member, it carries much weight, resolves many stresses. On the one hand, it reaches far back into preceding cantos, picking up for instance ("violet, sea green, and no name") the three pairs of differently colored eyes which figures so hauntingly and repeatedly in *The Pisan Cantos*, picking up also from *Rock-Drill* Canto 91 ("Help me to neede . . . Whuder ich maei lidhan") Brutus's prayer to Diana in Layamon's *Brut*, beseeching her to lead him to a new realm, the third Troy that Layamon identified with Albion. On the other hand, the passage also reaches forward, for instance to "the great acorn of light" in Canto 116. Among the matters thus picked up from quite far back in the poem, and then conveyed forward, is the matter of butterflies. For "the king-wings in migration" clearly "rhymes" (structurally) with the "far-falla" passage that we have looked at in Canto 92, and carries that forward to what may well be the last lines of the entire poem, among the "Notes for Canto CXVII et seq.":

        Two mice and a moth my guides—
        To have heard the farfalla gasping
                as toward a bridge over worlds.
        That the kings meet in their island,
                where no food is after flight from the pole.
        Milkweed the sustenance
                as to enter arcanum.

        To be men not destroyers.

For the Monarch butterfly *(Danaus plexippus)*, which does indeed live on the poisonous milkweed, in mid-September migrates southward, if not from the pole at least from arctic Canada, along skyways that have been mapped; and there are known locations where large flocks of them can be found resting, at staging posts on the migration. (The northward migration in spring is less marked, because apparently less marshalled.)

Thus, what in this way binds Canto 92 through Canto 106 with Canto 117 is a "rhyme" of *res*, not of *verba*. The only word-play involved is the easy substitution of "king" for "monarch." And so this transition can be (and should be, I think, for surely it is masterly) applauded as warmly by non-structuralists as by structuralists. The "borderline" cases come later in the passage when, if "king-wings in migration" have alerted us to the presence of butterflies, we ponder the lines:

> Selena Arsinoe
> So late did queens rise into heaven.
> At Zephyrium, July that was, at Zephyrium
> The high admiral built there;

For there is a butterfly called *Boloria selene* (the silver-bordered fritillary), and every one knows that there are butterflies called Admirals. One species of Admiral (the Viceroy) we have met already under the name *basilarch;* the other two species are named for or after a Greek goddess, whose name has resounded many times in the cantos and will resound even more loudly in the cantos that remain—they are *Limenitis arthemis* and *Limenitis arthemis astyanax*. So whoever the high admiral is in human terms (one thinks perhaps wrongly of Drake, for "Zephyrium" means "western promontory" and one promontory that might qualify is Circeo, with which Francis Drake was memorably connected in Canto 91), one cannot, and perhaps one should not, exclude the possibility that the admiral is as much insectile as human. If this is fanciful, a good deal less so is the nimbus or aura that hangs around "So late did queens rise into heaven." What this recalls first is a line from Canto 97, "Bernice, late for a constellation, mythopoeia persisting"; and another from Canto 102, "Berenice, a late constellation." A look into Lemprière will identify the Queen Berenice in question, and sketch the myth which transforms her, or rather the hair of her head, into a constellation. But what are we then to make of the perhaps unwelcome information from the invaluable Alexander Klots, that there is a Queen butterfly *(Danaus gilippus)*, which in many ways corresponds in the Southern states to the Monarch in more northerly latitudes; and that one sub-species of the Queen is called *Danaus gilippus berenice?* Are the queens, like the admirals, insectile as much as they are human, or mythologically divine?

What strengthens this alarmed or alarming supposition is that a few lines earlier has occurred ("caltha palistris . . . herys arachnites") what we may take to be an allusion to Linnaean botany—an important foreshadowing, if so, of the otherwise unheralded veneration to be given to Linnaeus in the *Drafts & Fragments*. For of course the classification of butterflies is itself

Linnaean, and some of the taxonomic namings (notably that of the Monarch) are credited to Linnaeus himself. When in the latest cantos Linnaeus is named for veneration along with Mozart and Ovid, is he in fact honoured as "natural scientist"? Is he not rather, or equally, honoured as a genius of language, a masterly inventor of and source for, interlingual punning *(logopoeia)* between Greek and Latin on the one hand, English and presumably Swedish on the other? According to Harry Meacham, in *The Caged Panther*, Pound's interest in Linnaeus dated from the St. Elizabeths years, and may have been prompted by the devotion to Linnaeus of the then Secretary-General of the United Nations, Dag Hammarskjöld. It would be interesting to know precisely the grounds on which Hammarskjöld venerated his great compatriot.

One of the rather few commentators who can help us in difficult speculations like these is Guy Davenport. His essay, "Persephone's Ezra" is illuminating for instance on the relation between tree and marble pillar which accounts, in the passage we have been considering, for

> trees open, their minds stand before them
As in Carrara is whiteness:

and

> Trees open in Paros,
> White feet as Carrara's whiteness.

And plainly, what we have more particularly been looking at is glossed when Davenport says in the same essay: "Pound cancelled in his own mind the dissociations that had been isolating fact from fact for four centuries. To have closed the gap between mythology and botany" (or, we may add, lepidoptery) "is but one movement of the process; . . ." However, when we return these sentences to their context we cannot help but wonder if the commonsense objections of a Michael Alexander are being given what is after all their due. For Davenport is quite uncompromising:

> To say that *The Cantos* is a "voyage in time" is to be blind to the poem altogether. We miss immediately the achievement upon which the success of the poem depends, its rendering time transparent and negligible, its dismissing the supposed corridors and perspectives *down* which the historian invites us to look. Pound cancelled in his own mind the dissociations that had been isolating fact from fact for four centuries. To have closed the gap between mythology and botany is but one movement of the process; one way to read the cantos is to go through noting the restorations

of relationships now thought to be discrete—the ideogrammatic
method was invented for just this purpose. In Pound's spatial
sense of time the past is here, now; its invisibility is our blindness,
not its absence. The nineteenth century had put everything
against the scale of time and discovered that all behaviour within
time's monolinear progress was evolutionary. The past was a
graveyard, a museum. It was Pound's determination to obliterate
such a configuration of time and history, to treat what had become
a world of ghosts as a world eternally present.

This is wonderfully eloquent, and phrase after phrase in these sentences
speaks justly to what we experience, and respond to, when we are reading
The Cantos at their best. Yet is it not clear that in this passage Davenport,
whether or not he intends it, is handing over the entire poem to the synchronic
or synchronizing vision of the structuralist? He speaks of Pound as cancelling
"the dissociations that have been isolating fact from fact"; but of course, as
any structuralist will point out with glee, it's not clear that *facts* figure in
any poetic discourse whatever. We can't any longer suppose, naïvely, that
a fact gets into a poem as soon as it is named there. For a fact, and the name
of that fact are different; and it is only the name, not the thing named, that
is at home in the verbal universe that is a poem. As John Steven Childs
remarks with obvious satisfaction, "modern poetry" (in which clearly he
includes *The Cantos*) "is based on the exploitation of non-referential discourse." If we do not share his satisfaction, if we want the discourse of *The
Cantos* to be in some ways or in some degree referential, the *res* that we look
for must be something different from what Guy Davenport means by "facts."
It must be, I have suggested, what Upward meant by the *forma;* and I glossed
this provisionally as a state of mind and feeling anterior to the making of
distinctions. Thus where Davenport speaks of the cancelling of dissociations
(which a Michael Alexander would surely, and with much reason, rephrase
as the blurring of distinctions), we might do better to speak of the post-
ponement, or the "willing suspension," of distinctions. And I think this is
more than nit-picking. For it permits of, and indeed requires, a *diachronic*
vision, such as we might expect of a poet who told Grazia Livi in 1962: "The
modern world doesn't exist because nothing exists which does not understand
its past or its future." (Guy Davenport, who quotes this with approval, must
be confident that it doesn't make against his reading of *The Cantos*, though
to my mind it certainly does.)

These difficult matters are best dealt with in relation to some particular
crux in our reading of the poem. Accordingly I will cite one more such crux,
from Canto 110, the first of the *Drafts & Fragments:*

The purifications
>are snow, rain, artemisia,
>also dew, oak and the juniper

And in thy mind beauty, O Artemis,
>as of mountain lakes in the dawn

The question is, very simply: Does it matter, for our reading of the poem aright, that we identify "artemisia" as wormwood? If it does not matter, then the link from "artemisia" to "Artemis" is a mere adventitious jingle of sound, and so obvious that we might justly call it "mechanical." Even if we take note of John of Trevisa in 1398 ("Artemisia is callyd moder of herbes and was somtyme hallowed . . . to the goddesse that hyght Arthemis"), we are still wholly in the realm of *verba* and moving from signifier to signifier by way of disputable etymology. If on the other hand we identify wormwood, and learn from *O.E.D.* that as early as 1535 wormwood was "an emblem or type of what is bitter and grievous to the soul," we have moved from *verbum* to *res:* and the link to Artemis accordingly takes on substance and specifity. For we are compelled to infer that the Artemis who is so markedly the presiding deity of these cantos is every inch the Artemis of Canto 30, she by whom we "maintain antisepsis," her special function the dispensing of what is, medicinally, "bitter and grievous to the soul." This means that the *forma* invoked and created in *Drafts & Fragments* is dark and tragically bitter in a way that, among the commentators, only Eva Hesse seems to have recognized. She must be right, I think, for if we move once more from *verbum* to *res*, we find the perception reinforced in those last lines where the Monarch butterflies "meet in their island":

Milkweed the sustenance
as to enter arcanum

It is only by ingesting that which is to all others bitter and poisonous that the kings can enter, or think to enter, arcanum.

I conclude therefore that, much as structuralist criticism can illuminate for us what is going on in many pages of *The Cantos*, and however much non-structuralist criticism must refine its assumptions so as to allow for this, yet in the end Pound's claim to attend to *res* not *verba* can be, and must be, vindicated; and that a thoroughgoing or dogmatic structuralism milks this text, as presumably any other, of human pathos and human significance.

CHRISTINE FROULA

The Pound Error: The Limits of Authority in the Modern Epic

We might begin an inquiry into the ideology of the errors and their correction by asking what it is about Pound's poem that has caused scholars to value literal accuracy with respect to its sources so highly. Coleridge, inspired by Milton's Mount Amara, could imagine his Mount Abora in "Kubla Khan" without moving his editors to enforce fidelity to his source. Keats could even substitute Cortez for Balboa in "On First Looking into Chapman's Homer," confusing the exterminator of the Aztecs with the first European to lay eyes on the Pacific, and still be excused by the editors of the *Norton Anthology*, who judge that this error "matters to history but not to poetry." What is acceptable in these texts, however, is unacceptable in Pound's. Indeed, the hundreds of "corrections" for the text of *The Cantos* proposed by scholars attests to the discomfiture which the errors in the poem cause some of its readers. Eastman expresses something of this discomfort in her discussion of alternative stances toward authorial error in *The Cantos:*

> One might contend that we cannot judge *The Cantos* as we would a piece of scholarly research or a prose argument from historical or literary sources because *The Cantos* is poetry. Therefore, once the printer's mistakes are corrected, the poet's really don't matter. This is itself an extraordinary assumption about aesthetics, equivalent to saying that the poetry is the "redeeming feature" of the work. Pound himself argued against such reasoning. . . . He did

From *To Write Paradise: Style and Error in Ezra Pound's* Cantos. © 1984 by Yale University. Yale University Press, 1984.

> not ask any special dispensation for his poem on the basis that
> poets are not expected to get their facts straight when they are
> giving the reader the facts. Rather, Pound earnestly believed that
> poets were the only ones who could. *The Cantos* is his testimony
> in the case. To grant special pleading for poetry is to ignore
> Pound's claims for it and to devalue his actual achievement in the
> poem.
>
> *(Ezra Pound's* Cantos: *The Story of the Text)*

While much of the unpublished evidence of Pound's views on textual matters
contradicts the position here attributed to him, Eastman's defense of the
corrective stance expresses the special urgency with which Pound's editors
press their remedies for deviance—exemplified in her attributing to Pound
an earnest belief that only poets can get their facts straight. That the editorial
judgment which, in Keat's case, finds that the poet's error matters to history
but not to poetry should, in Pound's case, become an extraordinary assumption about aesthetics points to the fact that *The Cantos* is a *qualitatively*
different kind of poem from Keats's or Coleridge's: an epic, not a lyric; a
self-proclaimed poem including history, not a fantasy of poetic power or a
literary rhapsody. It is a poem about public values which, as the early
manuscripts show, began in an effort to find a poetic form adequate to modern
history, and Eastman, though mistaken in thinking that Pound was committed to factual accuracy above all else, is entirely right to suppose that he
would have rejected an aestheticist defense of his errors.

   To resist accepting the errors on the grounds that they do not matter
to poetry is not necessarily to embrace a policy of correction on the grounds
that they matter to history, however. Indeed, the extraordinary assumption
about aesthetics which, according to Eastman, informs a conservative stance
toward authorial error is balanced by what seems upon reflection to be an
extraordinary assumption about history implicit in the corrective stance. To
suppose that correcting the errors would be equivalent to getting the facts
straight, and that straight facts would ensure a consensus about history,
implies belief that there is something called History which admits of perfection with respect both to its linguistic record and, by extension, to our
understanding of it. It implies, in other words, that History has an absolute
existence, independent of our experience and representation of it, which the
poetic text can capture. A claim for the possibility of such a perfect correspondence is implicit in conventional poetic forms, however complexly the
thematic ambiguities, counterplots, unfinishability and so forth of a particular
poem may subvert, or contradict it (*The Aeneid* is perhaps the preeminent

example). The experiment of *The Cantos*, while it originated in the desire to discover and explore some fundamental structures in human history, continually met with surprises, uncertainties, and contradictions that pointed to the necessity—and, no less, to the difficulty—of learning to conceive history apart from the certainty of story and the closure of form. As the compositional history of Canto 4 illustrates, the contingencies of history continually interrupted and overrode the designs of History—of the structuralist formal idea with which Pound replaced the story with its preordained ends, the "beautiful lie" of epic tradition. The epic task Pound undertook entailed creating a form and language which could register such incursions of history into History, of actual experience into ideas about the world; and for this reason, the historicity of *The Cantos* is not of a kind which precludes error. On the contrary, it is precisely the seriousness of the poem's engagement with the world that gives its errors a significance not found in Coleridge's divagation or Keats's mistake. Error, the root meaning of which is traveling or wandering, is integral to epic; Odysseus, Aenaes, Dante, Don Quixote, Spenser's Redcrosse, Milton's Adam and Eve all wander in and out of the errors, moral, tactical, and spiritual, that give their stories shape and meaning. In Pound's modern epic, in which the happening of history supercedes the closure of story and the author replaces the hero as exemplar of the self in the world, error remains the risk of trial and adventure. The difference between Pound's wanderings and those of the earlier epic heroes, however, is that theirs ultimately return them to a world of stable values. Odysseus's travels and travails end in his *nostos*, or homecoming. Aeneas's wanderings bring him from the timeless past of myth to the fiction of a historical origin invoked to endow with meaning all the events of human time to follow. Don Quixote's "sane" Christian recantation upon his deathbed reverses the effect of his parodistic wandering, in which begins the modern effort to wake from the dreams of authoritative stories to the uncertainties of history. Both Spenser's and Milton's epics endow wandering in history with meaning by imagining it as a progress toward a Christian paradise. All these epics are designed so that errantry ends in a paradisal home in which wandering ceases and all error is redeemed.

What makes Pound's epic both different and definitely modern is that its wandering is unclosed by any such redemption. The mutually mirroring salvations of aesthetic form and thematic paradise (conceived as the dream of a purpose which guides and justifies human history) are both ultimately renounced in *The Cantos*, because Pound had, as he said, "no Aquinas-map," no idea or philosophy from which to trace a governing design for his poem including history. His strategy, instead, was to record his own experience of that dialectic between desire and actuality that is the history of *The Cantos*, and simply to *wait* for the significance of that record to reveal itself. "When I get to end, pattern *ought* to be discoverable," he wrote to John Lackay Brown. "Stage set à la Dante is *not* modern truth. It may be O.K. but *not* as modern man's" [*Selected Letters*]. The history which the poem includes does not fall away like a scaffolding as a transcendent meaning emerges from it. The kind of meaning after which Brown was inquiring never does emerge from Pound's epic, not because the poem is unfinished or a failure but because the history of which it is made never did, in fact, redeem itself into a conventional story, a form in which "it all coheres." But its failure to resolve into a story, paradoxically, *is* its story. The poem is the history and the history is the poem: a record of a world without epistemological certainty, which offers no rest from wandering—a world in which error is all.

The authorial errors in the text of *The Cantos*, then, may be viewed as the "foot-prints" of the unfinished and unfinishable wandering which Pound's epic discovers—against its author's initial hopes as well as its readers'—to be modern history, modern experience. The editorial stances which it is possible to take toward these errors reflect in significant if indirect ways correlative stances toward error as such, for it seems likely that our discomfort with the small errors has more than a casual relation to our discomfort with the inconclusive form of the poem as well as with Pound's real-life errors. In the unresolvability of error or wandering in its three fields in *The Cantos*— letter, form, and, in the widest sense, the history of its making—the history of epic takes a radically different turn.

The Cantos, indeed, appears in certain crucial ways to be the epic to end all epics. In *The Cantos*, the symbolic collision of the Western epic tradition— and the alphabetic writing that carries it—with the metaphorical East invoked by the Chinese ideograms scattered through the text marks the limits of the Western *epos*, grounded since the *Iliad* in a tradition of conquest by violence. There can be very few readers for whom the Chinese characters ever become translucent signs. Their most powerful import remains, even after one learns their significations, the unassimilable difference with which their obscure and silent presence confronts the Western reader. Their alien mode of representation betokens all that exists beyond the closed culture celebrated by the Western epic tradition; their mere presence, apart from particular meanings, frames and limits the humanistic traditions of the Western epic, throwing into relief its ethnocentric conditions. The association of epic culture with speech, tale, and song—the meaning of the Greek *epos*, linked to Latin *vox*—becomes literally and graphically evident in Pound's juxtaposition of Western and Eastern forms of writing. The struggle of *The Cantos* to "make Cosmos" [*The Cantos of Ezra Pound* (New York: New Directions, 1975), Canto

116, p. 795; all further references will cite canto and page numbers only],
to further a new "civilization" in the twentieth century, is imagined in this
juxtaposition, in which the Western *epos* no longer appears as if circumscribing all universal, "human" value within the bounds of what Jacques Derrida
has termed its "phonocentric" and transcendentalist traditions. The Chinese
writing in Pound's text obscurely signals its anti-epical dimension: a symbolic
"going East" of the Western epic, an attempt to escape the correlated epistemological and symbolic models which have, since the *Iliad*, underwritten
in the name of "humanity" the traditions of cultural conquest to which Pound
opposed his modern epic. *The Cantos'* anthropological array of fragmented
images and its open form mark the end of the celebration of the closed
culture, with its "basis" in a single, coherent belief, not with the nostalgia
of which the poem is so often accused but in acknowledgment that this
tradition founded in violence can no longer be imagined as reconcilable with
"humane" values given the absolute destructive power which twentieth-
century technology has achieved.

To analyze fully the anti-epical dimensions of Pound's epic would require many pages, but it suffices for the textual question to suggest its
relevance to the diminishing value that Pound attached to the letter of his
text, its "literal" accuracy. We recall his rejoinder to a scholar's query about
standard transliteration of Chinese characters: "I refuse to accept ANY alphabetic display as final / AND the sagetrieb / different spellings used to
indicate the stream wherethru and whereby our legend came." Pound's insistence on the historical aspects of orthography reflects his awareness that
language is conventional, underwritten by historical and social factors and
not by a transcendent and absolute authority. On the other hand, the kinds
of changes Pound's editors made, against his own toleration of error in his
text, reflect the view that language and culture have "absolute," static, and
standard forms which the poem's mirroring preserves and which its devia-
tions threaten. This assumption is implicitly countered by Pound's advocacy
of sagetrieb, a true "philologer's" notion. Conceiving the forms of language
and culture as historical and therefore relative, and their authority as social
rather than transcendent, Pound's sagetrieb values the diachronic traces of
thought and language, the historical directions of their metamorphic flowing
and the paths of their dissemination, over standardized orthography. The
sagetrieb principle opposes a commitment to the ideal of a static, homogeneous, dominant culture identified with "standard" forms, as befits a poem
which, to fulfil its project of "including" modern history, must register not
one closed culture but a polyphonic global interpenetration of cultures, languages, and histories.

We may observe the relation between Pound's sense of the historical basis of culture and significant authorial error in his text in the Chinese History/John Adams diptych—Cantos 52–71, first published in 1940. His juxtaposition of Chinese history and Revolutionary American politics is a thematic rather than orthographical application of the sagetrieb principle, implying a line of descent from Confucian ethics through the French Enlightenment—via Jesuit sinologists such as Père Joseph-Anne-Marie de Moyriac de Mailla, whose *Histoire générale de la Chine, ou Annales de cet empire* (1777– 83) is the principal source for the Chinese History Cantos—to Adams and Jefferson, heirs of the Encyclopedists. Pound's giving over one hundred seventy pages of his poem to this complex exemplum, though unique in its particular form, participates in the heightened political urgency in American art of the thirties: his interest in China and in John Adams was for the sake of the present, not the past. And this context is reflected both in the poetics of the Adams Cantos, their hurried, fragmented, note-taking style, and in the many errors which scholars have identified in the text.

Pound's didactic motive is, by critical consensus, all too obvious in these cantos, which offer very little to conventional poetic taste. Pound was attracted to Adams as a "canonist," a social thinker who helped to institute the values of the new nation, and his presentation of Adams urges the importance of remembering his ground-laying thought in a period of social and economic crisis. Yet both the tortuous poetics and the errors in these cantos qualify Pound's canonizing of the canonist: the sequence is not a shrine but an "instigation," an effort to recover whatever value for the present there might be in a rich American past that had been in effect forgotten. The note-taking style issues from the fact that Pound is composing these cantos as he reads Adams's complete works for the first time; even as he wrote, he complained of the fact that Adams's work was out of print, observing testily that he could see no "regeneration of American culture while Marx and Lenin are reprinted at 10 cents and 25 cents in editions of 100,000 and Adams's and Jefferson's thought is kept out of the plain man's reach" [*Selected Prose*]. In a sense, then, Pound's errors are in keeping with the Adams Cantos' documentary expression of the obscurity into which Adams's work had fallen. (Ironically enough, the first American edition of the Adams Cantos billed them on the dust jacket as the "John Quincy Adams Cantos.") The errors also reflect Pound's historical position with respect to his material, qualifying his own canonizing stance. As [Donald] Davie shows [*Ezra Pound: Poet as Sculptor*], after his desperate political efforts of the thirties and early forties, Pound came to believe that the tradition of 1776 had failed for reasons inherent in its premises. Yet what is interesting about the Adams Cantos, composed in 1938–39, is how far their documentary poetics already limits their didactic intention. Their fragmenting mode presents neither historical fact nor authorial judgment in absolute terms, but rather situates the author in history. In the first Adams Canto, Pound pillories Alexander Hamilton, who, as first secretary of the treasury, established the Bank of the United States, tying governmental administration tightly to moneyed interests. In so doing, he explicitly circumscribes his own authority by locating it in history, in a specific time and place:

> and as for Hamilton
> we may take it (my authority, ego scriptor cantilenae)
> that he was the Prime snot in ALL American history
> (11th Jan. 1938, from Rapallo)
>
> [67:350]

This limitation of authority occurs implicitly as well, in the fact that the fragmentary notes of which the text consists do not transmit Adams's history effectively but rather come into existence as a gesture which connotes curiosity about the past for the interests of the present. Pound himself distinguished his intentions from the historian's, writing to one reader, "Epos is not COLD history. . . . The historian can add footnotes / in fact the philologers are busy already. Not there, the poem ain't, to explain the history, but to arouse curiosity." The poetics of Cantos 52–71 registers the incongruity of epic culture, conceived as a closed world view representable by a single, coherent voice, and the wilderness of modern history. As the modern "epos" is qualified, so is the concept of poetic authority: no divine muse guarantees the modern poet's authority, which must present itself as grounded in history rather than in transcendent truth.

Pound's historical qualification of his own authority in the Adams Cantos makes explicit what was implicit in his poetic modes all along. As early as Canto 4, he had begun to employ poetic strategies, such as the "ideogrammic method," in which meaning is not conveyed directly by signifying language but constructed in collaboration with the reader. If this collaboration fails, so does that dimension of meaning, along with the poetics of metaphor designed to create it. The "authority" of the text is thus diffused between author and readers, reflecting, again, its historical and social rather than transcendent ground. Pound in his modern epic replaces Odysseus as epic protagonist, but this substitution is not one of hero for hero. The noble, if fallible, hero of ancient Greek culture is replaced by a representative figure making its way through the perils of modern history. Whereas Odysseus, as king and captain, possessed for the Greeks a recognized social position and authority, and Homer, the bard, had the mystified and mythified social authority of the Muse for his tale, Pound as poet-protagonist can claim for his poem only the authority of experience. In this way, the "divine" authority of the Muse is returned to history and to the social agreement—or lack of it—that permits or refuses the reading of the poem.

Yet, though both thematically and through its poetics *The Cantos* subverts the traditional concept of epic authority, redefining it as a collaboration between author and readers, critical and interpretive responses to the poem have tended to assume precisely the models of history and authority which the poem puts in question. Several critics have argued that Pound's history-writing is biased. Both Ron Baar and Noel Stock, for example, analyze his treatment of the Bank War and judge that it favors Jackson's point of view; and Donald Davie, Harvey Gross, and others find his account of Confucianism wanting in historical accuracy and balance. On their own terms, these judgments have point, but they mistake the terms of Pound's engagement with history. As a writer of history, Pound was conscious that his own time and place determined his perspective on the past. For him, history-writing, like art, was always "local" (97:678), and he did not employ the forms of objectivity. More important, Pound's consciously polemical modes of history-writing do not simply reject an objective perspective but rather call into question the possibility of historical objectivity. As early as "Near Perigord," *Hugh Selwyn Mauberley*, and his brilliant rendering of the history of Sigismondo Malatesta in Cantos 8–11, Pound had designed poetic modes of history-writing to render the dynamic flux and chaos of events and the subjectivity of their narration. He had deliberately renounced the illusion of an accurate representation of historical events from a distanced, objective perspective for an illusion of events represented at first hand in all their immediacy, incompleteness, and doubtful meaning; as, for example, in the Malatesta Cantos, narrated by a composite voice which speaks at different moments from the vantage point of the chronicler Gaspare Broglio, of Sigismondo's brother Domenico, a soldier of his army, and of the poet confronting the traces of a past in its fragmentary documents.

Pound's history-writing, far from simply departing from an objective point of view, assumes the deeply problematic nature of the concept of historical objectivity, a fact which interpreters of his poetics have tended to overlook. Joseph Frank, for example, concludes his influential essay "Spatial Form and Modern Literature" with the observation that what occurs in modernist forms is "the transformation of the historical imagination into myth"; the modernists have abandoned "the objective historical imagination" and have created forms which strive to transcend history and temporality. Citing Mircea Eliade's view that modern literature is "saturated with nostalgia for the myth of eternal repetition, and, in the last analysis, for the abolition of time," Frank effectively silences the very considerable historical urgency of modern art and ignores its attempts to confront the *difficulty* of epistemological and communicative acts. In fact, however, Pound's modes of history-writing are informed by an insight into the profound interdependence of history and language. The history cantos' experimental forms embody the idea that, as Hayden White puts it, historical thought "remains the captive of the linguistic mode in which it seeks to grasp the outline of objects inhabiting its field of perception" [*Metahistory*]. This condition, analogous to the "Heisenberg microscopes" of quantum physics, encompasses objective or realistic literary modes no less than others. To identify historical objectivity with a temporally straightforward linguistic structure is to assume a model of history that is essentially linear and sequential, requiring for its representation a linear language capable of representing sequence and causality. But the modern physics that evolved alongside modern art has shown our assumptions about temporality to be precariously founded, suggesting that the forms of modern art do not imply an escape from history so much as they challenge the illusion that objectivity inheres in strictly linear and sequential forms of knowing. To complicate Frank's notion of "the objective historical imagination" with the awareness that language and representation are always moved by desire is to acknowledge that what has been said of Pound could be applied to all who write history: that he was the kind of historian who, loving his truth, was bound to distort his facts. To assert, then, as Baar does, that "Pound's *Cantos* lay claim to the validity of historical scholarship [and] claim to be truthful representations of historical events" ["Ezra Pound: Poet as Historian," *American Literature* (1972)] is to project upon Pound a historical idealism to which his poem does not subscribe. Indeed, it would be more accurate to say that he tailored his facts to abet his "truth." In the Malatesta Cantos, for example, Pope Paul II, in real life tall and so handsome that his conclave would not permit him to take the name "Formosus" for fear of his seeming vain, is nicknamed "fatty Barbo," "Little fat squab 'Formosus' " (11:51). Again, in Canto 11 the lines "And Vanni must give that peasant a decent price for his horses, / Say that I will refund" have their origins in a note which reads: "And don't let Giovanni get gypped in that horse deal." Neither of these distortions, however, makes Pound's portrait of Sigismondo any less accurate in its general import. In a more recent revisionary history, *The Malatestas of Reminini*, Philip J. Jones concurs with Pound's view that the pope's vilification of Sigismondo was politically inspired rather than founded in fact, and it is this revision of the record that Pound's portrait is designed to achieve. Had his purpose been

to present an accurate and straightforward account of the historical facts, he
would certainly have failed in it but, as it is interpretation and polemic that
inform his treatment of historical material, it is on a different plant that the
poem asks to be engaged. "It does not matter a twopenny damn," Pound
wrote in *Guide to Kulchur*,

> whether you load up your memory with the chronological se-
> quence of what has happened, or the names of protagonists, or
> authors of books, or generals and leading political spouters, so
> long as you understand the process now going on, or the processes
> biological, social, economic now going on, enveloping you as an
> individual, in a social order.

That it is historical "process" and not isolated facts which Pound aims
to represent in *The Cantos*, his divagations from his sources dramatize by
their very irrelevance. His concern was to make the reader aware through
the act of reading of the historical currents and contexts in which thought,
language, and poetic form are inextricably rooted. Norman Holmes Pearson
advocated corrections in the text "for those who wish to get history, and to
get it through Cantos," and Sanders recommends correcting "the documentary data of history" presumably for the same reason; but even with all the
factual errors in the text corrected, no reader could "get history" from *The
Cantos* in any sense that depends upon correctness in details. On the other
hand, to attempt to read the poem is immediately to become imaginatively
embroiled in the historical process to which Pound committed his poem from
the beginning. Some of the manuscripts for the historical cantos make this
point strikingly, giving evidence of Pound's concern to create the aura of
historical process in *The Cantos* even, sometimes, at the expense of the facts
surrounding the poem's literal process. As early as the Malatesta Cantos,
the documentary mode of *The Cantos* was at moments just that—a *mode*, a
technique, simulable pose rather than literal position, like the "trick / Of the
unfinished address" mentioned in "Three Cantos" (1:114). Later, in the
Adams Cantos, Pound placed documentary tags in the text—

18th assistant whereof the said Thomas Adams (abbreviated)
[62:341]

ten head 40 acres at 3/ (shillings) per acre
[62:341]

dash had already formed lucrative connections
[65:368]

—which indicate characteristics not of Pound's source but of his own note-book: "(abbreviated)," "shillings," and "dash" all refer to Pound's first draft, not to Charles Francis Adams's *The Works of John Adams*. By means of such "tricks," Pound makes the act of composing the poem continuous with its representation of history. Its artful self-representation makes the haste, the urgency, and the partiality of this act, its own historical contingency, a part of the record.

Elsewhere in *The Cantos*, Pound made it a point to leave "blanks in the record" for the things he didn't know or wasn't sure of, laying no claim to the absolute (or divine) authority bound up with straight declaration and underwritten by an epic muse. In *The Pisan Cantos*, where epic and lyric modes converge, his documentary technique becomes a poetic instrument of remarkable sensitivity, able to render lyric consciousness in—and as—its historical moment. In these cantos, written at a time and place where Pound had no books, no record but his memory, he often marks the blanks or fuzzy places with rhetorical brackets, as for example in remembering "the old Dynasty's music / as it might be at the Peach-blossom Fountain / where are smooth lawns with the clear stream / between them, silver, dividing" or "the grass on the roof of St What's his name / near 'Cane e Gatto' " or "somebody's portrait of Rodenbach / with a background / as it might be L'Ile St Louis for serenity" or an anecdote of Swineburne: "When the french fishermen hauled him out, he / recited 'em / might have been Aeschylus / till they got into Le Portel, or wherever / in the original" (84:538; 83:529; 80:512; 82:523).

The ease with which these lapses of memory are acknowledged could occur only in the exercise of a poetic authority antithetical to that claimed by Homer, Dante, or Milton. Implicitly, what the reader knows, loves, and remembers is as much to be valued as what the poet is remembering. Meaning resides not in the significations of his words but in their exemplary function; his memories are representative rather than constitutive treasures. The name of the port to which Swinburne was conveyed is of no importance; the particular memories only exemplify the comfort that their sustaining presence brings to the poet in the prison camp. In some sense, their "meaning" is that, as he puts it, "What thou lovest well remains / the rest is dross" (81:520–21).

Pound's demarcation of the historical limits of his own authority within the poem goes a long way toward explaining his tolerance of error in his text—how, for example, he could regard a mistake as a saving sign of the author's ignorance and insist on preserving it. His stance toward the errors in the text reflects a radical transformation of our three thousand year old Western tradition of epic authority, and it is this that accounts for the fact that we still tend to read the poem as though it claims, or ought to claim, the *kind* of authority on which our literary tradition is founded. The historical idealism that leads readers to value correct facts over grasp of historical process, to imagine anyone—the author or ourselves—as capable of taking up an objective vantage point outside history, is also what leads readers to expect from Pound a superior authority that the poem, in representing itself as a poem including history which is itself included in history, is at pains to reject.

It is possible, then, that our habitual assumptions about the intentions of *The Cantos* reveal less about the poem than about the unconscious expectations we bring to it. As a case in point, we may consider Ian F. A. Bell's recent remarks on Hugh Kenner's promotion of *The Cantos'* "curriculum" as a form of closure. Bell argues that

> Kenner's reading of "curriculum" as selection and concentration provides one of the clearest statements we have on the nature of authoritarian rhetoric: curricular concentration is inevitably a seeking after power, the power derived from a selective process designed to refine language for the purposes of manipulation and which always imposes "foreclosures" exactly in the disguise of "possibilities." The assumption of patterns of correspondence . . . becomes, for the modernist writer, a justification for omitting or denying the full range of discourse in favour of the stark solidity of objects which in effect stand on their own and merely signal silently towards the discourse of their hidden unity. This justification announces itself exactly as an ambition for the increased activity of the reader.

Bell's point is an important one, and to a great extent it is justified by the arduous demands *The Cantos* poses for any reader. Even it we understand the project of Pound's ideogrammic poetics as that of producing constellations of images that are transparent in meaning, the failure of his structuralist ideogram to be readable in this way creates the necessity of precisely that kind of reading that Bell decries: the laborious reconstruction of a plausible whole from the broken fragments on the page. But, whether or not one agrees with Bell that to read in this way is to capitulate to an obscure and dangerous exercise of power over the reader by the poet, this activity evades the central difficulty of reading *The Cantos* and its major challenge: that of understanding its form in relation to the historical conditions to which it responds, without denying or repairing its fragmentariness and its failure to conclude, and without smoothing over the difficulties it presents by substituting a reconstituted paraphrase of its sources for the thing itself.

In this light, the proper object of Bell's critique appears to be not so much the poem as certain habits of reading, grounded in long-established but fundamentally problematic assumptions about literary forms in relation to history. These assumptions underlie the reader's attempt to construct a whole from the fragments on the page, to assume and strive to make explicit "the discourse of their hidden unity." Oddly, Bell's misgivings concerning modernist forms seem to imply that nonmodernist aesthetics *can* somehow admit "the full range of discourse," which is to say that they have privileged access to something like truth (although he qualifies this implication in judging modernist forms more pernicious only in degree than "a domesticated history, a version of the past flattened out into the comforting fiction that conventionally representational art promises"). The relative merits of conventional and modernist forms aside, however, I would suggest that Bell's view takes insufficient account of the problematizing of truth implicit in the compromised success/failure of *The Cantos*' collaborative poetics. Pound's poetics of the fragment, I have argued, evolved as an experimental search for forms of order adequate to modern experience, forms that could endow experience with meaning and order without denying the impossibility of conclusion and completion. It is the impossibility of capturing the unity of things finally and totally in any discourse that informs this poetics which, as it is realized in the poem, gestures not toward *the* discourse of the fragments' hidden unity but toward the partiality and contingency of every effort to write history.

I would argue, then, that Bell's point too easily reduces the poet's purposes—and, indeed, those of "the modernist writer"—to a particular critic's at a particular moment. It fails, just as an uncritical adoption of the poem's curricular authority fails, to read *The Cantos* as the historical "record of struggle" Pound said that it was, both explicitly [*Guide to Kulchur*] and implicitly, in the errors, "blanks," and other markers of historical contingency in its text. For the purposes of this discussion, Kenner's and Bell's positions are not as far apart as they may seem: Kenner desires that the poem should be a locus of curricular authority so that he may affirm it as such, and Bell, that the poem should *claim* to be a locus of curricular authority so that he may reject it as such. Both, in other words, project upon the poem the authority of a sacred book, successful or failed.

In all fairness, both positions rest on aspects of Pound's poetics which appear to support them: Bell's on the structuralist ideology (exemplified in the composition of Canto 4) in which the "ideogrammic method" has its origin, and Kenner's, on the fact that Pound's historical qualification of his own authority was mixed with hopes that the poem would ultimately "cohere," still apparent in his late judgment of it as a "botch" and in "Canto 120." Neither, however, takes into account the experimental character of Pound's early poetics and the historical context of that experiment, and neither acknowledges the implications of its "failure." Kenner, perhaps, does not acknowledge the failure of the poem's original project at all, and Bell overlooks the fact that it is in the nature of the ideogrammic method to "self-destruct" if its premises are false: if, for example, a reader does not understand "red" in looking at a schematic juxtaposition of iron rust, a cherry, a sunset, and a flamingo, then the symbol's intended meaning fails. The practical difficulties presented by Pound's poetics are so great that it seems almost absurd to imagine it as arising from the desire to exert a limiting and con-straining power over the reader. To the contrary, I, for one, have found *The Cantos* the least teachable of books. Its poetics indeed demands collaboration, yet to conceive that collaboration as a mindless capitulation to a hidden agenda imagined to lie behind the apparent innocence of its fragments is to replace the historically grounded, *representative* authority which the poem implicitly and explicitly claims and enacts with the higher, or transcendent, authority attributed to all sacred books. As it is precisely such manipulability on the part of the reader that the ideogrammic method is designed to subvert, and as the power of so demanding a poetics to coerce the attention of a critical reader must be inconceivably small, the accusation that Pound's *Cantos* exert covert authority by linguistic manipulation appears less an accurate description of the poem than a new variation on an old theme in Pound studies: the critic's disappointment at not having found, after much effort, the hoped for center, totality, or power that would redeem such energies. In fact, fifteen years ago critics could reject the poem, as Bell does, for precisely opposite reasons. At that time, the common assumption was that Pound *ought* to present himself as "master of the situation" and that his poem ought to be analyzable as a structure of "sustained passages [joined] musically or any other way, into larger units, and thence into cantos, each one self-contained yet part of [a] whole" informed by "larger purpose"; and the common complaint—in this example, Noel Stock's—was that *The Cantos* fails to satisfy such expectations. What these opposite descriptions of the poem have in common is a localization of power, or authority, in text and poet, whereas the poetics of *The Cantos* assumes an illimitable and indeterminate diffusion of power/authority through the historical process which envelops author and reader alike. Both descriptions deny that very critical power that

Pound's poetics—the ideogrammic method no less than the documentary mode—sought not to coopt but to bring into play: "Properly, we shd. read for power. [One] reading shd. be [one] intensely alive. The book shd. be a ball of light in one's hand" [*Guide to Kulchur*]. However fundamental our scholarly tracing of sources and their interrelations is to study of *The Cantos*, it is not in itself the act of reading Pound designed, and it is finally only groundwork and prelude to the actual challenge his poem including history presents and, I think, rewards. Yet Bell's critique has great value in illuminating the extent to which its authoritarian Pound only mirrors the expectations of authority, the desire to be told what to think, feel, and value, that we as readers bring to the poem. The bad faith implicit in the act of reading, the easy abdication of critical authority, is exactly what modernist form challenges in exposing the difficulty of linguistic acts of understanding, meaning, and communication.

Pound's stance toward the errors in his text, then, has a heuristic value in leading us to reevaluate not only the achievement of his *Cantos* but our understanding of its project and the assumptions by which we judge it. The presence of the errors gestures toward a more difficult idea of paradise than the one with which Pound began his modern epic in 1915. Even then, taking up the perennial epic theme of war, Pound set his poem against the violence with which the *Iliad* so ambivalently inaugurates the Western tradition, the tradition of heroic tragedy whose continuing conditions now threaten the destruction not merely of cities but of that very earth which Homer could describe as breeding generations of warriors like leaves. One of the earliest gropings toward *The Cantos* was an image of the great error of World War I, represented in the uncomprehending soldier's monologue of MS Ur 1; that catastrophe instigated his search for constants of human experience which might unite diverse peoples at a level beyond their conflicting deities, as imaged in the Jesuit communing with Japanese sennin at the end of that early draft. Pound's ideogrammic method, his lifelong interest in the East, the historical relativism which transforms the concept of epic authority in *The Cantos*, all branch from this root. This dream of a common language gave urgency to his lifework, his effort to imagine a new "civilization"— defined, as he wrote in "Provincialism the Enemy," as "the enrichment of life and the abolition of violence" [*Selected Prose*]. Pound's effort in *The Cantos* to represent forms or patterns in history in the abstract was an attempt to discover a basis for truly universal human values in a world no longer served by its dominant traditions of war and conquest, a world which far exceeds the bounds of the Judeo-Christian theological imagination; and his hope was indeed, as he says in *Guide to Kulchur*, "totalitarian." But if Pound's dream

was of an ultimate order of human experience to which one could appeal in
seeking an end to intercultural violence and economic exploitation, his poem's
claim to greatness rests in its unretouched enactment of the failure of this
dream. Although the failure of his early dream eventually led him to carry
on a desperate campaign for an *instituted* order (evidenced in his interest in
such figures as Confucius, Adams, and Coke) and brought him to make
pernicious and disastrous political choices, in the poem in which he recorded
his own struggle through modern history that dream of wholeness and order
retains the form of desire. If Pound did not find what he was seeking, the
"natural" language of transparent metaphor posited in Fenollosa's poetics,
still his commitment to the unendingly diverse actualities of the world he
lived in kept him from imposing a linguistic and formal order he did not
find.

What is more, Pound's commitment to a poetics of history, to bringing
words and the world together, issued in his inventing a poetics which permitted him to find what he was not looking for: that difficult idea of paradise
that begins to emerge in *The Pisan Cantos*. There Pound records the anguish
of giving up the old paradises, old ideas of redemption:

> I don't know how humanity stands it
>   with a painted paradise at the end of it
>   without a painted paradise at the end of it
> the dwarf morning-glory twines round the grass-blade
>   [74:436]

But even as he suffers the "magna *NUX* animae" which his own errors have
brought upon him, fragments of brightness intrude from the Pisan landscape;
and with them the paradise gropingly designated by an aphorism of 1940—
"The essence of religion is the *present* tense" [*Selected Prose*]—begins to emerge
in his language. In saying this, I do not mean to sentimentalize the morning-
glory or to deflect attention from the seriousness of the misjudgments that
brought about the poet's incarceration in the prison camp. Rather, I want
to suggest that the wandering of attention from paradises lost to the grass-
blade traces a more profound movement toward a quite literal understanding
of paradise as "the present tense"; and of language, the trace of conscious
being, as history, heaven, and hell. The Pisan refrain, "Le Paradise n'est
pas artificiel / l'enfer non plus," resituates both paradise and hell in the here-
and-now: "unexpected excellent sausage," "the smell of mint under the tent
flaps," the minute observation of "an ant's forefoot," the recurring waves of
remorse, as "Les larmes que j'ai crées m'inondent." The extreme simplicity
of these images makes it easy to miss their import: the discovery of the

paradiso terrestre that Pound had sought so long and so erringly, in the inferno of the prison camp: in the moment, the "present tense," and in the unending miracle of life observed attentively, with weeping ("Dakruon, dakruon"), in the ant, the wasp, the "green midge half an ant size," the mint that "springs up again in spite of Jones's rodents." Only so simple a paradise, existing at once in history and beyond cultural difference, could answer Pound's earlier motive. As the threat of death made him feel the profoundly simple miracle of the earth, glimpsed in the metamorphoses of Canto 4, so our lately developed technological power to destroy this earth, achieved only months before he wrote *The Pisan Cantos*, gives epic significance to what he would later remember from Washington as "the Pisan paradise."

It is this paradise of the moment, this natural paradise, that Pound also evokes in what are now *The Cantos'* last lines in the American edition:

> I have tried to write Paradise
>
> Do not move
>   Let the wind speak
>   that is paradise.

The lines express the failure of the ("totalitarian") idea of paradise with which he began, the dream of an encompassing poetics, of a writing, an authority, adequate to "make Cosmos." Yet his refiguring of his former idea of the paradise of human desire in the natural paradise of the earth's unworded speech, even as it announces the failure of the dream that presided over *The Cantos'* beginnings, repeats an early moment in the poem's text and history, the words of the wind poem's king in Canto 4: "No wind is the king's." No longer, however, is the "wind's" power greater than the king's: what has changed in the fifty years separating these moments is precisely that relation of natural to human power that would, formerly, have rendered Pound's "Let the wind speak" a merely rhetorical, or "poetic," idea. Having lived through his life and his poem, Pound judged the failure of his dream harshly, asking forgiveness from "the gods" and from "those I love." But from a vantage point outside this epic autobiography, it is possible to see what Pound from within could not: that the fragments, both the "spezzato" paradise and the "errors and wrecks" that are the final poem, in their very partiality make cosmos more truly than any dream of totality could do.

The fragmentary paradise that Pound wrote, then, was not the one he intended at the outset to write; yet it seems in retrospect the only one possible to a modern poem including history. He began to write, as we usually begin to read, in the expectation that his fragments would eventually constitute a coherent whole, and in the end he still believed in a cosmos that "coheres all right / even if my notes do not cohere" (116:797). He never quite grasped the paradoxical truth uncovered by his epic wandering, of the necessary, inevitable, and ultimate partiality of all human experience and knowledge, the actual incompleteness, formal implications to the contrary, of all notes on cosmos. He judged the poem from the standpoint of a failed wish "To make Cosmos" (116:795) without realizing that he had done so, not *despite* the fact that, as he said, "my errors and wrecks lie about me" (116:796) but *because* his poem including history with its transformed and transforming language succeeds in representing the constitutive status of error, the partiality of vision, the diversity of experience, and the diffusion of social authority and power in modern experience. The poem that began as "drafts" in the expectation of an eventual wholeness—*A Draft of 16 Cantos, A Draft of Cantos 17–27, A Draft of 30 Cantos*—concludes in the volume of 1968, titled simply and finally *Drafts & Fragments of Cantos 110–117.*

The form of *The Cantos* thus challenges and defeats our fantasies of wholeness, completion, and authority, no less than it did its author's. If we are drawn to this modern epic as to an encyclopedic representation of modern culture, we discover not a sacred book but a "ragbag" full of errors, not divagations from a center but an epic wandering that never reaches home. The promise that lures us of an ordering force to constellate the bewildering fragments of history, experience, and tradition into "the rose in the steel dust" is not fulfilled. To read Pound's poem on these terms, which are in some ways its own, is to judge it a failure. But the drama of its struggle to renounce the "painted paradise," whether historicist or religious, and of its progress toward the fragmentary and compromised but possible paradise of history balances that failure with an unlooked for, and still hardly understood, success. I would, then, argue against the conclusion Michael André Bernstein reaches at the end of his fine study of the modern verse epic, his interpretation of *The Cantos'* fragments as "splinters of a redemptory wholeness" and as an "appeal, to a *potential* totality," which, as it were, patches back together the shattered hopes of the poet. The hope for "redemption" might attach itself instead to the "splinters" themselves, to the "spezzato" Pisan paradise that denies neither hell nor history and lays no claim to what Bernstein calls "a vision of an enlightened totality." The Pisan style, broken as it is and full of errors and "blanks," is yet an unsurpassed instrument for recording what it helps us to know as history. It is in essence a chronicler's style, not a historian's; a style which recalls Benjamin's remark that a "chronicler who recites events without distinguishing between major and minor ones acts in accordance with the following truth: nothing that has ever happened should be regarded as lost for history." And it is this metonymic Pisan style, alive to every chance and contingency—and not the metaphoric style of Canto 4—that best fulfills and "redeems" Pound's desire, early and late, to write Paradise. In the midst of an essay on the idyl, Schiller writes, "All peoples who possess a history have a Paradise." Insofar as the Pisan style delivers to us our own present, in the awareness that every act of consciousness makes history as it makes cosmos, it writes into literary history the different paradise Pound sought.

The authorial errors in *The Cantos*, then, and Pound's resistance to corrections (" 'Fang-Pearson' text as accurate as the natr of the goddam author permits), have a considerable heuristic value in precipitating the issue of authority in the modern epic. Indeed, given the exigencies of the modern epic, the errors, in their representative function, come to seem not a failure of poet and poem but rather an aesthetic and ideological necessity. Otto Rank has observed that in modern cultures, which lack a strongly unifying collective ideology such as Aquinas's and Dante's Christian cosmology, the struggle for the self-representation of the culture must be borne by the artist alone: "the great artist finally has to carry it personally, in artistic development and in human suffering"; "he does not practice his calling, but *is* it, himself, represents it ideologically." It is not incidental to the claims one can make for Pound's experimental and revisionary deployment of epic authority that he risked, made, recorded, and paid dearly for errors which were not solely his own but the crucial errors of twentieth-century history; and further, that his poem records them not simply as events but as modes of thinking and of using language.

But perhaps the greatest interest of the errors rests in the fact that in undermining the traditional conception of authority, transforming the poet from privileged diviner to representative, erring consciousness, they also dismantle even as they draw into play the dynamics of the powerful political reflexes of hero worship and scapegoating that are so deeply and dangerously engrained in Western humanism. This political psychology has played as striking a role in the reception of Pound's poem including history as in the history of poet and poem. In his hero worship of Mussolini and his scape-goating of Jews, which he was to judge his "worst mistake," Pound committed glaring, irrevocable, and consequential instances of the two most crucial errors of twentieth-century history. The two sides of this political coin recapitulate themselves, though in far weaker form, in the judging of Pound himself by readers and critics: not only in the relatively minor matter of stances toward error in the text (which correction idealistically denies and castigation scapegoats) but on the level of literary and social politics, almost

as though to confirm the representative status of Pound's modern epic. If
the dismantling of this dangerous political psychology is the final import of
Pound's epic, his poem including history, if the "foot-prints" of this representative—and, so Rank would suggest, sacrificial—epic autobiography are
followable to the end, where "worst mistakes" can be vicariously understood,
then the errors might indeed be thought paradisal inscriptions, leading its
readers as they led the poet to see the inevitable error of all ways, and so,
perhaps, teaching us to limit the field—technological as well as verbal—in
which our wandering takes its course.

MICHAEL ANDRÉ BERNSTEIN

Image, Word, and Sign: The Visual Arts as Evidence in Ezra Pound's Cantos

Great nations write their autobiographies in three manuscripts,—the book of their deeds, the book of their words, and the book of their art. Not one of these books can be understood unless we read the two others; but of the three, the only quite trustworthy one is the last.
                                        —JOHN RUSKIN, *St. Mark's Rest*

You can probably date any Western work of art by reference to the ethical estimate of usury prevalent at the time of that work's composition; the greater the component of tolerance for usury the more blobby and messy the work of art. The kind of thought which distinguishes good from evil . . . rises into the quality of line in painting and into the clear definition of the word written.
                                        —EZRA POUND, "Immediate Need of Confucius"

"All knowledge," so Ezra Pound repeatedly cautions his readers, "is built up from a rain of factual atoms." No matter how little confidence such an assertion may inspire as an epistemological slogan, it is true that one recurrent theme of regret rehearsed throughout art history primers is the absence of much detailed, factual knowledge about the lives of most pre-Renaissance masters. Thus it is hardly surprising that we still know so little about Giotto di Bondone, a painter sufficiently venerated during his own lifetime to be the only contemporary artist praised by name in Dante's *Divina commedia*

From *Critical Inquiry* 12, no. 2 (Winter 1986). © 1986 by The University of Chicago. The University of Chicago Press, 1986.

and to be called "familiaris et fidelis noster [our faithful and familiar friend]" by so powerful a monarch as King Robert of Naples. Perhaps, though, our ignorance really is more a relief than a cause for sorrow, since the documented facts that have survived are rather discouraging for a certain view of art, one with which Pound's *Cantos*—and this essay—are much concerned.

In his study of Giotto, Mario Bucci calls the painter an "out-and-out usurer," and even the more genteel academic rhetoric of American art criticism admits that Giotto "was not adverse to making money on non-artistic ventures." Virtually all the surviving contemporary documents concern Giotto's financial transactions, including his unpleasant habit of bringing legal action against those debtors unable to make timely payments on their loans. Now to be known as a usurer in fourteenth-century Florence is, considering the competition, no mean accomplishment, but, of course, the tale scarcely ends here.

Among the few extant fresco cycles from pre-Renaissance art, none is more perfectly achieved from a formal, aesthetic vantage point or more indicative of a dramatic, at times almost agonizing, awareness of the spiritual demands on daily life than Giotto's paintings in Padua's Arena Chapel. The most curious aspect of Giotto's work in Padua, for my purpose here, is that it was commissioned, according to most accounts, by Enrico Scrovegni to atone for the way his father, Reginaldo, had made the Scrovegni family Padua's wealthiest—that is, by a particularly harsh brand of usury. In fact, Reginaldo Scrovegni was so notoriously vicious a usurer that, like Giotto, he also figures prominently in Dante's epic—but his place is among the damned souls in the seventh circle of Hell.

The irony of a usurer creating a masterpiece of religious insight at the behest of a usurer's son is too obvious to detain us long, although to the edifying lesson of the Arena frescoes one might add, as a kind of grace note, an observation about another of Giotto's fresco cycles, now only partially preserved in the Bardi Chapel of Florence's Church of Santa Croce. Giotto devoted these frescoes to chronicling the life of a saint whose insistence upon total poverty so upset the *bien-pensant* churchmen of his day that for a time it was uncertain whether he would be a more likely candidate for canonization or for charges of heresy—the life of Saint Francis of Assisi. It is probably worth mentioning, however, that at least until the Counter Reformation, atonement for usury often provided a crucial impetus for the commissioning of a large number of artworks. Hence, if it is indeed true that, in Pound's words, "with usury" a citizen can have "no paradise [painted] on his church wall," one might, nonetheless, want to amend this claim to reflect the fact that guilt about usury, combined with the wealth amassed through usury, seems to have generated more public art projects than did lives of unparalleled rectitude among Italy's elite [*The Cantos of Ezra Pound* (New York, 1975), Canto 51, p. 250; all further references will cite canto and page numbers only].

But the tale doesn't stop with this simplistic, though rather unsettling, reversal either. For if the wealth of Florence—and especially of its greatest art patrons, the Medici—was based upon usury, then Pound has given us, in Sigismundo Malatesta, the exemplary figure of a different ruler, one opposed to the contrivances of bankers and the simony of priests and dedicated, instead, to doing "all that a single man could . . . *against* the current of power" (*Guide to Kulchur*). Today, any visitor to the Tempio Malatestiano in Rimini can still marvel at the artistic achievement Sigismundo brought into being and mourn the bankruptcy that doomed his original plans to only partial realization. The same visitor will undoubtedly also be led to the one major artwork remaining in the Tempio from its earlier incarnation as the Church of Saint Francis—that is, a magnificently painted crucifix left, according to tradition, by Giotto during his stay in the city, nearly 120 years before Sigismundo's reign. If that visitor's curiosity is whetted by the fortuitous conjunction of Giotto and Sigismundo within the same edifice, a little more probing begins to unfold a distinctly more melancholy narrative.

Sigismundo, as *The Cantos* tells us, had much trouble squaring his healthy paganism with the Christian orthodoxy of his time (nearly as much, say, as he had squaring his territorial ambitions with those of the papacy and of his other neighbors), but one unfortunate side effect of his impatience with the *Christianissime* artistic heritage decorating the walls of the church he converted into his Tempio was his decision to destroy most of its tangible reminders, including, so it is assumed, several more masterpieces by Giotto. I stress the term "masterpieces" because, according to Vasari at least, the works in question were reputed among the summits of Giotto's career and served as the chief inspiration for the subsequent flourishing of the Riminese school of painters—most of whose products suffered the same fate at Sigismundo's hands as had those of their teacher. So strongly do commentators like Vasari regret the destruction of these paintings that they have had some rather unkind words for Sigismundo as a wrecker of Rimini's cultural patrimony. And now, at last, this first part of my story does end, although without pretending to conclude, on the cautionary moral that Pound's "factive ruler" had indeed succeeded in wiping out the usurer's handiwork—and that we are all the poorer for his zeal.

II

Artists are the race's antennae. The effects of social evil show first in the arts.
—EZRA POUND, "Murder by Capital"

He [Pound] makes brilliant discoveries and howling blunders.
—JAMES JOYCE, Letter to Harriet Shaw Weaver

The question which I suspect might be troubling to readers is why I have chosen to situate my argument by means of a demoralizingly inconclusive series of tales. Certainly not to demonstrate that Pound got a few facts wrong, not even to suggest that he was deeply mistaken in his assumptions about the economic basis of art patronage in pre- and high-Renaissance Italy: that kind of exercise would be both banal and quite beside the point of furthering our knowledge of *The Cantos*. Before I answer the question, however, there are a few deliberately polemical premises that need to be stated explicitly, if only because Pound criticism has for so long tended to resist any debate about its own assumptions and methods.

1. To list Pound's triumphs of recognition in the realm of art, music, or literature is *by itself* no more enlightening than to catalog his oversights. Thus, for example, his instant and almost uncanny responsiveness to the work of Henri Gaudier-Brzeska is not more informative than his bizarre ranking of Francis Picabia's paintings above those of Picasso or Matisse. Clearly it is essential to know, with as much specificity as possible, exactly what Pound said about a particular work of art or literature and, equally important, given the frequent shifts of emphasis and interest throughout his long career, just when these opinions were first formulated. Like every reader of *The Cantos*, I am conscious of the enormous service rendered by Pound scholars whose research is giving us a more complete inventory of the poet's various statements and positions, and it would be foolish to take my point here as a derogation of such efforts. But a list, no matter how complete, is not an argument, and an inventory, no matter how scrupulously assembled, is not an explanation; a recurrent problem in Pound studies is that too often the compilation of discrete items of information is seen as a sufficient answer to problems of interpretation and understanding. In other words, I think it essential that discussions of Pound and the Visual Arts (or, for that matter, of Pound and History, Pound and Economics, and so forth) move beyond the quagmire resulting from still another rainstorm of "factual atoms" chronicling his various passions and dislikes.

2. Far from implying, however, that we must therefore simply accept

Pound's brilliant discoveries and pass over his "howling blunders," my position would emphasize the need to take his ideas seriously enough to confront them, to test them against the material to which they are a response and for which they often seek to provide an explanatory account. There are times, as I have argued in an analogous context, when it is less demeaning to give a man credit for his worst errors than to remove from him the capacity to err.

3. What we require, I believe, is less a catalog of all of Pound's specific statements about various artists, with each utterance assigned a positive or negative prefix depending upon our personal and currently sanctioned hierarchy of values, than a careful study of the place of those statements in the logic and texture of Pound's own work. The attempt to focus attention on *The Cantos'* network of artistic references—its invocation of masterpieces and privileged moments of cultural achievement—will yield only trivial results unless the inner dynamic linking Pound's various exampla and the actual role these play in the poem's argument become clearer in the process.

To reply, then, to the question I anticipated earlier, I did not mean in my discussion of Giotto merely to correct Pound's view of the destructive effects of high interest rates upon the arts; I also intended to suggest that when Pound wrote the celebrated "usura" passages, art had become less a specific, material creation with its own distinct historical developments than a sign, a particular instance of a position to which he was already committed for other and quite separable reasons. No matter how intense Pound's response to art was on its own terms, and irrespective of his skill in fashioning a poetic language able to transmit that intensity, the logical and thematic function of art in *The Cantos* is as "part of / The Evidence" brought forward to secure the "jury"-reader's conviction (46:234, 233). In his poem, the artistic image has been endowed with a uniquely authoritative speech: it is a kind of painted or sculpted word that can be heard to utter an unmediated, transparent truth about the fiscal conditions prevalent at the time of its creation. The decisive advantage of the work of art in this regard is that its truth lies literally on the surface, in fineness of execution, rareness of materials, and probity of line. Because the testimony of a work of art can be heard simply by studying it with sufficient attentiveness, its meaning is not vulnerable to the deliberate obfuscations, distortions, and erasures which Pound believes have sometimes compromised other kinds of historical documents. Since, presumably, we can see/read the truth of a painting merely by using our eyes, we are able to find tangible witnesses for the poet's historico-economic insights every time we look at a canvas.

It is essential to notice, by the way, that this belief has no implications about the *kind* of art under scrutiny, whether abstract or figurative, classical or postimpressionist. Accordingly, Pound could be a champion of the abstract impulse in Gaudier-Brzeska, Brancusi, or Picabia as readily as a celebrant of the delicate figural representation in Agostino de Duccio or Botticelli. Since it is largely the pure readability of the image that matters—its capacity to bear witness to "the degree of tolerance or intolerance of usury extant in the age and milieu that produced it"—the specific content of that image becomes a secondary concern (*Guide to Kulchur*). What is so striking about Pound's view here, quite apart from its degree of reliability in any given instance, is the insistence on a *direct* correlation between discrete phenomena. Pound was at once brilliantly alert to the connections between diverse realms—this is undoubtedly the reason for much of *The Cantos'* richness and one of the poem's major legacies to its successors—and utterly impatient of any notion of mediation between categories. If the production of art and the economic health of a culture are to be seen as linked, that link must be immediately registered and visible. I stress this point, because Pound's conviction that we must not treat art as something transcendentally outside our common world, as a fetish sovereignly indifferent to the circumstances of its production, is entirely salutary. But just as with his arguments linking international politics to the machinations of armament manufacturers and bankers, what vitiates Pound's insight about the role economics plays in the creation of works of art is his refusal to consider the mediations through which these connections are realized. Instead, Pound substitutes a universal and static formula (the rate of interest prevalent in a society = the chief determinant of its possibilities for creating works of enduring merit) for any analysis of the specific relationship between artistic practices, economic organization, and patterns of patronage in different historical circumstances. The problem, in other words, has nothing to do with the amount of research Pound did on the life and times of any particular painter but, rather, with the entire logic of interpretation to which painting is submitted in his poem's quest for convincing exempla.

The mistake, of course, would be to see this reading of art as a privileged social language as somehow unique to Pound or derived by him without theoretical foundation in his intellectual inheritance. In traditional Pound criticism, undoubtedly the most familiar source for the poet's convictions about art and social organization is found in the writings of Leo Frobenius (1873–1938). From his anthropological fieldwork, the notion of *Kulturmorphologie* took shape: the claim that all the essential characteristics of a civilization are discernible through examining a very restricted number of its artifacts. In fact, however, Frobenius himself only extended the technique of historical explanation pioneered by Jacob Burckhardt in his writings of the 1850s and 1860s. Like his teacher, Leopold von Ranke, Burckhardt wanted to reconstruct specific periods of the past by relying entirely upon firsthand, contemporary sources, but, unlike Ranke, he realized that such information need not be restricted to written documents. For Burckhardt, "any object from the past might be a 'source' with as good a title to the historian's attention as the written word. . . . It followed that works of art— buildings as well as paintings and sculptures and indeed musical composi- tions" might offer insights into an earlier epoch at least as revealing as more conventional archival material. Although Burckhardt applied his method- ology only to European culture, particularly in *The Age of Constantine the Great* (1852) and *The Civilization of the Renaissance in Italy* (1860), his funda- mental insight is indispensable for any study of a nonliterary society, and Frobenius's work would have been inconceivable without the prior example of Burckhardt's writings.

In Pound's account, however, Frobenius was able to derive his under- standing from a much smaller number of sources than Burckhardt would have considered necessary:

> Frobenius looked at two African pots and, observing their shapes
> and proportions, said: if you go to a certain place and there digge,
> you will find traces of a civilization with such and such
> characteristics.
>   As was the case. In event proved.
>
> [*Guide to Kulchur*]

So extreme an economy of evidence was, of course, particularly appealing to a poet engaged upon a project in which only a few, talismanic exempla could be introduced to substantiate an argument about the relationship be- tween art, money, and politics throughout history. To Frobenius's theory, Pound then joined what he regarded as the complementary insight, derived from the zoologist and geologist Louis Agassiz (1807–73): the conviction that a "scientifically" correct conclusion, even about such complex matters as "geological, racial and cultural characteristics," could be based upon the careful scrutiny of a few individual specimens. Together, Frobenius and Agassiz provided Pound with intellectual substantiation for a method of presentation that was not only consonant with his own intuitions but crucial in justifying his procedure in *The Cantos*.

Yet central as Frobenius and Agassiz undeniably were to Pound, I want to suggest that he was so receptive to their works because the ground had already been prepared by a much more familiar tradition—that of John

Ruskin. Several years ago, Hugh Witemeyer argued that "Pound's debt to the socialist economics and aesthetics of the Ruskin/Morris tradition needs to be examined much more closely than it has been to date." Although I think the term "socialist" should be used more carefully than Witemeyer's exhortation would imply, his plea seems to be both well taken and still awaiting a serious response. Indeed, I believe that Ruskin's kaleidoscopic polemics, especially *Unto This Last* and *Fors Clavigera*, are among the most striking nineteenth-century prose attempts at the kind of aesthetic-economic-historical-ethical synthesis underlying Pound's analogous impulse, expressed in *The Cantos'* idiom of high modernism. To summarize, albeit schematically, Ruskin's linking of artistic, ethical, and social arguments, I have extracted six main propositions from his various treatises, propositions whose uncanny similarity to some of Pound's own deepest-held beliefs will be obvious. Ruskin argues: (1) Artistic decay is the symptom of a disease infecting the whole social body. (2) The decline of art and taste is a sign of a general cultural crisis. (3) The conditions under which men live must first be changed if the sense of beauty and the comprehension of art are to be revived and strengthened. (4) Art is a public concern and its cultivation ought to be among the state's chief duties. (5) Art must not be regarded as the possession of an elite of privileged consumers but as the inalienable birthright of every member of society. (6) The work of an artist, work undertaken for the sake of inner satisfaction and resulting in products beneficial to the entire community, is the clearest example we have of the potential dignity of all human labor; as such, art provides a historically accessible paradigm which should serve as the model for every form of labor in an equitable society.

The tensions in Ruskin between aestheticism and moralism, between a highly dogmatic and authoritarian Epicureanism and a social doctrine which insists that real beauty is possible only in a just and nonexploitative commonwealth find echo in Pound's own works at almost every level of his argument. Both Ruskin and Pound began with a temperament and an intelligence preternaturally alert to the visual arts and the aesthetics of form, light, and water; they shared a unique ability to transpose the affective power of art into their own idioms; and both, reacting to the social exigencies of their epochs, were driven out of their aesthete's roles into that of social and economic reformers. As José Harris remarks, in a passage that might have been written with equal justice about Pound:

> Ruskin's condemnation of capitalism for estranging man from his
> noblest function was as savage as that of Marx, but his prescription was very different. The line of escape . . . lay not in socialism

and egalitarianism, but in the reconstitution of a morally legitimate hierarchical society based on a network of mutual obligations. Within such a society labour and its reward would be not
a question of utilitarian calculation but a creative act endowed
with transcendent purpose.

[*TLS*, August 31, 1984, p. 963]

The longing both Ruskin and Pound felt for a "morally legitimate hierarchical
society" lies at the heart of their proposed solutions to the social problems
of their times, and each of them united an unmistakable concern for the
economic hardship endured by much of the population with a profound
distrust of democratic institutions. In the event, Ruskin's Guild of Saint
George, founded to instigate the economic and spiritual regeneration of
England, was a harmless failure whose patent impracticality has occasioned
only amusement or mild scorn from commentators. Pound, on the other
hand, did not feel the same need to create his own organization able to
implement the desired new order, since, so he persuaded himself, Benito
Mussolini was already engaged in just such an effort. No doubt it is idle to
speculate upon how Ruskin would have regarded the Fascist program; nevertheless, it is difficult when considering Pound and Ruskin in this context to
suppress the thought that sometimes the worst fate that can befall an intellectual or artist turned social reformer is not to see his ideals dismissed as
eccentrically implausible but, on the contrary, to find a contemporary ruler
who appears to be putting those ideals directly "into action."

"Whatever economic passions I now have," Pound wrote as late as 1933,
"began *ab initio* from having crimes against living art thrust under my perceptions" ["Murder by Capital," *Selected Prose, 1909–1965*]. Both Ruskin and
Pound sought to relate beneficent economic and social practices to the production of the art they most valued, but since their methods of establishing
these relationships were essentially arbitrary, the actual financial life of such
cherished cultural centers as Florence, Venice, or Padua could not figure in
their analyses. The remarkable thing, however, is that Pound, unlike Ruskin,
never permitted the pressures of his economic or political dogma to compel
him to modify, let alone abandon, his earliest mental "catalogue of beautiful
objects." If Ruskin was notorious for revising his artistic judgments depending upon the exigencies of his economic, religious, or political convictions as well as upon the state of his psychological balance (witness, for
instance, his lavish praise for the work of Kate Greenaway), Pound never
swerved in his admiration for the artists who had first inspired him. The
intensities he venerated before seeing "usura as a murrain and a marasmus"

retained their talismanic authority and even became essential constituents of his subsequent socioeconomic preoccupations (*Guide to Kulchur*). The tragedy of both Ruskin's and Pound's positions is that in neither case, and for curiously similar reasons, could their social theories provide a convincing account of the relationship between art and economics, and the failed effort to resolve the contradictions between the aesthete and the political reformer did much to pattern the direction of both men's writings. Undoubtedly, this failure also helps account for the tone of frustrated anger that marks much of *Fors Clavigera* and some parts of *The Cantos*. But at the end, Pound was able to confront his "errors and wrecks" (116:796) and incorporate that confrontation into his work in a way Ruskin never managed, so that in the very splintering asunder of the poet's longing for a hierarchical totality, *The Cantos* could give voice to a plea for pardon articulated with an altogether rare inwardness and self-recognition:

> That I lost my center
> > fighting the world.
> The dreams clash
> > and are shattered—
> and that I tried to make a paradiso
> > > terrestre.
> > [Notes for 117 et seq.: 802]

> I have tried to write Paradise
>
> Do not move
> > Let the wind speak
> > that is paradise.
>
> Let the Gods forgive what I
> > have made
> Let those I love try to forgive
> > what I have made.
> > [120:803]

III

Color destroys perspective.
—PIERRE GAUDIBERT, *Ingres*

> *. . . the female*
> *Is an element, the female*
> *Is a chaos*
> *An octopus*
> *A biological process*
> —EZRA POUND, *Canto 29*

Surely one of the most puzzling pronouncements in *The Cantos* is the famous quatrain

> all that Sandro [Botticelli] knew, and Jacopo [del Sellaio]
> and that Velásquez never suspected
> lost in the brown meat of Rembrandt
> and the raw meat of Rubens and Jordaens
> [80:511]

It is, of course, true that anyone who has reached Canto 80 will already have encountered a canto of considerably more doubtful, at times clearly even eccentric, judgments—but almost without fail these will have concerned principles of statecraft, economics, and historiography rather than the artistic hierarchy asserted here. But again, what concerns me in these lines is not so much Pound's preference for, say, Botticelli's *La Calunnia di Apelle* over Velázquez's *Las Meninas* but rather the grounds upon which his preference is based. Essentially, Pound saw in the old line-versus-color argument an ethical contest in which firmness of line came to represent probity, craftsmanship, and clarity of vision, with ramifications that went far beyond any strictly painterly issues. This same perspective helps explain why Pound could so quickly acknowledge modern painters like Wyndham Lewis and Picabia, both of whose art is one of lines and forms rather than of color.

The treatment of line clearly offers the most readily measurable and unchanging standard of artistic excellence and hence can be evaluated in all of the different epochs included in *The Cantos'* argument. In fact, if we want to test artistic success and economic conditions against one another in an immediately verifiable and universally valid manner, *only* line can provide the illusion of a firm basis for comparative judgments, and only line can be clearly seen (that is, heard to speak) irrespective of the particular epoch in question or the specific mode of artistic practice. Insofar as art is to serve simultaneously as image, word, and sign, it requires the fixed contours of outline and edge upon which a stable definition depends.

One way to understand better the importance this distinction had for Pound is to consider that unlike line, which is always evocative of a tradition—which is, in fact, the embodiment par excellence of the memorializing aspect of art—color appears on the canvas without any immediate link to a tradition. Color, in other words, has no history and can evoke only itself; it thereby lacks the didactic element in representation which is so crucial to Pound's entire project in *The Cantos*. As Jean Starobinski has argued, in a cogent analysis of the line-versus-color debates at the time of the French Revolution, "Line, which determines things, is a symbol of moral determination. But line has a memory and refers to celebrated prototypes. . . . It figures forth an event, but the function of representation is paralleled by a dimension of reminiscence [*1789: The Emblems of Reason*].

Among the most striking aspects of the polemics about the importance of line in painting is how often the debates centered on issues seemingly remote from any purely aesthetic considerations. Conflicting positions about the individual's relationship to history, nature, and society found expression in the controversy over line and color, and scholars as diverse in their emphases as Starobinski and Karl Kroeber have shown how readily the rhetoric of such arguments acquired a moral and philosophical dimension. (In the British tradition, William Blake's annotations to *The Works of Sir Joshua Reynolds* provide a particularly vehement, but by no means unique, instance of this tendency.) Thus, it is scarcely surprising that for Pound, as well, adherence to the supreme importance of line has implications that extend considerably beyond determining the specific constellation of artists suitable for inclusion in his epic.

For the verse form of *The Cantos*, Pound created a dazzling repertoire of acoustic and metrical patterns, a repertoire that went much further than merely "break[ing] the pentameter" as the dominant rhythm of English verse (80:518). Yet for all the poem's justly praised metrical subtlety and inventiveness, it is striking how rarely Pound violates the autonomy of the line, seen as a single unit of verse composition. Throughout *The Cantos* there is remarkably little enjambment; rather than the complex interweaving of end-stopped and run-on lines characteristic of such otherwise quite distinct contemporaries as William Carlos Williams and Wallace Stevens, Pound's typical procedure was to compose in clearly separable lines, each often signaled by a spondaic or anapestic ending, as though to emphasize the elements of closure within an otherwise variable pattern. The link between the visual and the prosodic line and between the scrupulous tracing of the painterly line and the capacity of moral discrimination may seem more associative than logical, but it is nonetheless extraordinarily persistent, and it comes into play whenever the instructive or hortatory aspects of art are regarded as central, even in poets as seemingly distant from Pound's concerns as Alexander Pope.

Such a link helps explain, as well, why the ideogram proved so fruitful for Pound, since in terms of his understanding of the figure (and I am not concerned here with its accuracy as sinology), the ideogram is a speaking drawing, one based directly upon lines defining natural forces and, hence, immediately readable by a mind sufficiently alert to the vectors of energy found in an objectively guaranteed and eternally stable cosmos. Since the ideogram supposedly "pictures" directly what it signifies, it is the one form of writing free from the risk of ambiguity; it stands as a tangible microcosm of the order governing all of creation, and its drawing is possible only when the hand holding the brush traces the lines of ink in unbroken sympathy with the larger harmony.

Lastly, however, there is another aspect of Pound's commitment to the authority of the line, one which I think governs both Pound's artistic preferences and his astonishing description of "the female" that I quoted earlier and which touches the core of a seemingly quite disparate range of anxious utterances scattered throughout *The Cantos*. Although my claim may evoke considerable protest from those intent upon isolating the poem's various concerns from one another, I am increasingly convinced that it is the dissemination of meaning in a language freed from stable references, the "ungraspability" of an art of unbounded color, and the engulfing dangers of an ungovernable female sexuality, that are linked by Pound to his fears of social chaos and imaginative dispersal. Color, polysemy, and sexuality are certainly not condemned in *The Cantos*. Indeed, they are seen as vital components of a full human realization—but only as long as they are bounded and made serviceable by the shaping, linear, and phallic male order.

If, as I have argued earlier, the link between the painterly and the prosodic line itself participates in a long tradition of aesthetic and ethical speculation, my effort here to connect this theme both to Pound's longing for a stable, hierarchical society and to his ambivalence about female sexuality has, admittedly, no conventionally sanctioned provenance. As such, the linkage is far harder to demonstrate, and I realize that readers may take the connection as more mine than Pound's. But it seems to me that only by understanding how powerful the association was for Pound can we make sense of passages like those I've cited from Cantos 29 and 80 or the following words from Canto 47:

Two span, two span to a woman,
Beyond that she believes not. Nothing is of any importance.
To that is she bent, her intention
To that art thou called ever turning intention,

. . . .

> By Molü art thou freed from the one bed
> 　　　that thou may'st return to another
> The stars are not in her counting,
> 　　　To her they are but wandering holes.
> 　　　　　　　　　　　　　　　[47:237]

Throughout *The Cantos* eros and civilization are intimately, and often positively, associated. But if, in the poem, art must speak about the social order and if it must also speak to us about human desire, it must speak, so to speak, from a curiously missionary position. Beyond the "natural increase" based not on money's sinister capacity to breed itself but "on the growing grass that can nourish the living sheep" ["Banks," *Selected Prose*], beyond the stabilities of a transparent artistic image uttering its unchanging truth, beyond the energies of the line circumscribing the shapeless intensity of color, and beyond the phallic sexuality of the "factive" shaper and statesman is the "jungle" of greed (in all its senses), anarchic (that is, "female") urges, and ungovernable proliferation.

Already in the opening cantos Pound is careful to establish the central opposition between two kinds of female sexuality. The one leaves men empty of consciousness, transformed into a desolate bestiality as victims of Circe's random lust:

> When I lay in the ingle of Circe
> I heard a song of that kind.
> 　　　Fat panther lay be me
> Girls talked there of fucking, beasts talked there of eating,
> All heavy with sleep, fucked girls and fat leopards
> 　　　　　　　　　　　　　　　[39:193]

But the other is crystallized in an apparition compelling admiration ("Venerandam"), Aphrodite rising "with golden / Girdles and breast bands" as guarantor of a desire ennobled by its issue in city-founding Aeneas (1:5). Even in the Botticelli painting Pound so cherished, Venus emerges naked from the waters, but here her sexuality is simultaneously "civilized" and restrained by the golden lines of the metalworker's craft. It is a compelling image, at once traditional and highly personal, as are many of Pound's finest moments; and it succeeds in linking the motifs of an ordered and order-building eros, of color (Aphrodite's flesh, as well as the gold itself) contained within the "bands" that underline its perfect and stable form, and of a precious commodity that is used to serve an aesthetic rather than a mercenary end.

The description of Aphrodite clothed in bands of gold is, moreover, a common Renaissance topos, traditionally intended to signify the dual nature of sexual desire. As Robert Hollander has shown, when Venus is represented without her *ceston*, or girdle, she embodies illicit and destructive lust with "anti-social results," but when she is figured wearing the golden *ceston*, she stands for "positive sexual love, present in matrimony and resulting in the creation of offspring." Pound's description of Aphrodite in Canto 1 clearly draws upon the topos of the two Venuses to give us an image of the beneficent goddess as a kind of corrective-in-advance to her destructive incarnation as Helen of Troy in Canto 2, Eleanor of Aquitaine in Canto 7, and, most tellingly, as the Circe of Canto 39. If, in other words, both the visual and prosodic lines are linked to the idea of order and probity, then the image of Aphrodite wearing breast-bands and *ceston* is an entirely consistent, and even quite traditional, extension of the same constellation of associations.

So crucial, in fact, to Pound's entire vision is this initial image of a positive (that is, procreative) Aphrodite, that all of the terms introduced in Canto 1 are taken up again, only in an inverted fashion, when he subsequently proceeds to itemize the sins of usury: a humane economic and social order, a fruitful sexuality, and an art of clear lines are directly joined in Canto 45 as common victims of fiscal evil. "With Usura," Pound chants, "the line grows thick"; "wool comes not to market"; "None learneth to weave gold in her pattern"; "Usura slayeth the child in the womb / It stayeth the young man's courting" (45:229, 230).

In painting, color that is not strictly confined within the limits defined by a prior network of lines threatens to destroy the perspective necessary for a stable picture plane. How crucial the notion of a firm perspective—in every domain—is to Pound's argument scarcely needs emphasizing, but it does explain the strength of his resistance to a technique like Rembrandt's. Chiaroscuro, an art "not of outlines, but of . . . bodies made visible, in varying degrees, by the incidence of light," is, for Pound, genuinely dae-monic, an unmistakable sign of a world order that has lost its perspective and, with it, a proper reverence for hierarchy [H. W. Janson, *History of Art*]. Since, in chiaroscuro, even the principal figures tend to be partially shadowed by the dark, their "shapes remain[ing] incomplete, their contours . . . merely implied," the art of a Rembrandt or a Velázquez is not merely the result of a perverse decline in the painter's commitment to his craft but an unmis-takable sign of a society in which the shadowy devices of the usurer are beginning to triumph. Simultaneously, in the change from Botticelli's rep-resentation of the naked Venus to canvases like Ruben's *Angelica and the Hermit* or Rembrandt's *Danaë*, a radically different treatment of the female nude is apparent, a treatment which, to Pound, seemed, like a celebration of "raw meat" devoid of any spiritual content, seemed, that is, like the artist's abject surrender to the brazenly open sexuality of Circe.

By the 1930s, Pound had become convinced that the contagion was so widespread that only a leader with unrestricted authority could enforce a sufficiently rigorous cure. What Pound found, of course, was Benito Mussolini—"the Boss" in *The Cantos*' gratingly colloquial translation of *Il Duce*. We still lack a coherent account of Pound's years in Fascist Italy, but there is no doubting the extent of his loyalty to the regime or his approval of most of its programs. The Italian "New Orders" 's emphasis on the rights of the patriarchy over a woman's fertility, with a concomitant repression of all sexual activity not dedicated to procreation, its commissioning of pseudo-classic, monumental sculptures and canvases (fascist art is preeminently one of line and mass), and its attacks on the (supposedly Jewish) "international usocracy" would seem, were the historical consequences not so dreadful, like a grotesquely parodic version, a realization in the form of kitsch, of the ideals Pound had celebrated beginning *The Cantos*.

In a strange dialogue, narrated years later in Canto 93, Mussolini asks Pound why the poet wants to bring his ideas into a coherent order. As unlikely as the dictator's question may appear, Pound's response, in its implicit admission of a not yet successful struggle, is highly revealing: " 'Pel mio poema' "—"For my poem" (93:626). Considering the final shape of *The Cantos*, the poem's increasingly fragmentary narratives and its abandonment of any epic closure, is it too speculative to end with the suggestion that only someone deeply aware of his own tendency to dispersal and fragmentation (a tendency already explicitly confronted and ironized in the shifting tones and masks of *Hugh Selwyn Mauberley*) would have sought so strenuously to keep that disintegration at bay, would have longed so much for stable lines of authority neither his culture nor his own psyche could guarantee?

KATHRYNE V. LINDBERG

Rhizomatic America

Far too as her splendors shine, system on system shooting like rays, upward, downward, without center, without circumference—in the mass and in the particle, Nature hastens to render account of herself to the mind. Classification begins . . . and so, tyrannized over by its own unifying instinct, [the mind] goes on tying things together, diminishing anomalies, discovering roots running underground whereby contrary and remote things cohere and flower out from one stem.

—EMERSON, "The American Scholar"

A Pact
I make a pact with you, Walt Whitman—
I have detested you long enough.
I come to you as a grown child
Who has had a pig-headed father;
It was you that broke the new wood,
Now is a time for carving.
We have one sap and one root—
Let there be commerce between us.
—POUND, *Personae*

At times, Pound's desire for a compatible and legitimate tradition led him to renounce his Americanism and to abjure modernism altogether. Nevertheless, whether under the name of "Make it New" or "The American Risorgiamento," his historical and/or aesthetic project is articulated in terms which belie any simple desire to keep THE TRADITION intact. He wanted to *drill* a certain version of America into modern letters, to *graft* fragments

From *Reading Pound Reading: The Nietzschean Indirections of Modernism.* © 1986 by Oxford University Press.

of modern life onto the trunk of European art, and at the same time, to carve out an American heritage. I emphasize Pound's recurrent metaphors of grafting and drilling, of the organic and even the sculptural as against the architectonic. These figures, endemic to American poetics, at once ground and unsettle the edifice—or is it the system of poetic roots and shoots?—Pound hoped to erect or resurrect as an American tradition. One might note in passing that an American tradition, let alone one that combines the mutually exclusive models of the organic and the monumental, has always seemed oxymoronic if not downright impossible.

In "What I Feel About Walt Whitman," a note written in 1909 but left unpublished until 1955, Pound outlined a strange genealogical reconstruction in characteristically mixed metaphors and catachreses. Presenting the old saw, that is, "the family tree," perhaps too graphically, he says of Whitman that "the vital part of my message, taken from the sap and fibre of America, is the same as his" [*Selected Prose*]. This American tree, of which Whitman and Pound are parts, though not simply living trunk and branch, is indeed an unnatural one. Growing backward in time, it has not yet taken root. In fact, Pound suggests that both he and Whitman are misplaced and untimely. If Whitman was an imperfect beginning, Pound is the repetition of such a beginning. In this way, Pound marks both a repetition of and a revolution against Whitman, who, for better or worse, found himself in a similar position of at once taking up and overthrowing his European and American heritage(s).

Pound and Whitman are hardly alone in recognizing America's ambiguous cultural imperatives. Indeed, Henry Adams, for whom American culture was inescapably problematic, translated the search for roots into the broader and no less heterogeneous areas of pedagogy, medieval art history, and the new sciences of geology, genetics, and physics. Adams recognized that Americans' need for cultural legitimacy necessarily involved the breaking of discursive categories to say nothing of the laws of literary genre. This can be seen as much in the strange mixed genre of his own autobiographical history texts (*Mont-St.-Michel and Chartres* and *The Education*) as in his ironic treatment of the presumably pure disciplines out of which he created such heterogeneous and heterodox categories as "Conservative Christian Anarchism." I will have something more to say about Adams later, but first, it is necessary to look more closely at the relations between Pound and Whitman as a crisis of moment for modernism and Americanism in which current literacy theory, itself riddled with generic and genealogical anxieties, still has a stake.

Early and late, American writers have sung of themselves as additions

to or parasites upon an unbroken legacy of Western Art—marking both its completion and its unaccountable excess. Thus, not without quoting Whitman, Pound claims his American heritage and more: "I am (in common with every educated man) an heir of the ages and I demand my birth-right. Yet if Whitman represented his time in language acceptable to one accustomed to my standard of intellectual-artistic living he should belie his time and nation. Yet I am but one of his 'ages and ages' encrustations' or to be more exact an encrustation of the next age" [*Selected Prose*]. Whitman is honored there, as Pound would always honor him, for faithfulness to his time and language; like Dante in Italy and Chaucer in England, Whitman wrote in his native or vulgar tongue and thereby created the possibility of a new Poetry if not of an American language.

Pound is torn between refining the American, that is, the Whitmanesque, idiom and acquiring greater erudition and a more impressive ancestry. At the same time that he complains of Whitman's inadequacies, Pound approves his nativist project. Yet he does so by translating it into a series of metaphors—the organic and the destructive, the archeological and the archeoclastic, the genetic and the accidental—for that American mythos of history that has always been similarly befuddled. Thus Whitman is the encrustation upon as well as the founder of a still uncertain "American tradition" to which Pound turns in order to overturn. And Pound is part of the new which is an encrustation upon both the last and the next ages, only a moment of transition between two disjunct poetic and genealogical lines.

However "congenial" or genealogically amenable Pound insists he is to the more recognized precursors of the Eliotic Tradition, when he equates Dante and Whitman the earlier poet necessarily suffers an diminution. And, more importantly, the poetic hierarchy undergoes a leveling in which the privileged category of Poetry hardly remains intact. Pound both acknowledges and represses these difficulties in charting an ancestry which is, if geometry and genealogy permitted such aberrations, a series of intersecting parallel lines of poet-hybrids who cut across several languages, artistic genres, and historical periods.

Just so, "textbooks" such as "How to Read" and *ABC of Reading* privilege those writers who worked radical innovations *within* the very tradition Pound seems to propagate. Even as early as "I Gather the Limbs of Osiris" (1911-12) he proposes to anthologize and canonize the " 'donative' author who seems to draw down into the art something that was not in the art of his predecessors. If he draws from the air about him, he draws latent forces, of things present or unnoticed, or things perhaps taken for granted but never examined:" [*Selected Prose*]. Such an author/reader—let alone the modern reader who discovers and (re)positions him—automatically destabilizes the tradition by changing his inheritance and his legacy, that is, the "art of his predecessors."

Whitman, the acknowledged inventor of "free-verse" and of the "democratic epic," necessarily disrupts poetry's old generic categories. And Pound, while always dissatisfied with Whitman's characteristic lack of refinement, tended to praise his forebear for such violations and to affect such crudities in order to disturb the genteel tradition and inscribe his personal signature of the prodigal modern. Further, he proposes separating Whitman's meaning from his verse, thus performing an operation which rests on the assumption that *Leaves of Grass* is not an organic poem; it does not, unlike his favorite Provençal poems, require full quotation or "direct presentation." According to Pound, this is because Whitman was so open to history and to the nonpoetic that *Leaves of Grass* is as much history as it is poetry. If anything, Pound wants Whitman to be less "poetic"—at least along the old lines—and more iconoclastic.

Indeed, it is Whitman the reader of culture and the *scourge* of tradition Pound adopts as his American ancestor, as for instance, in *ABC of Reading*, when he says: "If you insist, however, in dissecting his language you will probably find out that it is wrong NOT because he broke all of what were considered [in] his day 'the rules' but because he is spasmodically conforming to this, that or the other . . . using a bit of literary language." However uneasy Pound might be about adopting the style of *Leaves of Grass* for his own poetic or pedagogical strategies, he never ceases acknowledging Whitman's *critical* (both crucial and interpretative) function of turning the European poetic tradition toward the broader area of (American) culture. As we will see, the replacement of "tradition," a word that must be associated with Eliot's fabrication of his conservative modernism, by "culture" and finally Pound's neologism, *Kulchur*, graphically as well as semantically marks disruption of the generic and genealogical orders.

Of his own relationship to Whitman, Pound says, "Personally I might be very glad to conceal my relationship to my spiritual father and brag about my more congenial ancestry—Dante, Shakespeare, Theocritus, Villon, but the descent is a bit difficult to establish. And, to be frank, Whitman is to my fatherland what Dante is to Italy and I at my best can only be a strife for a renaissance in America" [*Selected Prose*]. From a certain perspective, Whitman occupies the position of first poet, the flower of that belated and imported "American Renaissance" that originated in Emerson, or even the position of the disseminator of an American, in contrast to the English, poetic language. By these accounts, he is no more than an interloper in

Europe, especially the idealized Europe of pre-Renaissance Italy where Pound would situate himself and his American ancestor. Whitman is both the origin of American poetry and its unaccommodated original; perhaps because he was thus, like Americans generally, obsessed with origins yet compelled to be original in the exercise of individuality. At least Pound seems to say as much when he is at pains to decide where Whitman belongs in the greater scheme of things—as well as in the recent history of poetry.

Faced with a similar dilemma in the figure of that evolutionary glitch, the ganoid fish, *Pteraspis*, a still extant paleolithic species passed over by evolution, Henry Adams observed that "to an American in search of a father, it mattered nothing whether the father breathed through lungs, or walked on fins, or on feet." Surely Pound's choice of precursors is not quite that indiscriminate. Whitman's centrality to a nativist poetics is hardly in doubt; nevertheless, he resists incorporation into an organic tradition or literary history as fiercely as Adams's fish resists Darwin's neat taxonomy.

Yet Whitman himself had deliberately reorganized more than one category within the poetic tradition and the larger province he named "American culture," a recurrent phrase, if not a new and privileged idea, in his criticism as well as his poetry. In terms Pound would use in his poetry as well as his "culture criticism," Whitman had tried to redefine "culture" and his own European cultural inheritance. Not surprisingly, "culture" was a troublesome word for the egalitarian "rough" whose poetry and polemics were deployed against the narrow definitions of poetry and art advanced by "gentlemen of culture." In "Democratic Vistas," for example, Whitman asks how an American culture might be cultivated. One should note that his analysis proceeds by a series of agricultural metaphors resting on a pun:

> The writers of a time hint the mottoes of its gods. The word of the modern, say these voices, is the word Culture.
>
> We find ourselves abruptly in close quarters with the enemy. *This word Culture*, or what it has come to represent, *involves, by contrast, our whole theme*, and has been, indeed, the spur, urging us to engagement.
>
> Certain questions arise. . . . *Shall a man lose himself in countless masses of adjustment, and be so shaped with reference* to this, that, and the other, *that the simply good and healthy and brave parts of him are reduced and clipp'd away, like the bordering of a box in a garden?* You can cultivate corn and roses and orchards—but who can cultivate the mountain peaks, the ocean, and the tumbling gorgeousness of the clouds? Lastly—is the readily given reply that *culture only*

seeks to help, systematize, and put in attitude, the elements of fertility and power, a convulsive reply?
    I do not so much object to the name, or word, but I should certainly insist, for the purposes of these States, on a radical change of category, in the distribution of precedence [my italics].

Like Whitman, Pound felt uneasy about the limited and privileged term "culture," which he figures as both a continuum and a wearing down of classical unity into indistinct fragments. Here is one of his most quoted definitions of "culture," one which is nonetheless not granted the complexity and inconsistency it clearly presents: "European civilization or, to use an abominated word *'culture'* can best be understood as a *medieval trunk with wash after wash of classicism going over it.* That is not the whole story, but to understand it, you must think of that *series of perceptions, as well as of anything that has existed or subsisted from antiquity*" [*ABC of Reading*].

Pound has again resorted to catachresis, to mixed metaphors that jumble the classical inheritance with subsequent revivals or "perceptions" of it. In a fiction that does not resolve as smoothly as Eliot's "Tradition and the Individual Talent," culture is here imaged as both the perennial family tree and as a shore or even a painting effaced by waves or washes of color. Like "encrustations of the next age," washes cover over and, at least to all appearances, change what is underneath. In the case of white-wash or of watercolor washes, such simple distinctions as object and covering can become completely obscured. Furthermore, in Pound's model, "classicism," which should by rights precede the "medieval," comes later, as a series of additions to, rather than a revelation of, previous cultures. Thus belated, American literature which began in New England or Brooklyn, or, as Pound claims, in Virginia, was in a position to work a renaissance or a rejection of the old cultural forms—or perhaps to have it both ways, as Emerson and to some extent, Whitman hoped.

In speaking of an American culture, in repeating once again that American gesture of mapping a national history, Pound suggests that America should open art and literature to the nonliterary and the inartistic. In "The Jefferson-Adams Letters as a Shrine and a Monument," for instance, he insists that American literature originated or culminated in the fugitive journals and correspondence of John Adams, Jefferson, Franklin, and Van Buren. Pound denies any fall away from classicism and thereby endorses the heterogeneity characteristic of America and modernism, thus: "Our national culture can be perhaps better defined from the Jefferson letters than from any three sources and mainly to its benefice" [*Selected Prose*].

Jefferson and the other founding fathers are praised for repeating the ordered multiplicity Pound had uncovered in Dante. With regard to the Presidential correspondence, he recalls Dante's phrase, " 'in una parte piu e meno altrone.' " He translates the phrase as suggesting that Jefferson and Adams were polymaths who nevertheless maintained a sense of proportion and a scale of values. In describing the "palimpsest" of their "Mediterranean state of mind" as the best "intellectual filing system," Pound admits that the world and works of his favorite Americans contained "things neither perfect nor utterly wrong, but arranged in a cosmos, an order, stratified, having relations with one another." Despite the fact that here and in the "Jefferson/ Adams Cantos" Pound tends to focus on those details that refuse incorporation into any sort of organic whole, and on the infinitely interpretative relations among writers and writings rather than on monolithic Ideas, he memorializes the Jefferson/Adams letters in the following terms: "The implication is that they stand for a life not split into bits. Neither of these two men would have thought of literature as something having nothing to do with the nation, the organization of government" [*Selected Prose*]. Pound's category of American culture or the American "cosmos" (the unacknowledged adoption of the Whitmanesque term startles) is large enough to accommodate a great deal more than traditional art and literature, however miniscule Pound's quotations from the text of America eventually become.

Not without contradiction, then, Pound endorses the thrust of Whitman's change in the category "Culture," and thus tacitly approves the democratic and even the antipoetic elements of *Leaves of Grass*. Rather than smooth Whitman's roughneck image or remake his poem into a part of an epic continuity, Pound employs the earlier American as laborer against the conservative and elitist aesthetic which he nevertheless hoped to export intact back to America, as that "high modernism" he is credited with founding. His motives as well as his metaphors are mixed, and his translation of the European into an American culture is neither direct nor untroubled. Playing more on the architectonic than the organic, and in the name of Whitman as well as the names of more accepted figures, Pound issues a sort of Americanist manifesto: "It seems to me I should like to drive Whitman into the old world, I sledge, he drill—and to scourge America with all the old beauty . . . and with a thousand thongs from Homer to Yeats, from Theocritus to Marcel Schwob" [*Selected Prose*].

In his proposed destruction and reconstruction of the old beauty, Pound equates Whitman, Homer, Yeats, and the historian Marcel Schwob in a list he would supplement and reassemble throughout his literary career, adding, as time went on, writers from disparate ages and discourses. This was one strategy by which he would, as he said, "make all ages contemporaneous." But the cost of this ahistoricism or cultural relativism is a destabilizing of the poetic as well as the political hierarchies and privileges he never ceases claiming for Poetry, the acme of culture by his own definition(s).

Pound wanted both the stability of cultural monuments (though hardly Matthew Arnold's "touchstones") and the untameable action of new discoveries and unusual methods. Leo Frobenius's *Kulturmorphologie* and specifically the figure of *paideuma* satisfied Pound's conflicting desires for novelty and respectability. Under various names, *paideuma* runs throughout *Guide to Kulchur* and his other writings on American history. At one point, he says: "The history of culture is the history of ideas going into action." Later, in contrasting Frazer's mythography to Frobenius's archeology, Pound suggests that *paideuma* violates chronology in his favorite way; it turns the distant past into a new prospect: "His [Frobenius's] archaeology is not retrospective, it is immediate. . . . To escape a word or set of words [culture and tradition] loaded with dead associations Frobenius uses the term Paideuma for the tangle or complex of the inrooted ideas of any period."

It is not going too far to claim that Pound enlisted the quirky German anthropologist for his ongoing Americanist project of troping historical and cultural "retrospection" into nativist "prospect," or even a prospectus. After all, it was Emerson, that original American reviser, who began *Nature* with the familiar admonition: "Our age is retrospective, it builds the sepulchres of the fathers. It writes biographies, histories, and criticism. The foregoing generations beheld God and nature face to face; we through their eyes. Why should not we also enjoy an original relation to the universe." Pound articulated his similar concern about immediacy and originality in terms of original interpretations of the whole of culture. Yet, for all his efforts at erecting original and paradoxically *living* and *inrooted* "monuments" to Jefferson, Adams, Homer, Dante, *et alia*, Pound more than once echoes Emerson in defining his own project: "The reader, who bothers to think, may now notice that in the new paideuma I am not including the retrospect, but only the pro-spect" [*Guide to Kulchur*].

In spite of himself, Pound proposes to undermine, if not to dismantle, those artistic structures which had never been successfully transplanted onto American soil. This is to say that when Pound supplements American poetry with European beauty, he exaggerates the stability and coherence of the "American" as well as that of the "other" order he calls tradition. Yet he neglects to note Whitman's ambivalence toward the European tradition and thus he forgets the admixture of traditionalism and iconoclasm already stamped into "the American." His "feelings about Walt Whitman" are in fact characteristic of the schizophrenic loyalties the American writer has always felt toward the old and new worlds. A longer essay might consider other segments of the broken and often subterranean line that stretches from Emerson to those post-modern writers who still answer "The American Scholar's" call to an American poetics. But instead, I would like at this point to make a kind of European and post-modern detour, in order to call upon an even more recent commentary on what we have come to call Americn modernism. I will refer to a programmatic essay by Gilles Deleuze and Felix Guattari entitiled "Rhizome" [in *On the Line*, tr. John Johnston].

"Rhizome" was undertaken to explain the Frenchman's micro-political assaults upon such entrenched conventions of Western philosophical and literary discourse as the single author, the unified book, and the segregation of disciplines within the academy. The essay opens, for instance, with Deleuze and Guattari positioning—or, better, "deterritorializing"—themselves in the midst of an ongoing cultural exchange that will not admit of *their* own uniqueness. Their very insistence on shared and unaccountable authorship is an embarrassment to literature, psychology, and philosophy, all disciplines that privilege individual consciousness as primary to systematic and serious discourse. They begin thus, conscious of a belatedness that includes their own writings:

> We wrote *Anti-Oedipus* together. As each of us was several, that already made quite a few. . . .
>
> A book has neither subject nor object; it is made up of variously formed materials, of very different dates and speeds. As soon as a book is attributed to a subject this working of materials and the exteriority of their relations is disregarded. A benificent God invented geological movements. In a book, as in everything else, there are lines of articulation or segmentation, strata, territorialities; but also lines of flight, movements of deterritorialization and of destratification.

A similar and even more anxiety-ridden sense of belatedness has characterized American writing from Emerson to the present, and, as we have seen, applies even to Whitman, despite the critics' tendency to accept his immediate and "barbaric yawp" as a return to the primal voice. Marking this self-consciousness, which wants to preserve a genealogical sense of order yet claim a sense of individual identity in its own disruptiveness, is a gesture that Pound whimsically called, in a letter to William Carlos Williams, "the

American habit of quotation." Quoting and stealing, the American writer from Emerson to Poe on would "deterritorialize" his past. But this also meant subverting any claim to originality and authority over his own text.

Indeed, Pound [in *Guide to Kulchur*] calls into question his own authority if not his own authorship, as he persists in valuing the unstoppable exchanges of subjects and objects within the culture and its adequate history:

> We do NOT know the past in chronological sequence. It may be convenient to lay it out anesthetized on the table with dates pasted on here and there, but *what we know we know by ripples and spirals eddying out from us* and from our own time.
>
> There is no ownership in most of my statements and *I cannot interrupt every sentence or paragraph to attribute authorship* to each pair of words, especially *as there is seldom an a priori claim even to the phrase or half phrase* [my italics].

I do not wish to exaggerate the similarities between Pound and the two French writers who have no reason to think like the traditionalist/modernist/fascist writer, whom they instead have every reason to reject. Nevertheless, Pound, and Whitman as well, pushed against the limitations of books and logical discourse in much the same way as Deleuze and Guattari propose to do:

> A tiresome feature of the Western mind is that it relates actions and expressions to external or transcendent ends, instead of appreciating them on the plane of immanence according to their intrinsic value. For example, insofar as a book is made of chapters, it has its culminating and terminal points. What happens, on the contrary, with a book made of plateaus, each communicating with the others through tiny fissures, as in the brain? We shall call a "plateau" every multiplicity connectable with others by shallow underground stems, in such a way as to form and extend a rhizome. We are writing a book as a rhizome.

If such radical deployments of the problems inherent in writing remain—or have again become—surprising to the American critical ear, questions such as "What is an Author?" "What are the ends of philosophy?" and the like, have become thematic commonplaces in recent continental thought. Yet one might claim that they are native to American poetics and certainly to Pound's version of the modern, both of which unsettle categories of the Western literary tradition. Although they make no reference to Pound's modernist interventions, Deleuze and Guattari suggest as much when they say that Western culture, which they trace back to its roots in agriculture, has always privileged trees, if in a most ambivalent fashion: from the Edenic tree of knowledge to the family tree of Indo-European languages. Borrowing a disctinction from botany and amplifying its metaphoric resonance, they oppose the *arborescent* or tree-like culture to their own *rhizomatic* or weed-like writing. And, most important here, they find their precedent in America's weed-like multiplication of influences and tangled roots.

To summarize briefly the botanical definitions: trees have fixed roots and structural permanence; rhizomatic plants, which include most tubers, orchids, and such virulent weeds as the "Virginia creeper," lack fixed roots and instead have filamental shoots that grow horizontally just beneath the surface of the ground and sometimes project aeriel roots in all directions. Trees grow vertically; rhizomatic plants grow horizontally. With work, trees can be cut down, but rhizomes left in the ground can hide, hibernating and spreading subterraneously until they eventually give rise to new plants or more weeds, often in surprising locations and configurations. By extension, and to quote Guattari and Deleuze, "Arborescent systems are hierarchical systems comprised of centers of significance and subjectivization, of autonomous centers. . . . It is curious how the tree has dominated Western reality, and all of Western thought, from botany to biology and anatomy, and also gnosticism, theology, ontology, all of philosophy . . . the root-foundation, *grund*, fundaments."

Rhizomes can, however, masquerade as trees. Sometimes, as is the case with Pound and Adams, the grafting of a family tree of poetry and the other disciplines becomes a subtle parody of the search for origins. Or, as in Whitman, one cannot find the trees for all the individual, heterogeneous and heteroclite leaves of grass and of paper. Curiously enough, Deleuze and Guattari claim that "American literature," notwithstanding its perennial search for origins and originality, is the exemplary rhizomatic text, both for its origins of European and its writings about American culture. If the Frenchmen might be said to give "America's rhizomatic literature" a univocity *we all* know it lacks, they nevertheless expose the tangled themes of the Americanist problematic. I quote one particularly stunning segment:

> America should be considered a place apart. Obviously it is not
> exempt from domination by trees and the search for roots. This
> is evident in its literature, in the quest for a national identity,
> and even for a European ancestry or genealogy. . . . Hence the
> difference between an American book and a European book, even
> when an American sets off pursuing trees. A difference in the

very conception of the book: "Leaves of Grass." Nor are directions the same in America: the east is where the arborescent search and the return to the old world takes place; but the west is rhizomatic, with its Indians without ancestry, its always receding borders, its fluid and shifting frontiers.

Notwithstanding the rather complex and foreign, not to say subversive, character of Deleuze and Guattari's argument, it would seem that much of American writing has been involved with rhizomes, that is, with the wild weed-like growths that undermine the organic or agricultural order so fundamental to Western thought and its literature. Emerson, the putative founder of what is now recognized as a de-centered—if not a rhizomatic— American poetic tradition, has a good deal to say about the American underbrush which refuses to sustain trees or other rooted structures. One of his most striking and heuristic uses of the botanic metaphor takes the form of a self-conscious complaint against the very diffuseness and errancy epitomized by his own essays, journals, and miscellaneous notes. In a journal passage dated 1847, he says, "Alas for America as I must so often say, the ungirt, the profuse, the procumbent, one wide juniper, out which no cedar, no oak will rear up a mast to the clouds! It all runs to leaves, to suckers, to tendrils, to miscellany."

Guattari and Deleuze were probably not thinking of Emerson at all, nor were they embarrassed by Whitman's *Leaves of Grass* in quite the same way as were modern American poets like Pound, Eliot, and Williams. Yet what in "Rhizome" appears as a privileged, cross-discursive miscellany and the projection of a subterranean American counter-tradition (poetic counter-culture?) is related to the ambiguous nationalism of Pound's modernist program. Moreover, as we have seen with regard to Whitman's *sledging* and his *sap* of nativism, Pound's thoughts about American poetics are frequently conveyed in strained botanic metaphors.

Pound certainly set out "pursuing trees," if with the quixotic or at least the unnatural aim of grafting an ancient European genealogy onto the new growth of American literature to which Whitman was both precursor and product. Despite continual efforts to repair the rootlessness of *Leaves of Grass*, Pound's own long poem, and his criticism both in and out of that poem share much with the text Deleuze and Guattari somewhat cryptically identify as representative of "the American rhizome." Like Whitman's poem, *The Cantos* is heterogeneous, insistently incomplete or provisional; composed of fragments of various historical themes and poetic forms, it too changed over the history of its writing. Indeed, the further back in time and the farther

East Pound ventured in search of his "legitimate ancestry," the more fragmentary his poem became; that is, the more history Pound included in his
poem, and the more ancestors and antecedents he collated into metaphors
and models of his tradition, the more insistent became his questioning of
the fundamental concepts and figures comprising any nostalgic quest for
origins. Perhaps this contradiction is most pronounced in "The Chinese
Cantos," which record four thousand years of dynastic history in genealogical
tables which Pound interrupts with distracting and often idiosyncratic programmatic statements. This textual layering is conveyed by a mixture of
organic, economic, and architectural metaphors, comprising at best simulacra
of system or tradition.

"The Chinese Cantos," published with the "Jefferson/Adams Cantos"
and obsessed with order and systematization, are composed of virtually
unreadable fragments translated though French transliterations of often corrupt and incomplete records written by thousands of court historians whose
interested selections can hardly be considered the work of objective or accurate historiography; nor can their various styles and themes be gathered
into any sort of coherent book, let alone an organic American epic. Nevertheless, Pound was expressly attempting to use these texts to establish a
general economy or cultural paradigm that could in some way mark a continuity between the ancient agrarian civilization of China and such later
idealized cultural repetitions as Jeffersonian democracy. Despite the efforts
of sympathetic critics to translate Pound's stated intention into an organic
poem or an epic held together by such devices as "subject rhymes" and
"nodal repetitions," both in theme and form the text remains a kind of natural
hybrid (to use an oxymoron), exhibiting the sort of rootlessness and excess
Deleuze and Guattari call "rhizomatic." Perhaps more than any of the cantos
except for *Rock-Drill*, the Chinese sequence exceeds even the "wash upon
wash of classicism" that Pound both charted and descried. Moving away in
both directions from European Classical culture (east and backward in time
to China as well as west and forward in time to America), *The Cantos*, are
rhizomatic, that is, not rootless but, as Pound said, "the tangled and inrooted
ideas of any age."

Two examples from "The Chinese Cantos" will suffice to show that
Pound's own self-conscious metaphors undercut the organic or, more precisely, the "arborescent" tradition he set out to recover and, as it turned out,
to cut and graft into a different sort of growth. Canto 52 reintroduces and
augments the series of ostensibly architectonic metaphors and mythological
systems that weave through *The Cantos* like tendrils, surfacing only as new
sources and themes are introduced or old ones modified. At this point, Pound

signals a turn from sixteenth-century Venetian economics back to the mythic
founding of an agriculture in prehistoric China. Preceding the canto proper,
one of the poem's few prose notes announces the theme of the two decads
which encompass Chinese history and the Jefferson/Adams period of America. Here, Pound feels compelled to reflect on what impedes or disrupts his
own elucidation of this linkage.

After a table of contents more appropriate to a textbook like his own
Guide to Kulchur than to an epic, he makes his excuses in somewhat misleading
advice to the reader:

> Note the final lines in Greek, Canto 71, are from Hymn to
> Cleanthes, part of Adams' *paideuma*: Glorious, deathless of many
> names, Zeus eye ruling all things, founder of the inborn qualities
> of nature, by laws piloting all things. [*The Cantos of Ezra Pound*
> (N.Y: New Directions, 1975), Canto 51, p. 256; all further ref-
> erences will cite canto and page numbers only.]

On the one hand, he insists that the Eleusinian or agricultural Zeus serves
as a principle of order and exact repetition; on the other hand, he underscores
the problems inherent in translating proper names and ideas from one culture
into another and, by extension, the difficulties of substituting one set of
organizing or textual metaphors for another. Rather than mutually translat-
able or originary ideas of order, Pound offers a series of mixed metaphors,
which gain complexity as he traces them back through time and across
cultures: nature vies with classical poetry, agricultural myths with avant-
garde art, for preeminence in an "American paideuma," which names the
roots and shoots that form textual tangles rather than the permanent roots
and organized structures of (family) trees. While it seems to retain a ground-
ing in nature or vegetation myths, Pound's cultural history uses a different
organic/botanic model. In his repeated efforts at "clearing the underbrush"
and breaking ground aside, Pound seems always to focus on the wayward
and weed-like proliferation of words and translations.

In *The Cantos'* American *paideuma*, historical particularity and clear definitions give way to heterogeneity and lawlessness that might permit his
manner of grafting what had seemed independent and incompatible systems,
to the point where it is no longer possible to distinguish a main stem from
dependent offshoots. In the cultural exchange between revolutionary America and Imperial China, John Adams, like Pound's rather idiosyncratic Zeus,
figures centrally in the founding of both governmental and agricultural systems. Adams and Jefferson are praised for erecting monuments, including
statues of Washington, and for valuing the active and revolutionary over the
static and monumental. By way of reconstructing viable poetic and economic

programs for modern America—or creating them for the first time out of fragments of an old "American Dream"—Pound advances a wayward textual economy of multiplying references or, in his phrases, "spermatic thought" and "interpretative metaphors." His text embraces as many contradictions, and includes as many senses of "culture," as Whitman's.

As though to compound the disorder of his various systems, and to deny the fundamental principle of Imagism by which he rejected rhetorical ornament, Pound claims that his use of Chinese *ideograms* and all the other foreign quotations is almost purely supplementary and ornamental. In "The Chinese Cantos" one suspects that Pound's simply erroneous translations and transliterations border on irony, since he seems to know more about the complexities of cultural exchanges and translations than he practices. In the note preceding Canto 52, he seems to warn and yet to reassure the reader, aware at least that he is complicating linguistic and cultural matters: "Foreign words and ideograms both in these two decads and in earlier cantos enforce the text but seldom if ever add anything not stated in the English, though not always in lines immediately contiguous to these underlinings" (52:256).

Indeed, for most readers, the Chinese glyphs and Pound's other inter-polations add little to the English, though they are likely to erupt weed-like into the English text at places where their meaning remains indeterminate. Not only do Pound's foreign usages violate Imagist doctrine, but he also seems willing to court uncontainable metaphoricity, not to say rhetorical ornament, for the sake of inclusiveness and, perhaps, in order to appear "cultured" in a random sort of way. Chinese characters often stand as signs of the exotic, as metonymines for incompatible or irreducable systems, and, more to Pound's purpose, as impressive monuments to genealogical and state order. In this way, Pound complicates recurrent Classical references by interpolating into his text less congenial precursors of his ideal America— even in the very name of the Adams family line, and using Brooks Adams's notion of cultural/economic exchange. Pound is often self-conscious and always deliberate about his unorthodox procedures for fabricating what he will claim is an organic tradition.

The very claim that his text can be easily domesticated, that foreign borrowings contribute emphasis rather than meaning, involves Pound in a play of figures, a questioning of language, that he could not contain. Rather than "underlining" significant connections or tracing subterranean root sys-tems among the various langauges, arts, and sciences he wanted to appro-priate, his Chinese and other foreign inscriptions radiate tangled lines of force and influence in all directrions, jumping from plateau to plateau and following the "lawless laws" of rhizomes.

One of the more suggestive instances of these fertile outcroppings occurs in Canto 53, where Pound's nostalgic record of the agricultural and monetary reforms instituted by the founder of the ancient Shang dynasty is punctuated by that frequently cited modernist imperative, "Make it New." I quote: "In 1760 Tching T'ang opened the copper mine / (ante Christum) / made discs with square holes in their middles / and gave them to the people / wherewith they might buy grain. . . . Tching prayed on the mountain and / wrote MAKE IT NEW / on his bath tub. / Day by day make it new / cut the underbrush, pile the logs / keep it growing" (53:264-65). Pound's free translation of the imperial motto, which had been coined by Confucius roughly a millennium after Tching's reign, performs the same sort of destructive and/or reconstructive (one could nearly say de-con-structive) task for which the latter-day American enlisted Whitman as "drill." Thus, even in this most radical effort to affirm genealogical order, an absolute origin and continuity to culture, Pound uncovers the ubiquitous conflict of tradition and innovation in which history, science, and poetry must begin over again—and differently—every day.

Pound was compelled to reflect on the plethora of masterpieces, discourses, and traditions which lend to his poem a chaos of systems that cannot be reduced to a master system. Often his self-reflections on this palimpsestic structure involve an uneasy mixture of the organic and the architectonic; his reflections become inextricable from the textual machine he had set in motion. Especially in the later cantos, Pound addresses what we have been calling the American rhizome as against European and Asian arborescence. For instance, in Canto 85, the first poem of *Rock-Drill*, where he recalls the natural basis of sound economy and right government from the Shang dynasty to the present, Pound refers to the sacred ash of Norse mythology: "From T'ang's time until now / That you lean 'gainst the tree of heaven / and know Ygdrasil" (85:545).

A few pages later in the same canto, however, Pound tries to translate the myth of an originary unity, or transplant a rooted tradition, into the hostile climate of America. By his account, his native culture has "No classics, / no American history / no centre, no general root" (85:549). This particlar turn or translation back into the American literary scene ends one of *The Cantos* many catalogues of those nonliterary disciplines (including philology, geology, mathematics, biology, and publishing) from which Pound, rather like Henry Adams, borrowed tags and the proper names of culture heroes, though not system. Moreover, his very complaint places him in a certain pattern of anxiety-reaction to America's de-centeredness and miscellaneousness. As we have seen, Emerson, whose writings epitomize the very tendencies they dismiss, was already in this tenuous and, it would seem *American* position.

Finally, in the "Draft of Canto CXIII" Pound's own system-building culminates in an unsteady equation of three metonyms (rather improperly used proper names of the key figures from disparate arts) associated with the unrelated though internally coherent disciplines of music, taxonomy, and genetics. He depicts Paradise thus: "Yet to walk with Mozart, Agassiz and Linnaeus / 'neath overhanging air under sunbeat / Here take thy mind's space / And to this garden" (113:786). In this way, Pound's poem—for which a *baroque gallery* (a bust of Mozart here, a specimen chest in the style of Goethe's study there, and, in the midst of all these monuments, the artist creating new masterworks at an easel or writing desk surrounded by discarded drafts) would be a more fitting metaphor than even that untamed mental landscape or garden of the muses—collects fragments, tags, and whole strata of traditions and discourses.

The poet was not unconcerned about his tendency to miscellany. After all—and *after all*—he says, in the fragment of Canto 116, "I am not a demigod, / I cannot make it cohere. . . . Disney against the metaphysicals. . . . a nice quiet paradise over the shables." (116:786). If we take seriously Pound's sometimes tragic and sometimes more strategically ironic comments about the incoherence of his poem and of the culture which willy-nilly gave rise to it, we come to recognize that he poses fundamental challenges not only to poetry but to virtually all those western scientific and metaphysical traditions that have become the targets of current post-structuralist readings in the texts of Deleuze, Guattari, and certain wayward tendrils of recent American criticism.

Yet this deconstructive strain, this self-conscious tendency to subvert self-reflection, has always been present at least on the margins of American literature. No writer has been more crucial in this regard than Henry Adams, though one hesitates to name so insistently *marginal* a figure as central to America's critical—let alone its literary—tradition. As he visited the cultural shrines of Europe, Adams insisted that he was a tourist and an uncle, neither an expert nor the father of a new historiography or a new critical method. He discovered neither a continuous line of descent nor a completed circle of cultural achievements; instead, he multiplied genealogical anxieties until his recuperation of European culture became a parody of itself, a swirl of interpretations launched against the desire for *closure*—at least on the model of the hermeneutical circle of the autotelic test. His choice of literary and architectural monuments at least anticipates Pound's, even as it follows Hawthorne's *The Marble Faun* and a whole line if not a literary genre of travel romances that trace the pre-history of American culture. Adams was perversely fond of digging up problems such nostalgic texts are generally committed to avoiding. Meditating, for instance, on the edifice of Mont-Saint-

Michel, Adams recalls several conflicting accounts (some in tapestries, some
in poems) of the Battle of Hastings from which England dates its nationhood
and about which the record Mont-Saint-Michel tells another version. Not
only does he underscore the tangled heritage of England, and thus his Anglo-
American (or is it Franco-American?) inheritance, but he also shows that
the different interpretations of historical, architectural, and literary texts can
make cultural and artistic hierarchies tremble. He is at once "annoyed" and
motivated by an anarchical scepticism, one that in a particularly American
fashion, refuses to be destructive or simply affirmative as it finds metaphors
and interested interpretations where fundamental truths were supposed to
have existed:

> The feeling of scepticism before so serious a monument as Mont-
> Saint-Michel is annoying. The 'Chanson de Roland' ought not to
> be trifled with, at least by tourists in search of art. One is shocked
> at the possibility of being deceived about the starting point of
> American genealogy. Taillefer and the song rest on the same
> evidence that Duke William and Harold and the battle itself rest
> upon, and to doubt the 'Chanson' is to call the very roll of Battle
> Abbey in question. The whole fabric of society totters; the British
> peerage turns pale.

Yet doubt he would, and annoy his fellow Harvard historians with sceptical
analyses of facts and the empirical historicism by which culture and the
curriculum established their heritage and legitimacy. Rather than defer to
"science"—or to the "interpretative metaphors" Pound claims to have borrowed from science—Adams brings his criticism to bear on the modern
sciences and philosophy as simulated unities or systems to which the arts
have mistakenly turned. Adams uncovers the progressive complexity—indeed the original heterogeneity—that preceded the building of the first stra-
tum of such venerable textual and architectural palimpsests as Chartres and
Mont-Saint-Michel.

Since the full implications of the critical and parodic thrust of Adams's
writing has been glossed over by those readers who appreciate his genteel
prose and cultured sensibility more than his destructions of ideal genealogies,
it is worth noting his manner of reconstituting a texture of tissue of fragments.
He does not lament the ruined state of the churches and other "sacred places"
of medieval history. Quite the contrary, he takes advantage of the opportunity: using the flexible medium of his prose, he takes a striking piece from
the facade of, say, a Romanesque church and transposes it onto an incomplete, not to say stylistically incompatible, Gothic facade. By this method,

which is anathema to history and impossible for architecture, his various fragments become figures in an ever-growing construct that is grounded in complex synecdoches, in which details of various styles represent whole ages that are stitched into Adams's unique prose patchwork that never resolves into a whole book or even an exemplary beginning for a serious art historical study. The ideal edifice he erects is more modern than medieval, more a phantasmagoric exchange of images than a nostalgic recuperation of primitive or organic art:

> Here at Mont-Saint-Michel we have only a mutilated trunk of an eleventh-century church to judge by. We have not even a facade, and we shall have to stop at some Norman village—at Thaon or Ouistreham—to find a west front which might suit the abbey here, but wherever we find it we shall find something more serious, more military, more practical. . . . So, too, the central tower or lantern—the most striking feature of Norman churches—has fallen here at Mont-Saint-Michel, and we shall have to replace it from Cerisy-La-Foret, and Lessay, and Falaise.

Whether or not the modern poet had the proto-modern tourist in mind, the "mutilated trunk," to say nothing of its repair by further fragmentation and the mixing of genres into a sort of collage, anticipates Pound's poetic method. It is worth noting that, while medievalism and Provençal culture in particular were all the rage in Pound's college years, he was especially fond of "The Song of Roland" and granted to its writer and to such troubadours as Bertrand de Born a privileged place in his canon of innovators and other heretics. From *Personae* to *The Cantos*, he employed a method of construction that he claimed to have borrowed from Bertran de Born. We have already noted Pound's habit of carving out family trees and preferring "washes" of interpretation over rooted traditions; in this project of fragmentation, he goes a step further than Henry Adams (whom he fashioned the last of a long line of American politicians and active men whose lives were "whole"). He finds that the very poetics of the troubadours involved the piecing together of fragments into anything but an organic whole or an unmediated song. In early long poems, "Na Audiart" and "Near Perigord," for instance, Pound constructs a "composite poem" on the model of the "composite lady of the troubadours," who sent tributes to "real ladies" by analogizing [and] anthologizing the ideal features of renowned beauties immortalized by other poets. Thus, in American poems consisting of sometimes partially translated borrowings and stylistic parodies, Pound discloses that in poems written and performed at the same time that the great cathedrals and abbeys were slowly being erected, there was no simple relationship between art and life. No one planner, architect, or observer saw the completion of a cathedral, or even the final version of a poem in his lifetime. Furthermore, the most perfect songs were no more simple reflections of living women than Pound's new American poem, which was to be stitched together out of fragments already doubly textual because they were rooted in poems and not in Nature or Idea.

Pound's closest approach to Adams's architectural reconstructions is his admiration of Sigismundo Malatesta's Tempio (Cantos 13-21, *passim*), that textual layering of pagan/Christian/classical fragments which Pound called "both an apex and in a verbal sense a monumental failure" [*Guide to Kulchur*]. While Pound could accept the heterogeneity of Malatesta's late-Medieval (re)construction, he considered similar American attempts, including William Randolph Hearst's San Simeon, dangerous and inauthentic. When it came to an American Renaissance, he could brook no variety, no individuality. For his version of American culture, Pound chose the rigid, if no less ersatz, center of fascism. See, for example, his discovery of an Italian version of Jeffersonian agrarianism in *Jefferson and/or Mussolini*. The tangled roots of Pound's fascism can be read in—or back into—American history. But this is a subterranean line we cannot follow out here.

If Pound was more troubled by his American heritage, his mixed inheritance, Adams was bemused by the prospect of the *new* overtaking the old world. He too brought America with him, carrying his Adams and Quincy grandfathers from New England to his earlier continental ancestors—making, that is, a characteristically American version or reversal of the founding of Rome. In another passage that might be thought to adumbrate Pound's figure of the washes or waves of one culture over another, of modernism obscuring the clear demarcations of the European tradition, Adams confounds genealogy as well as history and geography. He discovers his native New England, as the trace of his own youth, even as he looks down under the foundation of Mont-Saint-Michel:

> From the edge of the platform, the eye plunges down, two hundred and thirty five feet to the wide sands or the wider ocean, as the tides recede or advance, under an infinite sky, over a restless sea, which even we tourists can understand and feel without books or guides. . . .
>
> One needs only be old enough in order to be as young as one will. From the top of this Abbey Church one looks across the

bay to Avranches, and toward Contances and the Cotentin—the Constantius pagus—whose shore facing us, recalls the coast of New England.

In both *Mont-Saint-Michel* and *The Education* Adams catalogues historical adumbrations and repetitions in the self-reflexive manner usually associated with the most disruptive and de-familiarizing sorts of modernism. The organic intersects with the architectural, as the critic ironically restages the fall into complexity that made possible his project of recasting culture into something more exciting because less homogeneous and more clearly marked by interpretation. Adams opens art to science, but to a science that has always been fragmented and in a state of flux. According to Adams, science became baroque or rhetorical after Aquinas, and the baroque is still becoming. And it is American.

Centuries before Adams wrote his idiosyncratic architectrural digest— that is, his autobiography of the growth of his own scepticism—there was no ultimate reference point for culture or the arts. Quite apart from his attraction to ruins and monuments, and the apparent nostalgia for the centering figure of the Virgin, Adams celebrates this multiplicity and dynamism. As he digs through layers of supplements to the ancient walls, he remarks the beginnings of the suspicion that organic unity was a mere dream. He suggests that modern science is only the natural—and we would have to say "rhizomatic"—outgrowth of a complexity as fundamental as the dream of organic art, which he criticizes as the "dogma" of orthodoxy and the central Idea. Of the birth of scientific skepticism out of medieval theology, he says:

> Modern science, like modern art, tends in practice to drop the dogma of organic unity. Some of the medieval habit of mind survives, but even that is said to be yielding before the daily evidence of increasing and extending complexity. The fault, then, was not in man, if he no longer looked at science or art as an organic whole or as the expression of unity. Unity turned itself into complexity, multiplicity, variety and even contradiction. All experience, human and divine, assured man in the thirteenth century that the lines of the universe converged. How was he to know that these lines ran in every conceivable and inconceivable direction, and that at least half of them seemed to diverge from any imaginable centre of unity?

American writers from Emerson to Whitman to Adams to Pound and beyond have naturally—or unnaturally—recognized this complexity and have nonetheless given life to a de-centered tradition, if not a culture, called *America* or American literature or, more simply, modernism. Neither centering nor de-centering has been without its poetic and political dangers.

GEORGE KEARNS

Reading Pound Writing Chinese:
A Page from Rock-Drill

A remark of Northrop Frye's about Blake's difficult later poems holds true for Pound's late cantos, those gathered as *Rock-Drill* (1955) and *Thrones* (1959): "If we read *Milton* and *Jerusalem* as Blake intended them to be read, we are not reading them in any conventional sense at all: we are staring at a sequence of plates, most of them with designs. . . . The artist demonstrates a certain way of life: his aim is not to be appreciated or admired, but to transfer to others the imaginative habit and energy of his mind." In place of Blake's designs, we have Pound's expressive typography, punctuated by more than 300 Chinese ideograms, as well as Egyptian hieroglyphs, troubadour music, pips from playing cards and stylized representations of temples. These later cantos, even more than the earlier ones, are presented to an ideal reader/ starer who is willing to say, as Pound says of his relation to the universe in Canto 95 [*The Cantos of Ezra Pound* (NY: New Directions, 1975, p. 646); all further references will cite canto and page numbers only]:

> Responsus:
> > Not stasis/
> > at least not in our immediate vicinage.

Pound (like Joyce, Eliot, Stein—it is one of the more attractive aspects of mandarin modernism) asks us to participate in his creation to an extraordinary degree. The demand raises questions about our attitude toward such "difficult" art, although the questions have been somewhat blunted now that

---

A revised version of "Section: *Rock Drill* (1955)" published for the first time in this volume. © 1986 by George Kearns.

we no longer hope, nor even wish, to make of a text a well-wrought urn. The Poundian text thrives under the banners of open field composition, dialogism, indeterminacy, inter-textuality, self-reflexivity, play of signifiers, polyvalency, *différance* and *supplément*. Many readers, I am one of them, have found great pleasures in *Rock-Drill* and *Thrones*, and it is the purpose of this essay to demonstrate something of the peculiar nature of those pleasures. Yet there can be no argument with readers who find these pages a preposterously arrogant gesture, a *reductio ad absurdum* of one of Pound's favorite sayings from Remy de Gourmont, "Sincerely to write what one thinks— the only pleasure of a writer." The absurdity may be seen in a list of books to be looked into by what Donald Davie calls "students, I'm afraid, rather than simple readers of the poem." A partial list would include: Couvreur's Latin translation of the Confucian histories, the *Shu Ching;* Senator Thomas Hart Benton's memoirs; Coke's *Institutes* of the Common Law; the seventeenth-century astrologer/alchemist/Neoplatonist John Heydon's *Holy Guide* (which Pound had Yeat's widow send to the Washington insane asylum where the later cantos were written); Charles de Rémusat's 1853 study of St. Anselm; and a Christian missionary's textbook edition of a salt commissioner's popular version of the emperor Yong Tching's expansion of his father's cryptic *Sacred Edict*. Moreover, it's possible to do your homework today but forget it when you take the examination.

It is perhaps too easy, after one has assembled (with pleasure and instruction) a set of notes on these cantos, to suggest what another reader might find just by reading with innocence and attention. Clearly, however, examples of beneficent rulers and other "paradisal" elements begin to predominate, although they continue to be set against the poet's irritations and denunciations, even as Dante, approaching the Empyrean, rails against the injustices of Florence. Unmistakable, too, is Pound's delight in what he has seen and his wit and skill in recording it:

> Above prana, the light,
>   past light, the crystal.
> Above crystal, the jade!
> The clover enduring,
>   basalt crumbled with time.
> "Are they the same leaves?"
>   that was an intelligent question.
>   [94: 634]

There are few places in the later cantos where dazzling changes of rhythm and voice do not move forward on the poet's pleasure and impatience to strike the next spark, to reach towards a simultaneous presentation that, indeed, strains the resources of the medium. Yet the obscurities are not those of a man talking to himself. On the contrary, the poem becomes more hermetic because of the poet's new sense of an audience: among the forces shaping the cantos written at St. Elizabeth's Hospital, not the least was the economics of American academic life. From about 1951 on, an enormous exegetical industry (in which the present essay participates) grew up around *The Cantos*, producing the Poundian journal *Paideuma* and, recently, Carroll Terrell's indispensible two-volume *Companion*. Pound writes with the confidence of a man who knows that if he uses a snatch from a Na Khi ceremony, someone will annotate it. The methods of the later cantos are an extension of methods he had been using for forty years, but an extension that makes a quantum leap.

Pound writes for an audience willing to share the intuition behind these later cantos, that of a "Confucian universe . . . of interacting strains and tensions," and the poetry has the merit of not attempting to make that intuition less complex than it is. A few years before he invented "Imagism," Pound was struggling with an analogy that is useful in thinking about the later cantos. He compares Blake on "line" in painting with Rodin's "belief that energy is beauty," which "holds thus far, namely, that all our ideas of beauty of line are in some way connected with our ideas of swiftness or easy power of motion." In *Rock-Drill* and *Thrones* especially, there is a "frame" of form in which each word modifies each other, and there is a universe of energies beyond, energies which enter and leave the frame. The analogy to Blake and Rodin brings us to the "swiftness" of these cantos, which Pound came to think of as *hilaritas*. This may help explain what often looks like an arbitrary choice and arrangement of materials: The line must be definite or it is nothing, yet it is drawn from the infinite possibilities of the idea of line. It could not be so arbitrary if its subject were something that can be *named:* Social Credit economics, the history of China, life in a hospital for the insane. The subject can only be named by reading each word in the poem: *Nomina sunt consequentia rerum*. If the "frame" of art, then, is not an impassible barrier, if it allows the passage of a force that extends beyond it, perfection of form, or communication in any ordinary sense, becomes less important, for even an imperfect poem may be a diaphan for the universe of energy:

> i.e. it coheres all right
> 　　　　even if my notes do not cohere.
> 　　　　　　　[116: 797]

Yet to claim that *Rock-Drill* and *Thrones* provide an image of, or an equation for Pound's Confucian universe leaves us with an unwieldy truth, one that may beg more questions than it answers.

As an example of what "reading" the later cantos entails, I offer the
following possibilities for the first page of *Rock-Drill* [85: 543]. You may take
these fourteen lines (if that is how you count them—a centrifugal sonnet?)
as a good example of a relatively separable Poundian ideogram, more prelude
or statement of themes for the 124 pages of *Rock-Drill* than part of Canto 85
proper. Immediately following these lines, the canto starts off on a long
reduction of the Confucian *Shu Ching*, or *History Classic*. Here is the page,
in fact a page plus a line:

LING^2

Our dynasty came in because of a great sensibility.

All there by the time of I Yin

All roots by the time of I Yin.

Galileo index'd 1616,

Wellington's peace after Vaterloo

                    chih^3

a gnomon,

Our science is from the watching of shadows;

That Queen Bess translated Ovid,

Cleopatra wrote of the currency,

Versus who scatter old records

ignoring the hsien^2 form

and jump to the winning side

The great LING[2] will be repeated seven times in the next two hundred pages, accumulating definition. That definition begins as the "sensibility" in the following line, connecting it with government and followed by examples of rulers who exemplify the sensibility to be invoked/defined throughout the twenty-five cantos of *Rock-Drill* and *Thrones* (this is Pound's "history," of course, not necessarily anyone else's): Wellington's wisdom and moderation, preventing overly-harsh reparations after the Napoleonic Wars; Cleopatra's attention to monetary policy; Elizabeth's literacy (with everything that "translation" and "Ovid" have come to stand for in the poem); the legendary minister I Yin's awareness of Confucian "process," and implicitly, by the tradition of Chinese historiography, that of all later ministers and emperors who remember and invoke him as a guide. (The second and third ideograms are his name, "one who rules.") These become points that define a periphery and suggest that a richness of sensibility/benevolence is possible in government. The defined sensibility becomes *chih*[3], something we can fasten to, a place to begin. The forms of rulers moving within the texts that record their accomplishments are shadows from which we may derive knowledge. Hence, obscurantism—any suppression of knowledge or "scattering" of records—is counter to the active, sincere intelligence necessary for civilization. Example: Galileo on the *Index Librorum Probibitorum*. Earlier cantos, however, have informed us that the Jesuits, in spite of the Church's silencing of Galileo, have introduced his thought to China. We have come to think of Galileo as a "scientist," but Pound wants us to think of him as a complete humanist, the author of verse, satire and literary criticism, a stylist whose principle "scientific" work is a dialogue among philosophers, a masterpiece of Renaissance prose. The final line of the passage implies a definition of *politics* opposite to that which guides most "politicians."

From the Chinese characters on the page, we may constuct a perfectly good line of poetry (the ideograms would read from top to bottom)

> ling[2]
> I
> Yin
> chih[3]
> hsien[2]

that, like each line in the Confucian *Odes*, can become the occasion for extensive commentary, but which may be rendered as: "The sensibility / spiritual forces registered by I Yin provide a point of reference for sincere and intelligent action." Beyond that, our gloss on this page / ideogram / Confucian ode takes us into the "pre-formed worlds" and submerged "ancient rivers of language" noted on the first edition dust jacket of *Rock-Drill*.

1. *Ling²*. The complete story behind this character would require an essay of some length. We may put together a brief version with only a little, and delightful, trouble, following Pound's autodidactic methods. If you have a transliteration of the ideograms (which is why Pound provides so many of them), you may look them up in Mathews's dictionary, where they are listed alphabetically. Karlgren's dictionary, with which Pound supplemented Mathews, is harder to use, but with some diligence you may find them there, with notes on early forms and root meanings. In Legge's editions of the Confucian classics (most of which are easily obtainable in paperback) there is an index listing each occurance of each ideogram, which leads to a series of contexts and to Legge's helpful commentaries. The only problem is finding them in the index, where they are listed by their "radicals," and that takes some searching. Yet some such process has produced the first four lines of *Rock-Drill*—carried out, of course, by

   chien⁴

the luminous eye. If we follow out the process, we see that Pound's way of defining *ling²* is essentially the Chinese way.

The character derives from the 173rd radical, "rain." The brushstroke at the top is sky/heaven, with clouds beneath it. The three "squares" at the center are enlarged raindrops, but may also have resembled, for Pound, the thirtieth radical, "mouth." The signs beneath show a ritual or ceremonial dance taking place upon the large brushstroke at the bottom, "earth, ground." Thus the ideogram suggests transfers of energy between heaven and earth, and an awareness (of the Process) necessary for good government.

The difficulty of supplying a Western equivalent for *ling²* may be seen in Couvreur, Mathews, and Legge. It is not a common character in the Confucian canon, not to be found in the *Unwobbling Pivot*, nor in the *Great Digest*, nor in the *Analects;* it occurs three of four times in the *History Classic*, not counting a few appearances as a phonetic ingredient in a proper name. It is used once in Mencius, but there it is a quotation from the *Odes*. We discover it in only four of the 305 odes, used quite differently each time, though always with a generally favorable connotation. For those four appearances in the *Odes*, Couvreur's definition is either desperation or a kind of buckshot ideogram: "*Esprit, merveille, merveilleux, puissant, grand, majestueux, bon, favorable.*" Mathews (4071) gives: "Spirit of a being which acts upon others. Spirit; spiritual; divine. Supernatural. Efficacious." At one point Legge gives up: "The *ling²*," he says, facing the complexities of *Ode* 3.1.8, "may be variously translated."

It must have been when he was translating that same ode at St. Elizabeth's that Pound was struck by its extraordinary uses of *ling*^{2}. (We might, by the way, expect to find in the *History Classic* something close to "Our dynasty came in because of *ling*^{2}," but we do not.) In the ode it undergoes a wonderful metamorphosis as it is used to describe first a tower, then a park, then a pond, all made by Wan, the great ancestor of the house of Tchou. Legge decides to translate it in all three cases as a simple adjective, "marvelous." But Pound, putting together everything he knows about the character—a rejected reading from Legge's notes, Karlgren's analysis, Courveur, *all* other appearances of *ling*^{2} in the Confucian canon, and what he sees just by looking at it—decides that the character attracts to itself the meaning of the entire ode, a lyrical presentation of a Tory paradise in which king, people, nature and music are in harmony and where pond-park-tower appear not to be a "real" place but rather signifiers of a civilization informed by the spirit of ancestral wisdom, or by "Heaven." When he translates *Ode* 3.1.8, he includes as much of this as possible with "spirit tower," "Park Divine," and "haunted pool."

Ling^2 juxtaposed with "Our dynasty came in because of a great sensibility" captures the spirit of what ministers and emperors say throughout the *Shu Ching*, from I Yin's own lecture to a young emperor (which we have heard in Canto 53) through the later dynasties that take I Yin as a guide to the spiritual-natural-social harmony that is an ideal for the wise ruler. At each appearance in *Rock-Drill* and *Thrones*, the character brings with it a new context to modify or extend the implications of *ling*^{2} in the lives of Elizabeth I, Coke, Senator Benton, the Irish revolutionary and minister Desmond Fitzgerald, and others whose sense of responsibility is "rooted" in awareness of natural order. (The list would have to include, indelible embarassment to Poundians, the poet's extraordinary misprision of Mussolini.)

2. *Chih*^{3}. As with *ling*^{2} the character is defined by the totality of its appearances in *The Cantos*. The reader saw it first at the end of Canto 52, where it could be taken in Pound's definition of it, in his translation of the *Analects*, as "hitching post, position, place one is in and works from." In its most common dictionary definition as "stop," it suggests something like "take action to bring to an end unfavorable conditions." It makes its final appearance in Canto 110, where it is juxtaposed again with "root," with the process celebrated in the Eleusinian mysteries (something like that pictured in *ling*^{2}) and with the warning "not with jet planes." Here, in Canto 85, it also suggests visually the gnomon casting its shadow.

3. *Gnomon*. An English word is no more a closed system than is *ling*^{2}. Fenollosa's essay on the Chinese written character taught Pound the dis-

tinction between word and ideogram, the latter retaining at least a ghost of picture or action in the brushstroke. Yet, Pound thought, if we assemble its roots and cognates, a word can be "almost" an ideogram. In *Guide to Kulchur* he decides that a word can be "aperient"—and immediately demonstrates what he means by inventing a definition for "aperient" that is not in the English dictionary, from roots in "uncovering, making accessible." This *aperient* occurs in the discussion of a word from Aristotle that cannot be translated by "any ready made current English," because Aristotle's word "lets in" not only its own roots and all its pre-Aristotelean history but also "all the Arabian commentators" and all related aspects of medieval theology. This Derridean openness is not quite Humpty Dumpty's way with words, but it implies that the meaning attracts to it anything we consider a legitimate application or extension.

No word can be more aperient than *gnomon* as we find it on this page from Canto 85. With roots in *perceive, know,* it becomes the pointer on the sundial, through whose shadow we know time and the position of the sun, and by extension any scientific instrument (like the many devised by Galileo) that acts as indicator. This page on which we find it exemplifies another meaning of *gnomon* as "saying, rule, canon of belief or action." Each line is a gnomon, a shadow or indicator of whole systems of light/wisdom/history and of a habit of Chinese thought that lasted for centuries and formed the basis for preserving, not scattering, old records. (At the end of Canto 85 we hear Confucius, who is supposed to have assembled the *Shu,* saying that he "had added nothing," that is, the roots of his teachings were "All there by the time of I Yin.")

This *gnomon* is casting a long shadow, yet there is one more meaning we should be aware of, for Pound is interested, as we hear explicitly in Cantos 95 and 105, in relations between "grammar" and "reality." If one were to translate the Confucian records into classical Greek, presumably it would require the use of the "gnomic aorist," a tense used to express "what once happened and has thereby established a precedent for all time." The feeling of that gnomic aorist is behind much of *The Cantos.*

4. *Science.* The word operates in its contemporary sense and in its root sense, "knowledge." Linked with *shadow,* through that great gnomic work the *OED,* it opens to "comparative darkness caused by the interception of light," "shades of the dead," "the faint appearance of something seen through an obscuring medium," and "symbol, type." Galileo's knowledge came literally through the watching of shadows. He had worked out his theory, but it remained necessarily speculative until the circle of proof was concluded at the moment when he looked through his telescope and saw that the moon

was not, as Aristoteleans claimed it must be, made of some smoother, purer substance than poor fallen Earth. What he saw, he tells us in his *Letter on the Liberation of the Moon*, were "the small shadows [*piccole adombrazioni*] dependent on the heights and cavities, visible only through the telescope." The dazzling precisions of Galileo's heirs are still calculated from the shadows of events (like the "history" on this page) which can not be observed directly. "Our science is from the watching of shadows" embraces the epistemology of Plato's cave, the *Shu Ching*, and this morning's discovery at MIT.

5. *Hsien²*. In Mathew's dictionary this *hsien²* is "virtuous, worthy, good." By now, Pound has presumably trained us not to settle for *that*. We can see the unwobbling pivot or balance in the upper-right corner. Combined with the strokes just beneath it, the sign for "heart," it becomes an ideogram common in the Confucian texts, meaning something like "good faith" or "sincere action from the heart." The component at the bottom is the active, "luminous" eye (sign for eye with running legs beneath). So this particular "virtue," by way of a Pound-Fenollosa way of reading, contains much of its own definition, something like "faithful action proceeding from a heart/eye/ sensibility aware of the Process." Certainly one possessing it would not scatter old records nor join the *turbae* (the next word in the canto), rabble who jump to the winning side.

Thus some of the difficulties of the later cantos and, I hope, an indication of arcane pleasures that may come with tracing them out, even as, in Donald Davie's words, they "defeat exegesis by inviting it so inexhaustibly." But there are other difficulties as well. Pound, after the defeat of the Axis, imprisonment at Pisa, and the incarceration at St. Elizabeths, still refused to join the winning side. Combined with the high idealism of which this first page of *Rock-Drill* is a manifestation, and with even stronger reaches toward the American Sublime elsewhere in *The Cantos*, there is that other Pound, starry fan of Mussolini and cracker-barrel anti-Semite, speaker in wartime of the broadcasts on Rome radio. Scurrilous, uninformed, incoherent, utterly impractical as communication, the broadcasts (and some of the letters) are surely the worst utterances by a great poet of which we have record. The Mussolini of these later cantos turns almost exclusively into a highly-edited version of the betrayed and desperate "Mussolini" of the Salò Republic. (The name really demands quotation marks, so far is it from actuality.) In the Washington years, as *Rock-Drill* and *Thrones* were composed, there were newly-ignorant flirtations with American and British right-wing fringes, which exist as (not always) suppressed presences and sources of inaccurate information for the later cantos. The anti-Semitism continued, softened in the poems but ugly in conversation and letters. There was to be,

in the poet's very old age, along with profound and moving self-recrimina-
tions, a recantation: "But the worst mistake I made was that stupid, suburban
prejudice of anti-Semitism." But *sero, sero*, too late, too late, and many readers
have, with arguable justification, closed the door on Pound. Where, in the
worst passages of his life, in the worst passages in his writing, were *ling*^{2},
hsien^3, and most of all *chung*^{1}, the unwobbling pivot, the balance? There is
the blindness that produces insight, and of that blindness Pound is master.
But there is a blindness that is only blind.

Chronology

1885 Ezra Loomis Pound is born on October 30 in Hailey, Idaho, to Homer Loomis Pound and Isabel Weston Pound. The family moves to Wyncote, Pennsylvania, 18 months later.

1901–5 Pound studies at the University of Pennsylvania (1901–3) and Hamilton College (1903–5). He earns a Bachelor of Philosophy from Hamilton in 1905.

1906 Earns a Master of Arts from the University of Pennsylvania and then tours Spain, Italy, and Provence with funds from a Harrison fellowship.

1907–8 Wabash College in Crawfordsville, Indiana, hires Pound and then dismisses him for having a woman in his room.

1908 Travels to Italy and publishes *A Lume Spento* in Venice. Later moves to London and publishes *A Quinzaine for This Yule*.

1909 Publishes two volumes of poetry: *Personae* and *Exultations*. (The 1926 *Personae* contains a selection of poems from both these volumes.)

1910 *Provenca; The Spirit of Romance.*

1911 *Canzoni.*

1912 Pound works as London editor of Harriet Monroe's magazine *Poetry*. Ernest Fenollosa's widow chooses Pound as editor of her husband's notebooks.

1914 Pound edits *Des Imagistes*, then writes on "vorticism" in *Fortnightly Review*, and contributes to *BLAST*, a journal edited by Wyndham Lewis. He marries Dorothy Shakespear.

1915 Pound begins work on *The Cantos*.

1916   *Lustra; Gaudier-Brzeska: A Memoir.* Working from Fenollosa's
        manuscripts, Pound completes *Certain Noble Plays of Japan* and
        "Noh," or, Accomplishment, A Study of the Classical Stage of Japan.

1917   Pound's first cantos appear as "Three Cantos" in the June
        issue of *Poetry.*

1918   *Pavannes and Divisions.*

1919   *The Fourth Canto.* "Homage to Sextua Propertius" appears in
        Quia Pauper Amavi.

1920   Pound moves to Paris and contributes to many journals and
        avant-garde reviews. *Hugh Selwyn Mauberley; Instigations; Um-
        bra: The Early Poems of Ezra Pound.*

1921   Cantos 4–7 appear in *Poems, 1918–21.* Eliot's *The Waste Land*
        is published with Pound's revisions.

1924   *Antheil and the Treatise on Harmony.* Pound establishes residence
        in Rappallo, Italy.

1925   Olga Rudge, a concert violinist, gives birth on July 9 to
        Pound's daughter, Mary. *A Draft of XVI Cantos.*

1926   Dorothy Pound gives birth to Pound's son, Omar, on Sep-
        tember 10. Omar is raised in London by his grandmother
        Olivia Shakespear. *Personae: The Collected Poems of Ezra Pound.*

1928   *Selected Poems; A Draft of Cantos 17–27.*

1930   *A Draft of XXX Cantos.*

1931   *How to Read.*

1933   *ABC of Economics.*

1934   *ABC of Reading; Make It New; Eleven New Cantos, XXI–XLI;
        Homage to Sextus Propertius.*

1935   *Alfred Venison's Poems; Social Credit: An Impact; Jefferson and/or
        Mussolini.*

1937   *The Fifth Decade of The Cantos; Polite Essays.*

1938   *Guide to Kulchur.*

1939   Pound visits the United States; receives an honorary D.Litt.
        from Hamilton College.

1940   Pound begins to broadcast for Radio Rome. *Cantos LII–LXXI.*

1943   The U.S. government indicts Pound for treason.

1944   *Oro e Lavoro.* The English version, *Gold and Labour,* is suppressed. Similarly, the English version of *L'America, Roosevelt e le Cause della Guerra Presente* does not appear until 1951, as *America, Roosevelt and the Causes of the Present War.*

1945   The U.S. Army arrests and imprisons Pound at the Disciplinary Training Center at Pisa from May through November, when he is flown to Washington, D.C.

1946   Committed to St. Elizabeth's Hospital on grounds of insanity.

1947   Pound's studies of Confucius lead to the publication of his "translation," *The Unwobbling Pivot & the Great Digest.*

1948   *The Pisan Cantos* and the first collection of all the cantos printed to date (70) are published. Olga Rudge publishes *If this be treason* . . . , a collection of six of Pound's wartime radio broadcasts.

1949   Pound receives the Bollingen Prize in poetry for *The Pisan Cantos.*

1950–52 *Patria Mia; The Letters of Ezra Pound, 1907–41; Money Pamphlets.*

1951   Translation of *Confucian Analects.*

1953   *The Translations of Ezra Pound,* selected by Pound, introduced by Hugh Kenner.

1954   *The Literary Essays of Ezra Pound,* collected and introduced by T. S. Eliot.

1955   *Section Rock-Drill, 85–95 de los cantares.*

1956   Translation of *Sophokles: Women of Trachis.*

1958   The treason charges against Pound are dismissed and he is released from St. Elizabeth's. Pound returns to Italy. *Pavannes and Divigations.*

1959   *Thrones: 96–109 de los cantares.*

1960   *Impact: Essays on Ignorance and the Decline of American Civilization,* edited and introduced by Noel Stock.

1962   *Love Poems of Ancient Egypt*, translated with Noel Stock.

1963   *E.P. to L.U.: Nine Letters Written to Louis Untermeyer by Ezra Pound.*

1965   *The Seafarer.*

1967   *Pound/Joyce*, edited by Forrest Read.

1969   *Drafts and Fragments of Cantos CX–CXVII*, dedicated to Olga Rudge. Pound makes his last visit to the United States.

1972   Pound dies in Venice.

Contributors

HAROLD BLOOM, Sterling Professor of the Humanities at Yale University, is the author of *The Anxiety of Influence, Poetry and Repression*, and many other volumes of literary criticism. His forthcoming study, *Freud: Transference and Authority*, attempts a full-scale reading of all of Freud's major writings. A MacArthur Prize Fellow, he is general editor of five series of literary criticism published by Chelsea House.

HUGH KENNER, Professor Emeritus of English at The Johns Hopkins University, is the leading critic of the High Modernists (Pound, Eliot, Joyce) and of Beckett. His books include *The Pound Era* and *The Stoic Comedians*.

EVA HESSE, a resident of Munich, has published a German translation of *The Cantos* and several other books on Pound. She is also the editor of *New Approaches to Pound* and a senior editor of *Paideuma: A Journal Devoted to Ezra Pound Scholarship*.

DANIEL D. PEARLMAN is the Chairman of the English Department at the University of Rhode Island. He is the author of *The Barb of Time: On the Unity of Ezra Pound's* Cantos.

LOUIS L. MARTZ is Sterling Professor Emeritus of English at Yale University. He is the author of several books on English seventeenth-century verse, including *The Poetry of Meditation*, and the editor of Pound's early poems and of the *Collected Poems, 1912–1944* of H. D.

MAX NÄNNY is Professor of English and American Literature at the University of Fribourg, Switzerland. He is the author of *Ezra Pound: Poetics for an Electric Age* and numerous articles on Pound.

FRED C. ROBINSON is Professor of English at Yale University. He has published many books and articles on the history of the English language, most recently *Beowulf and the Appositive Style* (1985).

213

DONALD DAVIE, Andrew Mellon Professor of Humanities at Vanderbilt University, is the author of *Ezra Pound: Poet as Sculptor, Dissentient Voice*, and *These the Companions: Recollections*. His *Collected Poems, 1950–1970* appeared in 1972.

CHRISTINE FROULA is Associate Professor of English at Yale University. She is the author of *A Guide to Ezra Pound's* Selected Poems and *To Write Paradise: Style and Error in the* Cantos *of Ezra Pound*. She is at present writing a book on gender and literary authority in Woolf and Joyce.

MICHAEL ANDRÉ BERNSTEIN is Associate Professor of English and Comparative Literature at the University of California, Berkeley. He is author of *The Tale of the Tribe: Ezra Pound and the Modern Verse Epic* and *Prima della Rivoluzione*. He is at present writing on the abject hero and literary genealogy.

KATHRYNE V. LINDBERG is Assistant Professor of English at Harvard University. Her article is excerpted from her forthcoming book, *Reading Pound Reading: The Nietzschean Indirections of Modernism*.

GEORGE KEARNS is Associate Professor of English at Rutgers. He is author of a *Guide to Ezra Pound's* Selected Cantos, and has published many articles on Pound.

Bibliography

Ackroyd, Peter. *Ezra Pound and His World*. New York: Scribner's, 1980.

Adams, Stephen J. "Musical Neofism: Pound's Theory of Harmony in Context." *Mosaic* 13 (1980): 49–64.

Alexander, Michael. *The Poetic Achievement of Ezra Pound*. Berkeley and Los Angeles: University of California Press, 1979.

Bacigalupo, Massimo. *The Forméd Trace: The Later Poetry of Ezra Pound*. New York: Columbia University Press, 1980.

Baumann, Walter. *The Rose in the Steel Dust: An Examination of The Cantos of Ezra Pound*. Coral Gables, Fla.: University of Miami Press, 1970.

Bell, Ian F. A. *Critic as Scientist: The Modernist Poetics of Ezra Pound*. London and New York: Methuen, 1981.

———, ed. *Ezra Pound: Tactics for Reading*. London and Totowa, N.J.: Barnes & Noble, 1982.

Berezin, Charles. "Poetry and Politics in Ezra Pound." *Partisan Review* 48 (1981): 262–79.

Bergman, Herbert. "Ezra Pound and Walt Whitman." *American Literature* 27 (1955): 56–61.

Bernstein, Michael André. "Identification and Its Vicissitudes: The Narrative Structure of Ezra Pound's *Cantos*." *Yale Review* 69 (1980): 540–56.

———. *The Tale of the Tribe: Ezra Pound and the Modern Verse Epic*. Princeton, N.J.: Princeton University Press, 1980.

Berryman, Jo Brantley. *Circe's Craft: Ezra Pound's* Hugh Selwyn Mauberley. Ann Arbor, Mich.: UMI Research Press, 1983.

Brooke-Rose, Christine. *A Structural Analysis of Pound's Usura Canto: Jakobson's Method Extended and Applied to Free Verse*. The Hague: Mouton, 1976.

———. *A ZBC of Ezra Pound*. London: Faber & Faber, 1971.

Bush, Ronald. *The Genesis of Ezra Pound's Cantos*. Princeton, N.J.: Princeton University Press, 1976.

Cantrell, Carol Helmstetter. "Obscurity, Clarity, and Simplicity in the Cantos of Ezra Pound." *Midwest Quarterly* 23 (1982): 402–10.

Chace, William M. *The Political Identities of Ezra Pound and T. S. Eliot*. Palo Alto: Stanford University Press, 1973.

Childs, John Steven. "Larvatus Prodeo: Semiotic Aspects of the Ideogram in Pound's *Cantos*." *Paideuma* 9 (1980): 289–307.

Chung, Ling. "Ezra Pound's Interpretation of 'Cheng Ming' and His Literary The-
ories." *Actes du VIIe Congrès de l'Association Internationale de Littérature Comparée:
II Comparative Literature Today: Theory and Practice*, 689–92. Stuttgart: Kunst &
Wissen, Ernst Bieber, 1979.

Davenport, Guy. *Cities on Hills: A Study of I–XXX of Ezra Pound's Cantos*. Ann Arbor,
Mich.: UMI Research Press, 1983.

Davie, Donald. *Ezra Pound*. New York: Viking, 1975.

———. *Ezra Pound: Poet as Sculptor*. New York: Oxford University Press, 1964.

Dekker, George. *Sailing after Knowledge: The Cantos of Ezra Pound*. London: Routledge
& Kegan Paul, 1963.

Dembo, Lawrence. *The Confucian Odes of Ezra Pound: A Critical Appraisal*. Berkeley
and Los Angeles: University of California Press, 1963.

Dennis, Helen M. "The Eleusinian Mysteries as an Organising Principle in *The Pisan
Cantos.*" *Paideuma* 10 (1981): 273–82.

Driscoll, John. *The China Cantos of Ezra Pound*. Stockholm: Almqvist & Wiksell, 1983.

Duffey, Bernard. "Ezra Pound and the Attainment of Imagism." In *Toward a New
American Literary History: Essays in Honor of Arlin Turner*, edited by Louis J.
Budd, Edwin H. Cady, and Carl L. Anderson. Durham, N.C.: Duke University
Press, 1980: 181–94.

Durant, Alan. *Ezra Pound, Identity in Crisis: A Fundamental Reassessment of the Poet and
His Work*. Sussex: Harvest Press; and Totowa, N.J.: Barnes & Noble, 1981.

Eastham, Scott. *Paradise and Ezra Pound: The Poet as Shaman*. Lanham, Md.: University
Press of America, 1983.

Emery, Clark. *Ideas into Action: A Study of Pound's Cantos*. Coral Gables, Fla.: University of Miami Press, 1969.

Espey, John J. *Ezra Pound's* Mauberley: *A Study in Composition*. Berkeley: University
of California Press, 1955.

Flory, Wendy Stallard. *Ezra Pound and* The Cantos: *A Record of Struggle*. New Haven:
Yale University Press, 1980.

Fraser, G. S. *Ezra Pound*. New York: Barnes & Noble, 1960.

Froula, Christine. *To Write Paradise: Style and Error in Pound's* Cantos. New Haven:
Yale University Press, 1984.

Furia, Philip. *Pound's Cantos Declassified*. University Park and London: Pennsylvania
State University Press, 1984.

Goodwin, K. *The Influence of Ezra Pound*. London and New York: Oxford University
Press, 1966.

Harmon, William. *Time in Ezra Pound's Work*. Chapel Hill: University of North
Carolina Press, 1977.

Hesse, Eva, ed. *New Approaches to Ezra Pound: A Co-Ordinated Investigation of Pound's
Poetry*. Berkeley and Los Angeles: University of California Press, 1969.

Homberger, Eric, ed. *Ezra Pound: The Critical Heritage*. London and Boston: Routledge & Kegan Paul, 1972.

Jackson, Thomas H. *The Early Poetry of Ezra Pound*. Cambridge: Harvard University
Press, 1968.

Kappel, Andrew J. "Ezra Pound in Heaven." *Hudson Review* 35 (1982): 73–86.

Kazin, Alfred. "Language as History: Ezra Pound's Search for the Authority of

History." In *The Problem of Authority in America*, edited by John P. Diggins and Mark E. Kann. Philadelphia: Temple University Press, 1981.

Kenner Hugh. *The Poetry of Ezra Pound*. Norfolk, Conn.: New Directions, n.d. [1951]; Millwood, N.Y.: Krauss, 1974.

———. *The Pound Era*. Berkeley and Boston: University of California Press, 1971.

Knapp, James F. *Ezra Pound*. Boston: Twayne, 1979.

Korn, Marianne. *Ezra Pound: Purpose/Form/Meaning*. London: Pembridge Press for Middlesex Polytechnic Press, 1983.

Kuberski, Philip. "Ego, Scriptor: Pound's Odyssean Writing." *Paideuma* 14 (1985): 31–51.

Lander, Jeanette. *Ezra Pound*. New York: Frederick Ungar, 1971.

Leary, Lewis. *Motive and Method in the Cantos of Ezra Pound*. New York: Columbia University Press, 1954.

Levin, Harry. "Ezra Pound, T. S. Eliot and the Idea of Comparative Literature." *Actes du VIIe Congrès de l'Association Internationale de Littérature Comparée: I Literatures of America: Dependence, Independence, Interdependence*, 545–52. Stuttgart: Kunst & Wissen, Ernst Bieber, 1979.

Levy, Alan. *Ezra Pound: The Voice of Silence*. Sag Harbor, N.Y.: Permanent Press, 1983.

Link, Franz H. "Pound's Imagist Alba: Myth as Cognitive Method." In *Poetic Knowledge: Circumference and Centre: Papers from the Wuppertal Symposium 1978*, edited by Roland Hagenbuechle and Joseph T. Swann, 128–40. Bonn: Bouvier Verlag Herbert Grundmann, 1980.

McDougal, Stuart Y. *Ezra Pound and the Troubador Tradition*. Princeton, N.J.: Princeton University Press, 1972.

Macleish, Archibald. *Poetry and Opinion: The Pisan Cantos of Ezra Pound; A Dialogue on the Role of Poetry*. Urbana: University of Illinois Press, 1950.

Makin, Peter. *Pound's Cantos*. London: Allen & Unwin, 1985.

———. *Provenance and Pound*. Berkeley, Los Angeles, and London: University of California Press, 1978.

Meacham, Harry M. *The Caged Panther: Ezra Pound at Saint Elizabeths*. New York: Twayne, 1967.

Miyake, Akiko. *Athematic and Structural Unity in Ezra Pound's Eleven New Cantos*. Kyoto: American Literature Society of Japan, 1971.

Nagy, N. Christophe de. *Ezra Pound's Poetics and Literary Tradition: The Critical Decade*. Bern: Francke Verlag, 1966.

———. *The Poetry of Ezra Pound: The Pre-Imagist Stage*. Rev. ed. Bern: Francke Verlag, 1960.

Nänny, Max. *Ezra Pound: Poetics for an Electric Age*. Bern: Francke Verlag, 1973.

———. "Oral Dimensions in Ezra Pound." *Paideuma* 6 (1977): 13–26.

Nassar, Eugene Paul. *The Cantos of Ezra Pound: The Lyrical Mode*. Baltimore: The Johns Hopkins University Press, 1975.

Nicholls, Peter. *Ezra Pound: Politics, Economics, and Writing: A Study of the Cantos*. London: Macmillan, 1984.

Nolde, John H. *Blossoms from the East: The China Cantos of Ezra Pound*. Orono: National Poetry Foundation, University of Maine, 1983.

Norman, Charles. *The Case of Ezra Pound*. Rev. ed. New York: Funk & Wagnalls, 1969 [first 1948].

———. *Ezra Pound*. New York: Macmillan, 1960.

O'Connor, William Van. *Ezra Pound*. Minneapolis: University of Minnesota Press, 1963.

Pearlman, Daniel D. "The Anti-Semitism of Ezra Pound." *Contemporary Literature* 22 (1981): 104–15.

———. *The Barb of Time: On the Unity of Ezra Pound's* Cantos. New York: Oxford University Press, 1969.

Pecorino, Jessica Prinz. "Resurgent Icons: Pound's First Pisan Canto and the Visual Arts." *Journal of Modern Literature* 9 (1982): 159–74.

Perloff, Marjorie. *Dance of the Intellect*. New York: Cambridge University Press, 1985.

Quin, Mary Bernetta. *Ezra Pound: An Introduction to the Poetry*. New York: Columbia University Press, 1972.

Rabaté, Jean-Michel. *Language, Sexuality and Ideology in Ezra Pound's* Cantos. London: Macmillan, 1986.

Rosenthal, Macha Louis. *A Primer of Ezra Pound*. New York: Macmillan, 1960.

———. "The Structuring of Pound's *Cantos*." *Paideuma* 6 (1977): 3–11.

Russell, Peter. *An Examination of Ezra Pound: A Collection of Essays*. n.p. [Norfolk, Conn.]: New Directions, 1950.

San Juan, E., Jr. *Critics on Ezra Pound*. Coral Gables, Fla.: University of Miami Press, 1972.

Schneidau, Herbert N. *Ezra Pound: The Image and the Real*. Baton Rouge: Louisiana State University Press, 1969.

Schulman, Grace, comp. *Ezra Pound: A Collection of Criticism*. New York: McGraw-Hill, 1974.

Sieburth, Richard. Instigations, Ezra Pound and Remy de Gourmont. Cambridge: Harvard University Press, 1978.

Stock, Noel, ed. *Ezra Pound Perspectives: Essays in Honor of His Eightieth Birthday*. Chicago: H. Regnery, 1965.

———. *Reading the Cantos: The Study of Meaning in Ezra Pound*. New York: Pantheon, 1966.

Sullivan, J. P. *Ezra Pound and Sextus Propertius: A Study in Creative Translation*. Austin: University of Texas Press, 1964.

Surette, Leon. *A Light from Eleusis: A Study of Ezra Pound's* Cantos. Oxford: Oxford University Press, 1979.

Sutton, Walter, ed. *Ezra Pound: A Collection of Critical Essays*. Englewood Cliffs, N.J.: Prentice-Hall, 1963.

Tay, William. "Fragmentary Negation: A Reappraisal of Ezra Pound's Ideogrammatic Method." *Chinese-Western Comparative Literature: Theory and Strategy*, edited by John J. Deeney, 129–53. Hong Kong: Chinese University Press, 1980.

Tucker, John J. "Pound, Vorticism, and the New Esthetic." *Mosaic* 16 (1983): 83–96.

Watts, Harold H. *Ezra Pound and* The Cantos. n.p.: Routledge & Kegan Paul, 1951.

Wilhelm, J. J. *The American Roots of Ezra Pound*. New York and London: Garland, 1985.

———. *Dante and Pound: The Epic Judgment*. Orono: University of Maine Press, 1974.

———. *The Later Cantos of Ezra Pound*. New York: Walter & Company, 1977.

Witemeyer, Hugh. *The Poetry of Ezra Pound: Forms and Renewal 1908–1920*. Berkeley and Los Angeles: University of California Press, 1969.
Woodward, Anthony. *Ezra Pound and The Pisan Cantos*. London, Boston, and Henley: Routledge & Kegan Paul, 1980.
Yip, Wai-lim. *Ezra Pound's Cathay*. Princeton: Princeton University Press, 1969.

Acknowledgments

"*Mauberley*" by Hugh Kenner from *The Poetry of Ezra Pound* by Hugh Kenner, © 1951 by Hugh Kenner. Reprinted by permission of the author and New Directions Publishing Corporation.

"The End of *The Cantos*" by Eva Hesse. © 1987 by Eva Hesse. Published for the first time in this volume.

"The Barb of Time" by Daniel D. Pearlman from *The Barb of Time: On the Unity of Ezra Pound's* Cantos by Daniel D. Pearlman, © 1969 by Daniel D. Pearlman. Reprinted by permission of the author and Oxford University Press.

"Pound's Early Poems" (originally entitled "Introduction") by Louis L. Martz from *Collected Early Poems of Ezra Pound*, edited by Michael John King, © 1976 by Louis L. Martz. Reprinted by permission of the author and of New Directions Publishing Corporation.

"Context, Contiguity, and Contact in Ezra Pound's *Personae*" by Max Nänny from *ELH* 47, no. 2, 1980, © 1980 by The Johns Hopkins University Press. Reprinted by permission of The Johns Hopkins University Press.

"Ezra Pound: America's Wandering Jew" by Daniel D. Pearlman from *Paideuma: A Journal Devoted to Ezra Pound Scholarship* 9, no. 3 (Winter 1980), © 1980 by the National Poetry Foundation, Inc. Reprinted by permission of the National Poetry Foundation, University of Maine, Orono, Maine.

" 'The Might of the North': Pound's Anglo-Saxon Studies and 'The Seafarer' " by Fred C. Robinson from *The Yale Review* 71, no. 2 (January 1982), © 1982 by Yale University. Reprinted by permission.

"*Res* and *Verba* in *Rock-Drill* and After" by Donald Davie from *Paideuma: A Journal Devoted to Ezra Pound Scholarship* 11, no. 3 (Winter 1982), © 1982 by the National Poetry Foundation, Inc. Reprinted by permission of the National Poetry Foundation, University of Maine, Orono, Maine.

"The Pound Error: The Limits of Authority in the Modern Epic" by Christine Froula from *To Write Paradise: Style and Error in Pound's* Cantos by Christine Froula, © 1984 by Yale University. Reprinted by permission of Yale University Press.

"Image, Word, and Sign: The Visual Arts as Evidence in Ezra Pound's *Cantos*" by Michael André Bernstein from *Critical Inquiry* 12, no. 2 (Winter 1986), © 1986 by The University of Chicago. Reprinted by permission of the author and The University of Chicago Press.

"Rhizomatic America" by Kathryne V. Lindberg from *Reading Pound Reading: The Nietzschean Indirections of Modernism* by Kathryne V. Lindberg, © 1986 by Oxford University Press. Reprinted by permission.

"Reading Pound Writing Chinese: A Page from *Rock-Drill*" a revised version of "Section: *Rock-Drill* (1955)" by George Kearns from *Guide to Ezra Pound's* Selected Cantos by George Kearns, © 1986 by George Kearns. Reprinted by permission of the author and Rutgers University Press.

Index